REMEDIES BEFORE THE INTERNATIONAL COURT OF JUSTICE

Understanding exactly how the International Court of Justice (ICJ) applies the remedies of international law is vital in order to determine its prioritisation of remedies and its rationales for resolving inter-state disputes. This analysis also shows whether the framework of remedies of international law, designed by the International Law Commission through the Articles on Responsibility of States for Internationally Wrongful Acts, is strictly observed by the International Court of Justice. This is among the few systemic studies in the field of remedies, contrasting the theoretical controversies with a complete survey of the large set of requests that have been submitted before the ICJ. International lawyers, agents of states and diplomats will be able to identify the relevant case law for each remedy in order to frame more effective requests to the Court. This study will also be of interest to researchers, practitioners, judges, policymakers and graduate students.

Victor Stoica is an international lawyer, working for the Ministry of Foreign Affairs of Romania. He is currently an assistant professor in public international law and international relations and organisations at the University of Bucharest and affiliate lecturer at the National University of Political and Administrative Studies of Romania.

Remedies before the International Court of Justice

A SYSTEMIC ANALYSIS

VICTOR STOICA
University of Bucharest

CAMBRIDGE
UNIVERSITY PRESS

University Printing House, Cambridge CB2 8BS, United Kingdom

One Liberty Plaza, 20th Floor, New York, NY 10006, USA

477 Williamstown Road, Port Melbourne, VIC 3207, Australia

314–321, 3rd Floor, Plot 3, Splendor Forum, Jasola District Centre, New Delhi – 110025, India

79 Anson Road, #06–04/06, Singapore 079906

Cambridge University Press is part of the University of Cambridge.

It furthers the University's mission by disseminating knowledge in the pursuit of education, learning, and research at the highest international levels of excellence.

www.cambridge.org
Information on this title: www.cambridge.org/9781108490825
DOI: 10.1017/9781108855006

© Victor Stoica 2021

This publication is in copyright. Subject to statutory exception and to the provisions of relevant collective licensing agreements, no reproduction of any part may take place without the written permission of Cambridge University Press.

First published 2021

A catalogue record for this publication is available from the British Library.

ISBN 978-1-108-49082-5 Hardback

Cambridge University Press has no responsibility for the persistence or accuracy of URLs for external or third-party internet websites referred to in this publication and does not guarantee that any content on such websites is, or will remain, accurate or appropriate.

To My Teachers

Contents

Foreword by Laurence Boisson de Chazournes	xi
Table of Cases	xiii
List of Abbreviations	xvii

Introduction		1
	1 The Context	1
	2 The Scope	4
	3 The Outline	7

1	**Jurisdiction**	9
	1.1 Introduction	9
	1.2 The Permanent Court of International Justice	10
	1.3 The International Court	11
	1.4 Conclusion	12

2	**Provisional Measures**	13
	2.1 Introduction	13
	2.2 The Permanent Court of International Justice	14
	2.3 The International Court	15
	2.3.1 The Binding Effect of Orders for Provisional Measures	15
	2.3.2 Orders for Provisional Measures Granting Remedies of International Law	16
	2.3.3 Remedies for Breaching Orders for Provisional Measures	18
	2.4 Conclusion	19

3	**Declaratory Judgments**	21
	3.1 Introduction	21
	3.2 Theoretical Perspectives	23

viii Contents

3.2.1 Declaratory Judgments and the Statute of the Court 23
3.2.2 The Definition and Function of
Declaratory Judgments 24
3.2.3 Types of Declaratory Judgments 25
3.2.4 Declaratory Judgments and Other Remedies 25
3.3 Practical Perspectives 32
3.3.1 Types of Declaratory Judgments 32
3.3.2 Declaratory Relief and the Subject Matter of
the Dispute 36
3.3.3 Declaratory Relief and the Manner in which the
Court is Seized 41
3.4 Conclusion 45

4 **Specific Performance** 46
4.1 Introduction 46
4.2 Theoretical perspectives 48
4.2.1 The Definition and Function of Specific Performance 48
4.2.2 The Availability of Specific Performance 49
4.2.3 Specific Performance and Other Remedies 52
4.3 Practical Perspectives 57
4.3.1 The Availability of Specific Performance 57
Conclusion 59

5 **Cessation, Assurances and Guarantees of Non-repetition** 61
5.1 Introduction 61
5.2 Theoretical Perspectives 63
5.2.1 Cessation 63
5.2.2 Assurances and Guarantees of Non-repetition 68
5.3 Practical Perspectives 72
5.3.1 Cessation As a Form of Reparation 72
5.3.2 The Obligation to Cease 73
5.3.3 Cessation, Guarantees of Non-repetition and Restitutio
in Integrum 74
5.3.4 The Meaning of Guarantees of Non-repetition 76
5.4 Conclusion 79

6 **Restitution in Kind** 81
6.1 Introduction 81
6.2 Theoretical Perspectives 83
6.2.1 The Definition and Function of Restitution in Kind 83

Contents

6.2.2 Types of Restitution in Kind	83
6.2.3 The Primacy of Restitution in Kind	84
6.3 Practical Perspectives	87
6.3.1 The Availability of Restitution in Kind	87
6.3.2 The Locus Classicus of Restitution in Kind	92
6.3.3 Restitution in Kind and Restitutio in Integrum	99
6.3.4 The Application of Restitution in Kind	101
6.4 Conclusion	105
7 Compensation	**108**
7.1 Introduction	108
7.2 Theoretical Perspectives	111
7.2.1 The Definition and Function of Compensation	111
7.2.2 Compensation and Damages	112
7.2.3 The Function of Compensation	113
7.2.4 Types of Compensation	113
7.2.5 Assessing Compensation	114
7.3 Practical Perspectives	115
7.3.1 Determined Compensation	115
7.3.2 Undetermined Compensation	118
7.3.3 Compensation and Reparation	121
7.3.4 The Implications of the Chorzów Factory Case	135
7.3.5 The Implications of the Corfu Channel Case	138
7.3.6 The Implications of the Diallo Case	140
7.4 Conclusion	143
8 Satisfaction	**145**
8.1 Introduction	145
8.2 Theoretical Perspectives	147
8.2.1 The Definition and Function of Satisfaction	147
8.2.2 Types of Satisfaction	149
8.3 Practical Perspectives	150
8.3.1 The Availability of Satisfaction	150
8.3.2 Non-pecuniary Satisfaction	152
8.4 Conclusion	155
9 The Case Law of International Courts and Tribunals	**157**
9.1 Introduction	157
9.2 Assessing Moral Damages	157
9.3 Pecuniary Satisfaction	159

x   *Contents*

9.3.1 The S.S. 'I'm Alone' Case	160
9.3.2 The Rainbow Warrior Case	160
9.3.3 The Lusitania Case	162
9.4 Conclusion	163

Conclusions   164

Appendices   171

1 *Requests Submitted before the Permanent Court of International Justice through Special Agreements*   171

2 *Judgments of the Permanent Court of International Justice in the Cases Submitted through Special Agreements*   174

3 *Requests Submitted before the Permanent Court of International Justice through Unilateral Applications*   177

4 *Judgments of the Permanent Court of International Justice in the Cases Submitted through Unilateral Applications*   183

5 *Requests Submitted before the International Court of Justice through Special Agreements*   187

6 *Judgments of the International Court of Justice in the Cases Submitted through Special Agreements*   191

7 *Requests Submitted before the International Court of Justice through Unilateral Applications*   196

8 *Judgments of the International Court of Justice in the Cases Submitted through Unilateral Applications*   245

Bibliography   275

Index   283

Foreword

This book is an important contribution to the understanding of how the International Court of Justice resolves interstate disputes and the mechanisms it uses for pursuing its contentious function. The focus of the book is on remedies in international law. There are in fact very few studies that have been conducted in this area. As such, Victor Stoica's book is most welcome as it offers a comprehensive assessment of the practice of the Permanent Court of International Justice and of its successor, as well as offering valuable insights from both theoretical and practice-oriented perspectives. Remedies are considered in the book as a distinct topic of international law as well as in relation to the broader conceptual framework of state responsibility.

Conducting an in-depth analysis of the judgments of the International Court of Justice, the written submissions and oral pleadings of the parties to the proceedings and a careful appraisal of academic writings on the topic, the author examines the manner in which the Court interprets and decides upon remedies.

At a time when there is a multiplication of international courts and tribunals, this detailed and refined analysis of how classical concepts and principles of international law are applied by the principal judicial organ of the United Nations sheds light on the features of the settlement of inter-state disputes and the challenges thereto. Of particular note is the way in which the book offers a nuanced understanding of some of the peculiarities attached to the resolution of disputes between sovereign entities. The book emphasises the unique approach of the Court in this area as well as the predictability it demonstrates in discharging its function 'to decide in accordance with international law' disputes brought before it.

Laurence Boisson de Chazournes

Professor at the Faculty of Law of the University of Geneva and Director of the Master in International Dispute Settlement (MIDS)

Table of Cases

CASES OF THE PERMANENT COURT OF INTERNATIONAL JUSTICE

Borchgrave 154
Certain German Interests in Polish Upper Silesia 23, 24
Denunciation of the Treaty between China and Belgium 15
Factory at Chorzow
  Jurisdiction 1, 5, 10, 11, 82, 86 92, 98, 108, 164
  Merits 4, 5, 10, 50, 81, 82 85, 88, 92, 93, 95, 96, 106, 111, 135, 136, 137, 138
  Provisional Measures 14
Free Zones of Upper Savoy and the District of Gex Judgment
  Judgment 10, 164
  Order 168
Interpretation of Judgments nos. 7 and 8 (Factory at Chorzów) ... 24, 28, 91
Legal Status of the South-Eastern Territory of Greenland 40
Lighthouses Case between France and Greece 7, 47, 51
Mavrommatis Jerusalem Concessions 27, 108
Mavrommatis Palestine Concessions 2, 132
S.S. 'Wimbledon' 1, 5, 10, 109, 123, 124

CASES OF THE INTERNATIONAL COURT OF JUSTICE

Aegean Sea Continental Shelf
  Application instituting Proceedings 32
Aerial Incident of 10 March 1953
  Application instituting Proceedings 115, 117
Aerial Incident of 7 October 1952
  Application instituting proceedings 115, 117
Diallo
  Application instituting Proceedings 116, 142
  Merits 5, 109, 110, 115, 118, 126, 127, 129, 130, 136, 141, 142, 158, 164

xiv   *Table of Cases*

Anglo-Iranian Oil Co
  Request for Provisional Measures 15
  Memorial 96
  Judgment 110
Application of the Convention on the Prevention and Punishment
    of the Crime of Genocide
  Application instituting Proceedings 151
  Merits 6, 18, 19, 89, 150, 151, 152, 153, 154
  Provisional Measures 18
Armed Activities on the Territory of the Congo
  Application instituting Proceedings 120
  Merits 94, 76
Arrest Warrant of 11 April 2000 .... 49, 55, 57
Avena
  Application instituting Proceedings 75
  Request for Preliminary Measures 17
  Preliminary Measures 17, 59
  Memorial 75
  Merits 48, 55, 62, 64
Barcelona Traction
  Application instituting Proceedings 101
  Merits 90
Questions of Interpretation and Application of the 1971 Montreal
    Convention Arising from the Aerial Incident at Lockerbie
  Application instituting Proceedings 35
Right of Passage over Indian Territory
  Application instituting Proceedings 33
  Merits 11
Aerial Incident of 27 July 1955
  Application instituting Proceedings 115, 117
Aerial Incident of 4 September 1954
  Application instituting Proceedings 115
Application of the Convention of 1902 governing the Guardianship
    of Infants
  Application instituting Proceedings 35
Northern Cameroons 23, 167
Temple of Preah Vihear
  Application instituting Proceedings 33
  Merits 27, 38, 56, 81, 82, 100, 102
Certain Activities Carried Out by Nicaragua in the Border Area
    and Construction of a Road in Costa Rica along the
    San Juan River
  Compensation 132, 133, 134
Certain Iranian Assets
  Application instituting Proceedings 110, 119
Certain Phosphate Lands in Nauru
  Application instituting Proceedings 94

Table of Cases

Certain Property
Application instituting Proceedings 119, 122
Colombian–Peruvian Asylum 28, 49
Continental Shelf
(Libyan Arab Jamahiriya/Malta) 26, 43
(Tunisia/Libyan Arab Jamahiriya) 26, 39, 43
Corfu Channel
Order appointing Expert 6, 139
Oral Proceedings 88
Counter-memorial 150
Merits 2, 5, 6, 11, 29, 78, 108, 124, 139, 147, 150, 151, 153, 155
Compensation 4, 5, 109, 110, 125, 132, 139, 140, 148, 153
Delimitation of the Maritime Boundary in the Gulf of Maine Area
Order appointing Expert 140
Dispute regarding Navigational and Related Rights
Application instituting Proceedings 100
Memorial 127
Merits 65, 70, 73, 128
Électricité de Beyrouth Company
Application instituting Proceedings 120
Elettronica Sicula S.P.A. (ELSI)
Application instituting Proceedings 119
Memorial 120
Fisheries Case
Application instituting Proceedings 120
Fisheries Jurisdiction
Jurisdiction and Admissibility 2
Merits 128
Frontier Dispute
(Benin/Niger) 26
(Burkina Faso/Republic of Mali) 26, 37
Gabčíkovo–Nagymaros Project 4, 6, 57, 58, 89, 108
Haya de la Torre 28, 49
Immunities and Criminal Proceedings
Application instituting Proceedings 119
Kasikili/SeduduIsland 26, 39
LaGrand
Application instituting Proceedings 70, 77, 120
Memorial 77, 78, 79, 82, 120
Merits 16, 55, 62, 78, 154, 155
Land and Maritime Boundary between Cameroon and Nigeria 40
Legal Consequences of the Construction of a Wall in the Occupied
    Palestinian Territory
Advisory Opinion 82, 89, 103
Pleadings 103
Maritime Delimitation in the Black Sea
Application instituting Proceedings 33

xvi   *Table of Cases*

Maritime Dispute
   Application instituting Proceedings 33
Military and Paramilitary Activities in and against Nicaragua
   Application instituting Proceedings 73
   Request for Preliminary Measures 17
   Memorial 74, 94, 118
   Merits 7, 11, 52, 62, 74, 94
Minquiers and Ecrehos
   Special Agreement 43
   Merits 26, 37
North Sea Continental Shelf 26, 39, 43
Nottebohm
   Application instituting Proceedings 94, 116
   Memorial 94, 96, 116
   Merits 93, 115
Oil Platforms 122
Passage through the Great Belt
   Application instituting Proceedings 34
Pulp Mills on the River Uruguay
   Application instituting Proceedings 104
   Memorial 105
   Merits 105
Delimitation of the Continental Shelf between Nicaragua
      and Colombia beyond 200 nautical miles from the
      Nicaraguan Coast
   Application instituting Proceedings 34
Request for Interpretation of the Judgment in the Avena Case
   Order of Provisional Measures 59
Sovereignty over Certain Frontier Land 26, 37
Sovereignty over Pedra Branca/Pulau Batu Puteh, Middle Rocks
      and South Ledge 26, 37
Sovereignty over Pulau Ligitan and Pulau Sipadan 26, 37
Territorial and Maritime Dispute
   Application instituting Proceedings 33
   Reply 122
   Merits 40
Vienna Convention on Consular Relations
   Application instituting Proceedings 99, 100
   Memorial 99

OTHER COURTS AND TRIBUNALS

Opinion in the Lusitania Cases 110, 158, 162, 163
S.S. 'I'm Alone' 159, 160
Rainbow Warrior 161, 162

Abbreviations

ECHR	European Court of Human Rights
ed/eds	editor/editors
ICJ, International Court, Court	International Court of Justice
ICSID	International Centre for Settlement of Investment Disputes
ILC	International Law Commission
ILC Articles	International Law Commission's Articles on Responsibility of States for Internationally Wrongful Acts
No./nos.	number/numbers
p./pp.	page/pages
PCIJ, Permanent Court	Permanent Court of International Justice
Rep	Report
RIAA	United Nations Reports of International Arbitral Awards
UK	United Kingdom of Great Britain and Northern Ireland
UN	United Nations
UN Doc	United Nations document
USA	United States of America
v	versus
vol	volume

Introduction

1 THE CONTEXT

The manner in which states perform international obligations contributes towards and influences the development of international law. Further, international law is interpreted and clarified by international institutions, designed for various purposes, including the resolution of disputes between states. Even if the clarification of international law is not the primary function of the International Court of Justice, this judicial body provides constant and relevant insight with respect to the interpretation of international law, and, consequently, with respect to its evolution.

The Court's function is uncontroversial, and prescribed by Article 38 of its Statute, which provides that it is mandated to *'decide in accordance with international law such disputes as are submitted to it'*. Through the exercise of its function, the Court contributes not only to the development of international law but also towards the maintenance of peace among states, in its capacity as the principal judicial organ of the United Nations. In the exercise of its contentious function, the Court renders a judgment at the end of its proceedings, through which the effects of the breaches of international obligations suffered by the applicant state are sought to be totally or partially repaired, by certain mechanisms designed for this purpose. The mechanisms that are meant to re-establish the situation as it existed prior to the occurrence of the illegal act are referred to as *'remedies of international law'*. The final resolution of a dispute implies a judgment on remedies, without which the dispute would not be settled in its entirety. The Permanent Court has confirmed this conclusion in several of its judgments,[1]

---

[1] *Case concerning Factory at Chorzów (Germany v Poland)* [1927] (Jurisdiction) PCIJ Rep Series A No. 9, 4, 21; *Case of the S.S. 'Wimbledon' (Britain et al v Germany)* [1923], PCIJ Rep Series A,

2 *Introduction*

these findings being further substantiated by the International Court throughout its case-law.[2]

By submitting a dispute before the Court, states seek the resolution of their
disputes in the manner set out in the prayers for relief within their pleadings.
The documents submitted by parties, such as special agreements, applications,
memorials, counter-memorials and rejoinders, include express references to
the specific remedies that the Court is called upon to grant. The judgments of
the Court clarify the legal arguments and controversies of a given case, with
respect to the relevant breaches of international law and the interpretation and
application of the provisions related to the dispute. However, the Court
generally provides few details regarding the interpretation of the applicable
remedies. Consequently, while findings of principle make up the bulk of the
judgment, the Court's analysis of remedies and their interpretation remains on
its fringes. A systemic study of the various perspectives regarding the remedies
of international law, as applied by the Court, is therefore relevant for determining the meaning and characteristics of the related notions.

The remedies that are available under international law have been, in a
general manner, analysed by scholarly writings and by specialised international bodies. Authors like James Crawford[3] and Christine Gray[4] have
provided relevant insight regarding the remedies of international law and they
conclude that the scope of remedies, available before the Court, has been
rather ignored by the Court and by academic writing as well. In that sense, a
comprehensive analysis of remedies is still outstanding and necessary with
respect to a variety of issues.

International bodies such as the International Law Commission or the
Institute of International Law have contributed to the interpretation and
clarification of the remedies that are available under general international
law, and thus, for proceedings before the Court. The customary rules
regarding the particular remedies, usually granted by international bodies,
have been best described through the ILC Articles, which contain several
provisions that treat remedies as part of the wider notion of reparation.[5] These

---

No. 1; *The Mavrommatis Palestine Concessions Case* (*Greece v United Kingdom*) [1924] PCIJ
Rep Series A, No. 2.

[2] *Corfu Channel Case* (*Great Britain v Albania*) (Merits) [1949] ICJ Rep 4; *Fisheries Jurisdiction Case* (*Germany v Iceland*) (Jurisdiction and Admissibility) [1973] ICJ Rep 49, 54.

[3] James Crawford, *State Responsibility: The General Part* (Cambridge University Press 2013) 506–536.

[4] Christine Gray, *Judicial Remedies in International Law* (Clarendon Press 1990) 59–119.

[5] ILC, 'Articles on Responsibility of States for Internationally Wrongful Acts', UN Doc A/56/83 (2001) 95–107.

provisions represent a synthesis of the customary international rules with respect to the available remedies under international law. Moreover, the ILC has also adopted a Commentary, which interprets and clarifies the notions provided through the ILC Articles. As such, to say that there is no analysis regarding the remedies of international law would be an exaggeration and an underestimation of the relevant work that currently exists. However, even though the above-mentioned references clarify the remedies available under international law, there is no precise theory of remedies, under international law, that applies before the Court. The judicial body generally takes into consideration the principles that describe the remedies of international law, but contextualises them by observing the particularities of the disputes that are submitted before it. In this respect, the ILC Articles represent a general instrument that is not intended to provide a clear determination of the manner in which the prescribed remedies should apply before the Court. The conclusion regarding the generality of the ILC Articles is also reflected and confirmed by the preamble of this document, which provides that it seeks to formulate the basic rules of international law concerning state responsibility.[6]

There is, therefore, a need for a more focused and targeted study regarding the manner in which the Court applies said remedies of international law. Its practice is useful for contextualising and developing the basic rules provided by the ILC Articles. The proliferation of international courts and tribunals, which occurred during the past decades, justifies the wide approach of the ILC towards remedies in international law. A general theory of remedies of international law might also be suitable for the multitude of international legal situations occurring in the world today, such as human rights disputes that are resolved by the ECHR, interstate disputes resolved through arbitration, investment disputes resolved through ad hoc or institutional arbitration, such as ICSID, and interstate disputes resolved by the Court. All these dispute resolution institutions might need a specific application framework of remedies, depending on various elements such as the affiliation of the institution, the appearing parties, or the subject matter that the said institution is competent to decide upon. Each judicial body has the power to interpret and apply the principles of reparation, which involve remedies, in accordance with its own functions. Thus, even if the said institutions do not necessarily need a substantially different set of remedies, the manner in which the remedies apply

---

[6] ILC, 'Articles on Responsibility of States for Internationally Wrongful Acts', UN Doc A/56/83 (2001) 31.

4   *Introduction*

before each institution might differ.[7] This is the justification for which a systemic analysis of the remedies of international law applied by the Court is relevant.

2 THE SCOPE

For a relevant determination of whether a particular set of rules is applicable before a particular international body, the general framework of remedies available under international law should be tested, by observing how the said international body applies them. The focus of the book is the International Court and the consequences that the disputes before this international body produce in the context of remedies.

Consequently, the primary research material is represented by the submissions of the parties before the International Court, and by the judgments and orders of the judicial body, with respect to remedies. The book provides a systemic and detailed analysis regarding the remedies available before the Court and it endeavours to determine whether the general theory of remedies provided through the ILC Articles, as currently interpreted by academic writings, is applicable or not before the International Court. The current interpretation of the remedies of international law before the International Court is concentrated on interpreting their characteristics through the lens of landmark cases, loci classici on the point. Examples such as the Chorzów Factory Case,[8] the Corfu Channel Case[9] and the Gabčíkovo–Nagymaros Case[10] contain clarifications regarding the applicable remedies before the International Court. The conclusions provided by the Court in these cases have been guised as findings of principle, or obiter dicta, which have established the customary interpretation of certain concepts. However, these findings are not without flaws, and are interpreted differently by scholarly writings and by the Court throughout its subsequent practice.

The first relevant issue with respect to the subject matter of the book is the manner in which the Court clarified its competence to decide upon the applicable remedies, even if states did not expressly grant the Court the power to decide upon the application of a particular remedy.[11] The issue of the

---

[7] James Crawford, 'Flexibility in the Award of Reparation: Role of the Parties and the Tribunal' in Rüdiger Wolfrum, Maja Seršić and Trpimir Šošić (eds), *Contemporary Developments in International Law: Essays in Honor of Budislav Vukas* (Brill/Nijhoff 2016) 693.

[8] *Case concerning Factory at Chorzów (Germany v. Poland)* (Merits) [1928] PCIJ Rep Series A No. 17.

[9] *Corfu Channel Case (Great Britain v Albania)* (Compensation) [1949] ICJ Rep 244.

[10] *Gabčíkovo–Nagymaros Project (Hungary/Slovakia)* (Judgment) [1997] ICJ Rep 7.

[11] Gray, *Judicial Remedies in International Law*, 57.

competence of the Court to decide upon issues related to remedies was first clarified by the Permanent Court, through judgments such as those in the Wimbledon Case[12] and the Chorzów Factory Case,[13] in which applicant states raised preliminary objections regarding the competence of the Permanent Court to grant remedies. The question has arisen in other cases as well, but the Court has maintained and confirmed its findings from the Chorzów Factory Case,[14] where it concluded that it has jurisdiction to decide upon the applicable remedies, in this situation. No less important is the competence of the Court to grant remedies of international law through its orders on provisional measures.

Restitution in kind is one of the most controversial remedies that have been requested before the Court. Issues regarding its availability and application mainly originate from the alleged primacy of this remedy. Not only is the primacy of restitution in kind before the Court disputable, but its availability is also questionable. Commentators conclude, in this respect, that uncertainties exist regarding the application of restitution in kind in international law,[15] indicating that this argument is further substantiated by the recent case-law of the International Court. The controversies regarding this remedy go as far as to the question of the definition of restitution in kind and its interaction with the wider concept of restitutio in integrum.

Compensation is a remedy that has been interpreted by the Court in a rather restrictive manner. The Court's judgments regarding compensation are few and provide even fewer details related to the interpretation and clarification of this remedy. It is telling that monetary compensation has been granted by the Court in a handful of cases, the most referred to being the Corfu Channel Case[16] and the Diallo Case.[17] Further, moral damages have been granted only in the Diallo Case. However, in the same manner in which the Permanent Court provided certain findings of principle related to restitution in kind, the International Court has pursued this approach as well, and issued judgments related to compensation, further clarifying the characteristics of

---

[12] *S.S. 'Wimbledon' (Britain et al v Germany).*
[13] *Factory at Chorzów (Germany v Poland)* (Merits).
[14] *Case concerning Factory at Chorzów (Germany v Poland)* (Jurisdiction) [1927] PCIJ Rep Series A No. 9; *Corfu Channel Case (Great Britain v Albania)* (Judgment on Preliminary Objection) [1948] ICJ Rep 15, 29; *United States Diplomatic and Consular Staff in Tehran (USA v Iran)* (Judgment) [1980] ICJ Rep 3.
[15] Christine Gray, 'The Choice between Restitution and Compensation' (1999) 10:2 European Journal of International Law 413.
[16] *Corfu Channel Case (Great Britain v Albania)* (Compensation) 250.
[17] *Ahmadou Sadio Diallo (Republic of Guinea v Democratic Republic of the Congo)* (Merits) [2010] ICJ Rep 639.

6   Introduction

this remedy. The very right of states to claim compensation has been confirmed by the Court in the Gabčíkovo–Nagymaros Case.[18] The Corfu Channel Case further established the Court's authority to use experts for the verification and determination of the amounts of compensation that were requested by the applicant state.[19] The Diallo Case is unique in its findings with respect to moral compensation before the International Court.

The meaning attributed by the International Court to satisfaction, and the mechanism through which it grants this remedy throughout its case-law, contribute to the idea that the ILC Articles have no application before it with respect to this remedy. While the ILC Articles prescribe that satisfaction should be ordered by the Court and further provided by responding states, when they are responsible for internationally wrongful acts, the International Court has taken a different approach. As such, in the Corfu Channel Case, the Court concluded that declaratory judgments represent appropriate satisfaction.[20] The approach that the Court has taken with respect to satisfaction in the Corfu Channel Case has been confirmed by its subsequent case-law,[21] and this has led certain members of the Court to conclude that satisfaction should no longer be considered as a veritable remedy before it.[22]

Cessation is a remedy that has raised a number of controversies in the past, which have not yet been completely resolved. While cessation is clearer, as a concept, than other remedies, its interaction and relationship with other forms of relief leads to certain confusions. For example, the interplay between cessation and assurances and guarantees of non-repetition is the reason for which the ILC Articles and the case-law of the Court treat them as complementary, without necessarily implying that they should be requested together, or that a request for only one of the two would be inappropriate.

The manner in which the Court applies cessation and specific performance, due to their final scope of fulfilling an obligation, has also led to differences of opinion among authors and rather harsh reactions from some, particularly because the case-law, in this respect, is not very clear. Firstly, the Court never used the nomenclature of 'specific performance', even though it granted it in several of its judgments, such as the ones in the Case concerning

---

[18] *Gabčíkovo–Nagymaros Project* (*Hungary/Slovakia*) (Judgment) 81.
[19] *Corfu Channel Case* (*Great Britain v Albania*) (Order) [1949] ICJ Rep 237–238.
[20] *Corfu Channel Case* (*Great Britain v Albania*) (Merits) 4, 36.
[21] *Application of the Convention on the Prevention and Punishment of the Crime of Genocide* (*Bosnia and Herzegovina v Serbia and Montenegro*) (Judgment) [2007] ICJ Rep 43, 195.
[22] *Corfu Channel Case* (*Great Britain v Albania*) (Merits) (Dissenting Opinion of Judge Azevedo).

3 *The Outline* 7

Military and Paramilitary Activities in Nicaragua,[23] the Lighthouses Case,[24] the Serbian Loans Case[25] and the Iranian Hostages Case.[26] Nevertheless, cessation suffers the same fate as specific performance with respect to the lack of clarity and consistency with which the Court has treated this remedy.

The above-mentioned remedies are far from having been completely developed by the Permanent Court, in the past, by the International Court, presently, and by academic writings. This conclusion is substantiated by the fact that, in accordance with the jurisprudence of the Court, states, and the judicial body, are more comfortable with requesting and granting declaratory relief. This is perhaps because the system in which the Court activates takes due consideration not only of legal relationships but of political ones as well. The impact of the political relationship between states is justified in these circumstances, considering that the Court is the principal judicial body of the UN. As such, generally, the Court does not pursue a coercive approach to order actions, but rather decides upon the legality of a certain approach, allowing states to pursue, through diplomatic mechanisms, the manner in which the situation, as it existed prior to the occurrence of the internationally wrongful act, would be restored.

Another relevant issue that has arisen before the Court, and which has contributed to the current understanding of remedies, is that states often request multiple remedies. The manner in which the above-mentioned remedies interact with each other is also relevant for their proper interpretation. The book describes and clarifies the particularities of the remedies of international law available before the International Court.

3 THE OUTLINE

The book is divided into nine chapters that assess the contemporary interpretation of each remedy of international law, with the aim to provide an overview of the manner in which they are understood and applied before the Court. Presently, the Court applies a determined set of remedies, which contain several characteristics that have evolved due to their interpretation and clarification. Generally, the Court follows the framework of the ILC Articles, in the

---

[23] *Case concerning Military and Paramilitary Activities in and against Nicaragua (Nicaragua v USA)* (Merits) [1986] ICJ Rep 14.

[24] *Lighthouses Case between France and Greece (France v Greece)* (Judgment) [1934] PCIJ Series A/B No. 62, 312.

[25] *Case concerning the Payment of Various Serbian Loans in France (France v Yugoslavia)* [1929] PCIJ Rep Series A, No. 20.

[26] *Diplomatic and Consular Staff in Tehran (USA v Iran)* (Judgment).

sense that the remedies provided therein are found within the judgments of the Court. Nevertheless, the Court has its own perspective regarding the application of the remedies provided by the ILC.

As such, the structure of the book follows, in general lines, the procedure before the Court and the remedies provided by the ILC Articles. It will firstly focus on issues regarding the jurisdiction of the Court to give judgment regarding the applicable remedies (Chapter 1). Secondly, it will assess the availability of remedies at the provisional measures stage (Chapter 2). Following these two procedural chapters, the book focuses on the substantial analysis of the remedies of international law. The remedies that are most versatile in their application and interpretation – the declaratory judgment and specific performance – which have been granted by the Court of Justice in the majority of the cases that were submitted to these judicial bodies, shall be firstly addressed. In other words, the next two chapters focus on the remedies that are well represented before the Court. Chapter 3 shall focus on declaratory judgments and Chapter 4 on specific performance. The next chapters address the more coercive remedies of cessation and assurances and guarantees of non-repetition (Chapter 5), restitution in kind (Chapter 6) and compensation (Chapter 7). Lastly, satisfaction, and its characteristics, is evaluated (Chapter 8). This chapter completes the spectrum of the remedies of international law applied by the Court, it being the remedy that is most unclear with respect to the form in which the judicial body applies it. The chapters that focus on the remedies of international law from a substantial point of view are structured in two sections. The first (Section 2.2, 3.2 and so on – Theoretical Perspectives) will address the manner in which the doctrine has interpreted the remedies of international law, as applied by the Court, from a theoretical point of view. The second (Section 2.3, 3.3 and so on – Practical Perspectives) will focus on the practice of the judicial body, by addressing requests of states and judgments of the Court. The justification of this two-pronged structure is designed so as to demonstrate the convergences and divergences between the theoretical and practical perspectives on the interpretation and clarification of the remedies of international law. A final chapter (Chapter 9) addresses the manner in which the judgments of other courts and tribunals influenced the clarification of the remedies of international law, as applied by the International Court of Justice.

1

Jurisdiction

1.1 INTRODUCTION

States often challenged the jurisdiction of the judicial body to grant remedies, especially at the historical beginning of the activity of the Permanent Court. In this sense, a recurrent issue raised by applicant states was whether the Court had the jurisdiction to grant a particular remedy, in situations in which states did not provide an instrument that would confer such powers to it. The nature of its competence to give judgment on the remedies of international law, in cases in which its jurisdiction is derived from an agreement that does not include any provision in this respect, merits brief assessment, as without such competence the Court might not have the power to resolve the dispute in a final manner. Commentators have concluded that Article 36(2) of the Statute of the Court provides that states can recognise its competence, regarding the nature and extent of reparation,[2] and that, in such a situation, the scope of the power of the Court to grant remedies is not necessarily defined in international law.[3]

Evidently, it is possible for states to include a provision in a treaty granting the Court the power to order a remedy in case of a breach of an international obligation. Even if the scope of the Courts' power to order remedies is not necessarily clear in international law generally, the Permanent Court and the International Court have manifested clear views regarding their competence to grant remedies, even in the absence of an agreement in this respect.

---

[1] Gray, Judicial Remedies in International Law, 59.

[2] Malcolm N. Shaw, 'The International Court, Responsibility and Remedies' in Malgosia Fitzmaurice and Dan Sarooshi (eds), *Issues of State Responsibility before International Judicial Institutions* (Hart Publishing 2004) 19, 21.

[3] Shaw, 'The International Court, Responsibility and Remedies' 19, 21.

1.2 THE PERMANENT COURT OF INTERNATIONAL JUSTICE

The Permanent Court first addressed, albeit implicitly, the issue regarding its jurisdiction to grant remedies in the 'Wimbledon' Case.[4] It delivered a judgment that included an order for compensation within its dispositif, even though the treaty did not contain any express provision related to remedies.[5] In its later judgments, it reached the same conclusion regarding its power to order reparation. Illustratively, the case concerning the Free Zones of Upper Savoy and District of Gex[6] is similar in this respect, as the Permanent Court issued an order through which it concluded that the responding state should perform certain acts in order to fulfil its international obligations.[7]

Though the Permanent Court had previously granted remedies in disputes where the underlying treaty was silent in this respect, it was in the Chorzów Factory Case that the Permanent Court concluded, as a matter of principle, that it has the power to order remedies. This case is one of the first in which the issue of jurisdiction to order remedies was legally addressed by the Permanent Court. Here, Poland argued that the clause through which the parties agreed to refer the dispute to the Court did not provide for remedies and that, therefore, their consent did not extend to granting remedies.[8] Poland, thus, interpreted the dispute resolution clause in a restrictive manner, and requested the Permanent Court to approach the issue accordingly. The Court decided to pursue a different path, and concluded that the parties to the dispute did not need to include a provision regarding its competence to grant remedies because *'it is a principle of international law, and even a general conception of law, that any breach of an engagement involves an obligation to make reparation'.*[9] The Permanent Court further analysed the potential negative effects of a restrictive interpretation, and found that an isolated decision on a point of law, without a subsequent judgment regarding reparation, would amplify the dispute rather than resolve it, thus creating the possibility of future disputes.[10]

---

[4] *S.S. 'Wimbledon'* (*Great Britain et al v Germany*).
[5] *S.S. 'Wimbledon'* (*Great Britain et al v Germany*) 33.
[6] *Free Zones of Upper Savoy and District of Gex* (*France v Switzerland*) (Judgment) [1932] PCIJ Rep Series A/B No. 46.
[7] *Free Zones of Upper Savoy and District of Gex* (*France v Switzerland*) (Judgment) [1932] PCIJ Rep Series A/B No. 46, 80.
[8] *Factory at Chorzow* (*Germany v Poland*) (Jurisdiction) 20.
[9] *Factory at Chorzow* (*Germany v Poland*) (Merits) 29.
[10] *Factory at Chorzow* (*Germany v Poland*) (Jurisdiction) 25.

1.3 The International Court

The conclusion reached in the Chorzów Factory Case was that the jurisdiction to resolve a particular dispute implies the jurisdiction to resolve and determine any related issues involving the applicable remedies. In other words, not only is the Court empowered to state whether a certain remedy was applicable as reparation, but it also has the competence to determine if, in that case, reparation is due.[11]

1.3 THE INTERNATIONAL COURT

The conclusion that the Court has implicit jurisdiction to grant remedies has been maintained and confirmed throughout its jurisprudence, in cases in which the question was raised by responding states, for similar arguments to the ones in the Chorzów Factory Case. One such example is the Corfu Channel Case, in which Albania requested the Court to find that it had the jurisdiction to decide on the available remedies, but that it did not have the power to decide upon the specific amounts due. In other words, Albania argued that the Court had partial jurisdiction to declare that compensation was due, but that it lacked the jurisdiction to decide upon the quantum of the compensation. The Court rejected this argument and concluded that, should it accept it, an important part of the dispute would not be fully resolved.[12] The reasoning of the International Court in the Corfu Channel Case was, therefore, not as drastic as that of the Permanent Court in the Chorzów Factory Case, which concluded that a decision devoid of remedies would amplify the dispute. This approach has been maintained throughout the years, in cases such as the Iranian Hostages Case,[13] the Nicaragua Case[14] and the Right of Passage Case.[15]

While this issue has arisen in different forms, the Court has constantly reiterated its finding from the Chorzów Factory Case, that the jurisdiction to resolve the dispute implies the jurisdiction to decide issues regarding reparation. Perhaps the most unequivocal statement is seen in the Nicaragua Case, in which the Court bluntly concluded that '[i]n general, jurisdiction to determine the merits of a dispute entails jurisdiction to determine reparation'.[16]

---

[11] Factory at Chorzow (Germany v Poland) (Jurisdiction) 33.

[12] Corfu Channel Case (Great Britain v Albania) (Merits) 26.

[13] Diplomatic and Consular Staff in Tehran (USA v Iran) (Judgment).

[14] Military and Paramilitary Activities in and against Nicaragua (Nicaragua v USA) (Merits).

[15] Case concerning Right of Passage over Indian Territory (Portugal v India) (Merits) [1960] ICJ Rep 6.

[16] Military and Paramilitary Activities in and against Nicaragua (Nicaragua v USA) (Merits) 142.

1.4 CONCLUSION

Even if the jurisdiction of the Permanent Court and of the International Court to grant the remedies of international law has been challenged in the past, presently this issue is settled. The Court has the competence to give judgment on the remedies of international law, in situations in which the agreement of the parties is silent in this respect.

As such, the Court has the inherent jurisdiction to grant remedies, to decide on the specific manner in which a remedy is capable of restoring the status quo ante, and on the manner in which said remedy should be implemented by states. This outcome is, to a certain degree, an exception from the principle of consent, as it implies that the agreement of states regarding the remedies of international law is presumed by the judicial body. Nevertheless, this presumption is not absolute, and states have the possibility to derogate from it, through a specific reference in their agreement. In other words, there is nothing in the jurisprudence of the Court that would lead to the conclusion that states do not have the possibility to opt out of the application of certain remedies of international law.

As such, the necessary conclusion is that, generally, the dictum of the Chorzów Factory Case is applicable, in the sense that the Court has an inherent competence to decide on the application of the remedies of international law, in cases in which special agreements or compromissory clauses are unclear. However, if the said instruments are clear in the sense that states agreed to exclude the application of any given remedy, the Court would necessarily observe the principle of consent.

2

Provisional Measures

2.1 INTRODUCTION

The competence of the Court to grant provisional measures is provided through Article 41 of its Statute, which prescribes that the judicial body has the power to indicate, *'if it considers that circumstances so require, any provisional measures which ought to be taken to preserve the respective rights of either party'*. The above-mentioned provision allows the Court to apply the necessary mechanisms that would preserve the rights of the parties. The procedure related to provisional measures is further regulated through Article 61 of the Rules of the International Court, which contains provisions similar to Article 41 of its Statute. It is relevant to note, in this sense, that the Institute of International Law has issued a Draft Resolution through which it concluded that *'the availability of provisional and protective measures is a general principle of law in international law and national law'*.[1] Further, commentators have concluded that *'the indication of provisional measures constitutes in itself a form of remedy'*,[2] inasmuch as the orders provided by the Court in this respect have binding effect. Nevertheless, orders containing provisional measures might include, at times, the remedies of international law, prescribed through the ILC Articles.

It should be noted, from the outset, that the International Court has concluded, through its Practice Direction XI, that it *'has noticed the increasing tendency of parties to request the indication of provisional measures'*.[3] In this context, one issue that remains is whether the orders for provisional measures

---

[1] Yearbook of Institute of International Law – Session of Hyderabad 2017, vol 78, Deliberations, 3.

[2] Juan Jose Quintana, *Litigation at the International Court of Justice: Practice and Procedure* (Brill/Nijhoff 2015) 656.

[3] Press Release of the ICJ No. 2004/20, Annex, 1.

issued by the Court can include the remedies of international law, and if so, what remedies might fulfil the scope of this procedural mechanism. The question is relevant especially because this procedure is an exceptional one,[4] and characterised by the diligence of the Court not to prejudge the merits of the case.[5] As such, a brief assessment of its competence to grant remedies of international law, through orders of provisional measures, is relevant.

2.2 THE PERMANENT COURT OF INTERNATIONAL JUSTICE

One case regarding the application of the remedies of international law, through orders for provisional measures, is the Chorzów Factory Case. In this instance, Germany sought compensation as a mechanism through which its rights would be preserved, and requested the Court to order an interim measure, in the form of a *'sum to be paid immediately'*.[6] The justification of this claim was that if the sum would not be paid, as an interim measure of protection, the amounts that would result from the breaches of international law would increase and the prejudice caused would become irreparable.[7]

The question that the Permanent Court had to answer, in these circumstances, was whether this remedy of international law had the capability to preserve the rights of the state claiming it. Its answer was in the negative, in the sense that compensation could not be ordered as a provisional measure, as, in this case, it would equate to an interim judgment in favour of one of the parties.[8] Thus, it could be concluded that the Court may not grant remedies of international law at the provisional measures stage, if the order granting it would amount to an interim judgment. There is no definitive argument of the Permanent Court that would lead to the conclusion that compensation is not applicable de plano, as a mechanism through which an order for provisional measures could be granted, even if it would seem that compensation is not a suitable remedy to be granted as a provisional measure.

---

[4] Cameron A Miles, *Provisional Measures before International Courts and Tribunals* (Cambridge University Press 2017) 476.

[5] Inna Uchkunova, 'Provisional Measures before the International Court of Justice' (2013) 12:3 Law and Practice of International Courts and Tribunals 396.

[6] *Factory at Chorzów (Germany v Poland)*, Request for an Interim Measure of Protection of 14 October 1927, 6.

[7] *Factory at Chorzów (Germany v Poland)*, Request for an Interim Measure of Protection of 14 October 1927, 6.

[8] *Case concerning the Factory at Chorzów (Germany v Poland)* (Order) Measure on Interim Protection [1927], 10.

As such, subject to the limitation prescribed by the Court in the Chorzów Factory Case, the Permanent Court has issued several orders for provisional measures, the Sino-Belgian Treaty Case, in which the Court concluded that certain measures of interim protection related to nationals, property and shipping and judicial safeguards should be granted,[9] being an example that confirms the power of the Court to grant remedies of international law as safeguards of rights.

2.3 THE INTERNATIONAL COURT

Generally, the power of the Court to grant provisional measures does not deserve special analysis. Nevertheless, it is important to note, at this juncture, that the first case in which the Court granted provisional relief was the Anglo-Iranian Oil Co Case, in which the meaning of Article 41 of its statute was clarified in the following terms:

> Whereas the object of interim measures of protection provided for in the Statute is to preserve the respective rights of the Parties pending the decision of the Court, and whereas from the general terms of Article 41 of the Statute and from the power recognized by Article 61, paragraph 6, of the Rules of Court, to indicate interim measures of protection proprio mottu, it follows that the Court must be concerned to preserve, by such measures, the rights which may be subsequently adjudged by the Court to belong either to the Applicant or to the Respondent.[10]

The issuance of an order for provisional measures is, therefore, left at the discretion of the Court and, as such, its justifications are not necessarily limited by the submissions of the parties. The case-law of the Court is vast in its granting of provisional measures. As such, in the following subsections, relevant findings of the Court regarding the application of the remedies of international law at the provisional measures shall be analysed.

2.3.1 The Binding Effect of Orders for Provisional Measures

The increase in requesting provisional measures is justified, to a certain degree, by the finding of the International Court in the LaGrand Case, through which it concluded, for the first time, that its orders for provisional

---

[9] Denunciation of the Treaty of 2 November 1865 between China and Belgium (Belgium v China) (Order on Provisional Measures) [1927] PCIJ Rep, 7–8.

[10] Anglo-Iranian Oil Co Case (United Kingdom v Iran) (Request for Provisional Measures) [1951] ICJ Rep, 93.

measures have binding effect. The arguments of the USA in this sense are relevant from the perspective of the remedies of international law, as the binding nature of such an order is linked with the measures of redress granted by the Court. As such, the USA requested the Court to conclude that *an order of the International Court indicating provisional measures is not binding and does not furnish a basis for judicial relief*.[11] This distinction is relevant because an order granting remedies of international law, which is not binding, might prove procedurally irrelevant, as states receiving it could ignore its findings. Assessing the questions posed by the parties in this sense, the International Court concluded that its orders for provisional measures have binding effect, and that this conclusion is in line with the interpretation of Article 41 of its Statute, in accordance with the VCLT.[12]

This finding of the Court represents a clear precedent[13] in this respect, as it has acted as an important clarification in the sense that the judicial body has the competence to order binding provisional measures. As mentioned, the result of this finding is that an order for provisional measures may include remedies of international law, which must be performed by the state breaching an international obligation, in order to preserve the rights that the Court adjudicates at the merits stage.

2.3.2 Orders for Provisional Measures Granting Remedies of International Law

Once established that compensation is not necessarily applicable as a remedy contained in orders for provisional measures, as long as it would lead to an interim judgment, it is worth mentioning, at this juncture, that the International Court has granted, throughout its case-law, several remedies of international law which, in the Courts' view, contributed to the preservation of the rights of the parties in dispute. The Court has granted restitution in kind through its provisional measure order in the Tehran Hostages Case, in which the applicant requested the issuance of an order for provisional measures, in the following terms:

> *That the Government of Iran immediately release all hostages of United States nationality and facilitate the prompt and safe departure from Iran of these*

[11] *LaGrand Case (Germany v USA)* (Judgment) [2001] ICJ Rep 466, 479.
[12] *LaGrand Case (Germany v USA)* (Judgment) [2001] ICJ Rep 506.
[13] Jorg Kammerhofer, 'The Binding Nature of Provisional Measures of the International Court of Justice: The "Settlement" of the Issue in the LaGrand Case' (2003) 16 Leiden Journal of International Law 67.

2.3 The International Court

persons and all other United States officials in dignified and humane circumstances.[14]

The Court granted the request of the applicant and concluded that the Republic of Iran should ensure that the premises of the Embassy of the USA are restored to its possession and that all persons of its nationality should be immediately released.[15]

Cessation has also been ordered by the Court, through orders for provisional measures. Illustratively, in the case concerning Military and Paramilitary Activities in and against Nicaragua, the applicant requested that the Court grants cessation by declaring and ordering that the USA should *'immediately cease and desist'*[16] from breaching its international obligations and that it should perform certain acts in this sense. The Court granted the request of the applicant state and unanimously decided that the USA should *'immediately cease and refrain from any action restricting, blocking or endangering access to or from Nicaraguan ports, and, in particular, the laying of mines'.*[17]

In the same manner in which the Court granted restitution in kind and cessation, at the provisional measures stage of the dispute, the Court has also issued orders through which it granted specific performance. One case in which this remedy was granted is the Avena Case, in which the applicant requested the Court to find that the obligations and rights contained in Article 36 of the VCCR were breached and to order the USA to perform the said obligations, pending its judgment on the merits.[18] The Court accepted the arguments raised by the applicant and issued its order on provisional measures, unanimously.[19]

As such, a brief conclusion regarding the jurisprudence of the Court regarding the application of remedies at the provisional measures stage would

---

[14] *United States Diplomatic and Consular Staff in Tehran (USA v Iran)*, Request for the Indication of Provisional Measures of Protection Submitted by the Government of the USA [1979], 12.

[15] *United States Diplomatic and Consular Staff in Tehran (USA v Iran)*, Order for Provisional Measures [1979], 21.

[16] *Military and Paramilitary Activities in and against Nicaragua (Nicaragua v USA)*, Request for the Indication of Provisional Measures of Protection Submitted by the Government of Nicaragua [1984], 29.

[17] *Military and Paramilitary Activities in and against Nicaragua (Nicaragua v USA)*, Order for Provisional Measures [1984], 22.

[18] *Avena and Other Mexican Nationals (Mexico v USA)*, Request for the Indication of Provisional Measures of Protection Submitted by the Government of the United Mexican States, 8.

[19] *Avena and Other Mexican Nationals (Mexico v USA)*, Provisional Measures, Order of 5 February 2003, [2003] ICJ Rep 96, 19.

18   2 Provisional Measures

be that it has the power to order, with a binding character, any remedy of
international law that is capable of preserving the rights of states throughout
the resolution of their disputes before the judicial body, as long as through
such an order it does not issue an interim award.

2.3.3 Remedies for Breaching Orders for Provisional Measures

A relevant question answered by the Court relates to the remedies of international law applicable for breaching orders for provisional measures. The
locus classicus in which the Court answered this question is the judgment of
the Court in the Application of Genocide Convention, in which the applicant
requested the Court to conclude that reparation is due for a breach of its
orders regarding provisional measures. In this context, it could be reasonably
concluded that the explicit finding regarding the binding character of orders
for provisional measures of protection, pronounced by the Court in its judgment of the LaGrand Case, was foreseen within its prior jurisprudence.

It is relevant to point out, at this juncture, that in the mentioned Genocide
Convention Case, the Court had issued two orders for provisional measures.
The order issued by the Court on the date of 8 April 1993 contained the
remedies of specific performance and cessation,[20] while the order issued by
the Court on the date of 13 September 1993 contained the remedy of specific
performance. In these circumstances, the Court concluded that it was its
previous order that should be immediately and effectively implemented and
not the obligations contained in the Genocide Convention.[21] Bosnia
requested the Court to determine that the responding state breached its
previous orders through which it granted binding provisional measures.
Further, in similar terms to the ones raised by Germany in the Chorzów
Factory Case, Bosnia requested the International Court to order the remedy of
compensation for breaches of its order for provisional measures, as a means to
provide symbolic reparation, the specific amounts to be determined by the
Court.[22] It could be concluded that the above-mentioned request is, in fact,

---

[20] *Case concerning Application of the Convention on the Prevention and Punishment of the Crime
of Genocide (Bosnia and Herzegovina v Serbia and Montenegro)*, Provisional Measures, Order
of 8 April 1993, [1993] ICJ Rep 15.

[21] *Case concerning Application of the Convention on the Prevention and Punishment of the Crime
of Genocide (Bosnia and Herzegovina v Serbia and Montenegro)*, Provisional Measures, Order
of 13 September 1993, [1993] ICJ Rep 28–29.

[22] *Case concerning Application of the Convention on the Prevention and Punishment of the Crime
of Genocide (Bosnia and Herzegovina v Serbia and Montenegro)*, [2007] ICJ Rep 33.

not a request for compensation but for pecuniary satisfaction. The Court reached the following conclusion regarding the effects of the breach of its orders granting provisional measures.

> *The Court will however include in the operative clause of the present Judgment, by way of satisfaction, a declaration that the Respondent has failed to comply with the Court's Orders indicating provisional measures.*[23]

The Courts' finding confirms the view that satisfaction was, in fact, applicable in this case, albeit not in a monetary form, but in the more established manner provided by the Court in the Corfu Channel Case. The Court, therefore, presently appreciates that symbolic damages cannot be granted for breaches of its provisional orders. This finding is in line with the jurisprudence of the Court regarding the remedy of compensation for moral damages caused directly to states, even if in this particular instance the moral damages which originated from the breaches of its order through which it granted provisional measures could have been caused to individuals as well, as long as the obligations contained in the applicable treaties referred to genocide.

2.4 CONCLUSION

The procedure that allows states to request, and the Court to grant, orders containing provisional measures of protection is currently established, and it is not necessarily controversial. Nevertheless, the interpretation, clarification and application of the remedies of international law at this procedural stage are not without controversy. First, the jurisprudence of the Court demonstrates that a rather secondary function of the remedies of international law is that of preserving the rights of the parties, pending the judgment of the Court on the merits of the case. Second, it is currently rather unclear whether all the remedies prescribed through the ILC Articles have the potential to preserve the rights of states. While the Court has ordered restitution in kind, cessation or specific performance, as capable remedies, it is for its future judgments to determine whether other remedies such as compensation or assurances and guarantees of non-repetition might be included in the scope of its orders for provisional measures. It is also apparent that the breaches of the Courts' orders

---

[23] *Case concerning Application of the Convention on the Prevention and Punishment of the Crime of Genocide (Bosnia and Herzegovina v Serbia and Montenegro)*, [2007] ICJ Rep 33, 197.

for provisional measures are currently repaired through declaratory relief, rather than more coercive remedies such as compensation. Nevertheless, there is nothing in the jurisprudence of the Court that would lead to the conclusion that coercive remedies are not available for breaches of orders granting provisional measures.

3

Declaratory Judgments

3.1 INTRODUCTION

The declaratory judgment is the most versatile remedy that states request when submitting a dispute before the Court, mainly because it has the potential to play multiple roles.[1] The versatility of this remedy led commentators to conclude that it is the most common remedy sought before the Court and further rendered in its judgments.[2] This conclusion is relevant, because states often include requests for declaratory judgments within their prayers of relief, as the sole remedy or in conjunction with others, such as restitution in kind, specific performance or compensation. This versatility has led commentators to conclude that the *word "declare" is content free and a declaratory judgment may be directed to almost any subject or object imaginable*.[3] This inherent flexibility of the declaratory judgment could be the reason for which it has been labelled by some commentators as convenient but unreliable.[4] This conclusion might have arisen because declaratory relief is the most requested remedy before the Court for various types of disputes, which range from territorial cases to cases addressing expropriation. Other authors conclude that the declaratory judgment is an appropriate remedy in international law because it brings balance between third-party dispute settlement and state sovereignty,[5] especially in cases in which injury is directly caused to states.[6]

---

[1] Quintana, Litigation at the International Court, 1167.
[2] Gray, Judicial Remedies in International Law, 96.
[3] Juliette McIntyre, 'Declaratory Judgments of the International Court of Justice' (2012) 25 Hague Yearbook of International Law 107–108.
[4] Ian Brownlie, 'Remedies in the International Court of Justice' in Robert Yewdall Jennings, Vaughn Lowe and Malgosia Fitzmaurice (eds), *Fifty Years of the International Court of Justice: Essays in Honour of Sir Robert Jennings* (Cambridge University Press 1996) 559.
[5] Gray, Judicial Remedies in International Law, 98.
[6] Gray, Judicial Remedies in International Law, 99.

Nevertheless, the interpretation of the declaratory judgment might meet the same fate as other remedies: being dogged by controversy regarding its substance.

Declaratory relief is the remedy that applicant states frequently seek before the Court, as the wide majority of the disputes contained requests for this remedy. Further, the judicial body itself seems most comfortable with rendering declaratory judgments, rather than coercive remedies, such as restitution in kind or compensation. The instrument through which the Court is seized with the dispute is relevant for providing the perspective of the states, because, at the initiation of proceedings stage, the judicial activity of the Court is incipient. The special agreement or the unilateral application represent the first acts through which states refer, in a general manner, to the remedies applicable to their claims. Article 40(1) of the Statute provides the procedural means through which states seize it, either through a notification of the special agreement or through a written unilateral application. These two mechanisms impact the manner in which the dispute unfolds before the Court. It is significant that, from the outset, states reach an agreement related to the existence and scope of their dispute. In this situation, they are able to find common ground regarding the resolution of their contradictory views towards a certain factual and legal situation.[7] The consensus of the parties related to the necessity of resolving a determined dispute through the International Court instils a positive[8] and cooperative relationship between the states involved.

This is one reason for which cases brought before the Court through the notification of a special agreement are procedurally less complicated than cases initiated through a unilateral application. Since states have already reached agreement prior to the Court being seized of their dispute, the procedure is not interrupted, for instance, by preliminary objections towards the jurisdiction of the Court. Similarly, the way in which the parties frame their requests regarding the remedies is influenced by the fact that they have reached an agreement regarding certain aspects of their dispute. Further, the subject matter of the dispute is also relevant to the analysis of the remedies that are sought by states. Thus, certain matters call for requests for restitution in kind, and others for compensation, satisfaction or specific performance. Nevertheless, most of them seem to call for declaratory relief, which are best

---

[7] Shabtai Rosenne, *The Law and Practice of the International Court 1920–2005* vol 2 (4th edn, Martinus Nijhoff Publishers 2006) 168.

[8] Peter Tomka, 'The Special Agreement' in Nisuke Ando, Edward McWhinney and Rüdiger Wolfrum (eds), *Judge Shigeru Oda: Liber Amicorum* vol 1 (Kluwer Law International 2002) 691.

3.2 Theoretical Perspectives

categorised as i) declarations of rights, ii) declarations of title and iii) declarations of responsibility.[9]

3.2 THEORETICAL PERSPECTIVES

3.2.1 Declaratory Judgments and the Statute of the Court

The Statute of the International Court defines its judicial function without expressly mentioning the remedies it can apply through its judgments. However, a wide interpretation of the Statute could lead to the conclusion that the Court has discretionary power regarding the mechanism through which it decides to resolve the dispute, including by means of a declaratory judgment, if considered appropriate.[10] The competence of the Court to grant remedies is prescribed through Article 36 paragraph 2 of the Statute, which provides that it can give judgment with respect to the interpretation of a treaty, to any question of international law, to the existence of any fact, which would constitute a breach of an international obligation and to the nature and extent of reparation for the breach thereof. The power to issue declaratory judgments also stems from Article 38 of the Statute, which provides that the Court can *'decide, in accordance with international law such disputes as are submitted to it'*. Further, Article 59 prescribes that *'the decision of the Court has no binding force except between the parties and in respect of that particular case'*. These provisions do not specifically address the remedies that lie within the Court's jurisdiction and, hence, arguments might be raised against its competence to grant declaratory relief. It could also be asserted that a declaratory judgment is too abstract to be considered a remedy, the argument in this sense being that a declaratory judgment could not have res judicata effect, as prescribed by Article 59 of the Statute of the Court. Objections of this nature have been resolved by the Permanent Court.[11] The International Court has addressed similar objections,[12] and concluded that it cannot be disputed that it can deliver declaratory judgments, in certain cases.

The conclusion provided by the Permanent Court in the Chorzów Factory Case is relevant in this respect, as in this case it concluded that the scope of a declaratory judgment is the recognition of a situation of law, *'once and for all,*

---

[9] McIntyre, 'Declaratory Judgments' 131.

[10] Tomka, 'The Special Agreement' 691.

[11] *Certain German Interests in Polish Upper Silesia (Germany v Poland) (Merits) [1926] PCIJ Series A, No. 7,* 4, 18–19.

[12] *Case concerning the Northern Cameroons (Cameroon v United Kingdom) (Preliminary Objections) [1963] ICJ Rep* 37.

and with binding force'.[13] The Permanent Court also held, in the Polish Upper Silesia Case, that Article 59 does not exclude declaratory judgments.[14] Authors have confirmed this finding and concluded that the possibility of a judgment of the Court to entail a purely declaratory nature is foreseen in Article 63 and Article 36 of the Statute of the Court.[15] To sum up, the fact that the declaratory judgment is a remedy under international law cannot be validly challenged,[16] as it represents a mechanism through which the Court brings the disputes submitted before it to an end.

3.2.2 *The Definition and Function of Declaratory Judgments*

The declaratory judgment has been defined as being *'a jurisdictional decision interpreting a point of law, independently of the concrete consequences of that interpretation in the circumstances of a particular case'.*[17] Commentators have concluded that the declaratory judgment is a veritable act of dispute settlement, which has res judicata effect and, thus, resolves disputes.[18] This latter definition is preferable, as it identifies the elements that a declaratory judgment has and clearly distinguishes it from an advisory opinion. In this context, the main characteristic of the declaratory judgment is not that it interprets points of law, as the first definition might suggest, but that it resolves legal disputes, as suggested by the latter definition.

The main function of the declaratory judgment is that it confirms the pre-existing rights of states, with no coercive decree.[19] The fact that the declaratory judgment does not necessarily have a coercive character, in the sense that it does not always imply a specific act on behalf of the disputing states, does not take away from its efficacy as a remedy. As mentioned above, by virtue of Article 59 of the Statute of the International Court, the declaratory judgment is binding upon the parties in the dispute, even if it does not have an executory character.

---

[13] *Case concerning the Interpretation of Judgments nos. 7 and 8 concerning the Case of the Factory at Chorzów (Germany v Poland)* [1927] PCIJ Rep Series A No. 13, 37.

[14] Shabtai Rosenne, *The Law and Practice of the International Court 1920–2005* vol. 1 (4th edn, Martinus Nijhoff Publishers 2006) 1579.

[15] Quintana, Litigation at the International Court, 1167.

[16] McIntyre, 'Declaratory Judgments' 109.

[17] Hersch Lauterpacht, *The Development of International Law by the International Court* (Cambridge University Press 1982) 250–252.

[18] McIntyre, 'Declaratory Judgments' 131.

[19] Edwin Borchard, 'The Declaratory Judgment – A Needed Procedural Reform' (1918) 28 Yale Law Journal 105, 149 (as cited in McIntyre, 'Declaratory Judgments' 107, 113).

3.2.3 Types of Declaratory Judgments

Some authors consider that declaratory relief is often abused,[20] in the sense that states often characterise as declaratory their claims related to first-stage proceedings, legal entitlements, acts of implementation of an award, satisfaction or applicable principles. Other authors have categorised declaratory judgments by stating that through this mechanism the Court clarifies '(i) the meaning of certain legal norms, (ii) the significance of certain facts in relation to the applicable law, (iii) the legal scope and bearing of a given situation or (iv) the rights and obligations of the parties involved in a particular legal relationship.'[21]

The above-mentioned categorisations seem convoluted in certain respects, as they endeavour to cover a wide variety of rights and obligations involved in defining this remedy. As such, a general, broader categorisation would be more suitable. In this respect, other commentators[22] have concluded that declaratory judgments can be divided into three main categories: i) declarations of rights or title; ii) declarations of applicable law and iii) declarations of responsibility.

3.2.4 Declaratory Judgments and Other Remedies

The interaction between declaratory judgments and other remedies is of relevance for the determination of its characteristics. Often, states seek declarations of illegality, from the International Court, in conjunction with other remedies such as compensation or restitution in kind. This approach towards declaratory judgments has led to relevant conclusions in this respect, provided below.

3.2.4.1 Declaratory Judgments and Compensation

The declaratory judgment did not have the nature of a separate remedy in the disputes submitted before the Permanent Court.[23] The reasoning behind this approach was that declaratory judgments were interpreted as judicial determinations with a preliminary character. Authors have concluded, in this respect, that in decisions granting coercive remedies such as damages, the

---

[20] Brownlie, 'Remedies in the International Court of Justice' 560.
[21] Robert Kolb, *The International Court of Justice* (Hart Publishing 2013) 755.
[22] McIntyre, 'Declaratory Judgments' 132.
[23] Gray, Judicial Remedies in International Law, 97.

first stage was the determination of responsibility, through a declaratory judgment, and the second was the assessment of reparation.[24]

Nevertheless, even if in certain cases states request declaratory relief at the preliminary stage, this procedural circumstance should not lead to the conclusion that this remedy cannot exist by itself. An example that confirms this conclusion is that in the majority of cases that were referred to the Court by means of a notification of a special agreement, the parties jointly requested the Court to exclusively deliver declaratory judgments.[25] Consequently, the declaratory judgment, even if used at a separate stage by most states, should not be interpreted as being strictly preliminary, since this stage is independent from the future procedural steps related to monetary relief.

It should be noted, at this juncture, that the relationship between declaratory judgments and requests for more coercive remedies is not the same as the relationship between the preliminary objections stage and the merits stage. If the declaratory judgment is interpreted as being limited to the stage where the existence of responsibility is determined,[26] a relevant conclusion would necessarily be that this stage is primary rather than preliminary and the stage related to monetary compensation is auxiliary. Thus, the first determination that the Court must make in order to grant compensation or restitution is a finding of illegality, or, as the ILC Articles provide, a finding regarding the existence of an internationally wrongful act committed by a state.[27] In this context, it has been correctly stated that the declaratory judgment represents a remedy for which the Court and the parties work, during the proceedings and after the judgment is given.[28] Consequently, it is the monetary relief stage that cannot stand on its own, without a declaratory judgment regarding the existence of international responsibility.

---

[24] Gray, Judicial Remedies in International Law, 97.

[25] *The Minquiers and Ecrehos Case (France v United Kingdom)* (Judgment) [1953] ICJ Rep 47; *Case concerning Sovereignty over certain Frontier Land (Belgium v Netherlands)* (Judgment) [1959] ICJ Rep 209; *Sovereignty over Pulau Ligitan and Pulau Sipadan (Indonesia v Malaysia)* (Judgment) [2001] ICJ Rep 575; *Frontier Dispute (Benin/Niger)* (Judgment) [2005] ICJ Rep 90; *Frontier Dispute* (Burkina Faso/Republic of Mali) (Judgment) [1986] ICJ Rep 554; *Sovereignty over Pedra Branca/Pulau Batu Puteh, Middle Rocks and South Ledge (Malaysia/Singapore)* (Judgment) [2008] ICJ Rep 12; *North Sea Continental Shelf (Germany/Netherlands and Germany/Denmark)* (Judgment) [1969] ICJ Rep 3; *Continental Shelf (Tunisia/Libyan Arab Jamahiriya)* (Judgment) [1982] ICJ Rep 18; *Continental Shelf (Libyan Arab Jamahiriya v Malta)* (Judgment) [1985] ICJ Rep 13; *Kasikili/Sedudu Island (Botswana v Namibia)* (Judgment) [1999] ICJ Rep 1045.

[26] Gray, Judicial Remedies in International Law, 98.

[27] ILC, '2001 Articles on Responsibility of States for Internationally Wrongful Acts', UN Doc A/56/83 (2001).

[28] Kolb, The International Court of Justice, 755.

A telling example is the Mavrommatis Case, in which *'the Court decided that as there had not been any loss to M. Mavrommatis, the claim for damages must fail'*[29] and granted declaratory relief,[30] determining, albeit indirectly, that a declaratory judgment was sufficient for resolving the dispute. As a consequence, the declaration regarding the existence of responsibility is a veritable remedy of international law, which is not restricted in its interpretation or application by material consequences, such as compensation or restitution in kind.[31]

3.2.4.2 Declaratory Judgments and Specific Performance

As highlighted in the previous section, a declaratory judgment is a complete remedy under international law[32] and is independent from a request for damages or restitution in kind. To reiterate, the role of the Court is to resolve *'legal disputes'* in accordance with Article 38 of its Statute and therefore, any declaratory judgment of the Court is binding as provided by Article 59 of the Statute. Two strands of opinion exist with respect to the possibility of the declaratory judgment to prescribe future behaviours of states. One argues that the declaratory judgment should contain an inherent obligation which would provide that states should act in a certain manner. The other argues that a declaratory judgment can be issued without the need for prescribing future acts.

Several arguments have been expressed regarding the power of the International Court to prescribe a certain behaviour within the declaratory judgments' dispositif. In this respect, a prescriptive declaratory judgment might be interpreted as embodying certain characteristics of restitution in kind, specific performance or other coercive remedies. The Court, on occasion, has included in the dispositif of its judgments the conduct that should follow the rendering of a declaratory award. For instance, in the case concerning the Temple of Preah Vihear, the Court concluded that Thailand was under an obligation to remove its military forces that were stationed by the Temple and to restore to Cambodia any object of the kind specified by Cambodia in its submissions.[33] The finding of the Court in this case

---

[29] Gray, Judicial Remedies in International Law, 100.
[30] *The Mavrommatis Jerusalem Concessions (Greece v United Kingdom)* (Judgment) PCIJ Rep Series A No. 5, 51.
[31] McIntyre, 'Declaratory Judgments' 114.
[32] Brownlie, 'Remedies in the International Court of Justice' 560.
[33] *Case concerning the Temple of Preah Vihear (Cambodia v Thailand)* (Merits) [1962] ICJ Rep 6.

demonstrates that the declaratory judgment can be the cornerstone of restitution in kind or specific performance.

The express request for a certain conduct might prove superficial in cases such as 'Serbian Loans, Lighthouses and Socobelge, where the court declared that a contract has been duly entered into and is binding on the parties'.[34] In such cases, future conduct is implied and must be complied with.[35] These distinctions have been drawn by the Permanent Court when deciding upon the Certain German Interests Case, in which it concluded that its judgment was issued 'to ensure recognition of a situation at law, once and for all and with binding force as between the parties; so that the legal position thus established cannot again be called in question'.[36] This is another example that demonstrates that a call for action might prove superfluous, since the mandate of the Court is to determine, in a binding manner, if a certain situation exists. In the Haya de la Torre Case,[37] the Court was requested to give guidance as to the manner in which its judgment in the Asylum Case[38] should be performed. The parties requested the judicial body to state the manner in which they should execute a former judgment and the Court concluded that their intention was to determine a declaration as to the course through which the asylum should have been terminated.[39] The Court did not assess whether the performance of its judgment is implied or not, its argument for rejecting this plea being that it only had the competence to decide questions submitted to it in the earlier proceedings.[40] It was, thus, held that the choice regarding the specific mechanisms through which its declaratory judgments should be implemented are not based on legal considerations but on practical ones, and, thus, that such a determination is outside the judicial function of the Court.[41]

As such, a definitive answer to the question of its power to decide the manner in which states shall implement its decision was rather evaded. In effect, the Court rejected the submissions of the parties regarding the performance of its previous judgment. Commentators have expounded further upon this issue and concluded that, traditionally, requests for declaratory judgments

---

[34] Gray, Judicial Remedies in International Law, 98.

[35] McIntyre, 'Declaratory Judgments' 118.

[36] Interpretation of Judgments nos. 7 and 8 concerning the Case of the Factory at Chorzów (Judgment), 20.

[37] Haya de la Torre Case (Colombia v Peru) (Judgment) [1951] ICJ Rep 71.

[38] Colombian–Peruvian Asylum Case (Colombia v Peru) (Judgment) [1950] ICJ Rep 266.

[39] Crawford, 'Flexibility in the Award of Reparation' 696.

[40] Gray, Judicial Remedies in International Law, 99.

[41] Haya de la Torre (Colombia v Peru) (Judgment) 79.

and for judgments through which a certain action is prescribed are distinct judicial mechanisms.[42] Others consider that without a prescription of future conduct, the declaratory judgment might lose its procedural value and might be assimilated to an advisory opinion.[43] Nevertheless, a declaratory judgment is authoritative for all involved, as it is binding pursuant to Article 60 of the Statute of the Court, which provides that such decision shall be final and without appeal. It has been rightly stated that *the impact of any decision shall range far and wide*'[44] and, thus, declaratory judgments are not *mere opinions devoid of legal effect*',[45] even if the dispositif does not contain provisions with respect to future conduct. To conclude, the essence of the declaratory judgment rests not in the fact that it contains an order for the parties, but in the final statement as to the legality of a certain legal relationship.

3.2.4.3 *Declaratory Judgments and Satisfaction*

One form in which the Court uses declaratory judgments is to assimilate this remedy with satisfaction. The case that is most often referred to when discussing this topic is the Corfu Channel Case, in which the Court declared that the action of the British Navy constituted a breach of sovereignty[46] and that its declaratory judgment in this respect constituted, in itself, satisfaction for Albania.[47]

It is important to note, at this juncture, that the Court partially followed the submission of Albania, which requested a declaration that Albania had the right to request satisfaction from the United Kingdom. As such, the issue of whether the declaratory judgment could morph into the remedy of satisfaction still remains, since the Court did not necessarily explain the reasons for which it considered that this was the case. It is relevant to point out that even if Albania sought the usual form of satisfaction, i.e. an apology to be given by an official or head of state,[48] Judge Azevedo concluded that this procedure is outdated.[49]

---

[42] Karel Wellens, *Negotiations in the Case Law of the International Court of Justice – A Functional Analysis* (Routledge 2014) 288.

[43] Gray, Judicial Remedies in International Law, 100.

[44] Malcolm N Shaw, 'A Practical Look at the International Court of Justice' in Malcolm Evans (ed.), *Remedies in International Law: The Institutional Dilemma* (Hart Publishing 1998) 27.

[45] McIntyre, 'Declaratory Judgments' 117.

[46] *Corfu Channel Case (Great Britain v Albania)* (Merits), 35.

[47] *Corfu Channel Case (Great Britain v Albania)* (Merits), 36.

[48] Arnold Pronto and Michael Wood, *The International Law Commission 1999–2009 Volume IV, Treaties, Final Draft Articles and Other Materials* (Oxford University Press 2010) 288.

[49] McIntyre, 'Declaratory Judgments' 144; *Corfu Channel Case (Great Britain v Albania)* (Merits) (Dissenting Opinion of Judge Azevedo).

30   3 *Declaratory Judgments*

Whether the Court can deliver declaratory judgments that represent satisfaction is debatable. It has been remarked that the declaratory judgment in the Corfu Channel Case is not satisfaction, understood in its usual formulation, because this remedy should be provided by the responding state and not by the Court.[50] Opinions could also be made in the sense that the Court should not offer remedies on behalf of states, and, consequently, that it should order states to provide satisfaction, rather than assimilating this remedy with the judgment itself. In other words, satisfaction should be performed by the losing party, after the dispute has been resolved, and not by the Court through its judgment. Thus, even if the Court has not necessarily been consistent in its approach towards the issue of declaratory judgments as satisfaction, the practice indicates that this remedy is geared towards the parties and, hence, the Court should carefully approach this remedy, so that the injured state is satisfied with its judgment.

3.2.4.4 *Declaratory Judgments and Advisory Opinions*

The view of Lauterpacht[51] with respect to the danger of declaratory judgments being used by states to obtain advisory opinions deserves attention, since such a risk indeed exists. It is useful, however, to look at the main differences between these two manifestations of the Court's jurisdiction. The fundamental difference between declaratory judgments and advisory opinions is that the immediate scope of the advisory function is not the resolution of disputes.[52] This is based on the teleological interpretation of Article 65 of the Statute, which provides that the Court may give advisory opinions on legal questions, and Article 36 of the Statute, which prescribes that the Court has the power to resolve legal disputes. In this context, the existence of a legal dispute is essential to the Court's competence to render a declaratory judgment[53] and the word '*declare*' bears more meaning than it appears to, at first blush.

Commentators have concluded that one main differentiator between the advisory opinion and the declaratory judgment is their relationship with time in the sense that the advisory opinion relates to the future, while the

---

[50] McIntyre, 'Declaratory Judgments' 144.
[51] Gray, Judicial Remedies in International Law, 100.
[52] Philippe Couvreur, 'The Effectiveness of the International Court of Justice in the Peaceful Settlement of International Disputes' in AS Muller, David Raic and JM Thuranszky (eds), *The International Court of Justice: Its Future Role after Fifty Years* (Martinus Nijhoff Publishers 1997) 113.
[53] McIntyre, 'Declaratory Judgments' 120.

declaratory judgment relates to the past.[54] As such, declaratory judgments target precisely the application and interpretation of a legal relationship as being in accordance with international law, thus having a retroactive character. This distinction could seem superficial and has been criticised, since the International Court has issued declaratory judgments for the future.[55] More so, it could be validly argued that states could seek the interpretation of a treaty through the issuance of a declaratory judgment, provided that this interpretation is *'not too far divorced from the factual situation pertaining to the relevant State, such as to render it abstract'.*[56] Therefore, another distinction between a declaratory judgment and an advisory opinion appears to rest upon its degree of abstractness or concreteness.

One instance where this argument was discussed was before the Permanent Court in the German Interests Case, in which Poland challenged the jurisdiction of the Court to issue a declaratory judgment because the relief that Germany sought was too abstract.[57] However, the Permanent Court dismissed this argument and proceeded with the case, on the basis of the *'broader normative effect that such a declaratory judgment might have'.*[58] This reasoning is in conflict with Ritter's interpretation, as presented by Gray, who argues that *'to the extent that a declaratory judgment goes beyond the consideration of the past, it is no longer a judgment but a method of proclaiming a norm',*[59] which is not what the Court is mandated to do. This appears to be the interpretation that the Court has given to the notion of declaratory judgments in rendering the decision in the Northern Cameroons Case. Here, the Court concluded that even if it had jurisdiction, it could not exercise its judicial function given the fact that the instrumentum upon which the relationship of the parties was based, i.e. the treaty, was no longer in existence.[60] Gray agrees with the conclusion of Judge Morelli expressed through a Separate Opinion, that if the Court found that a dispute is in existence, it should have issued a judgment to settle the said dispute.[61]

Nevertheless, the Court cannot issue a declaratory judgment where the level of abstractness is so high that it becomes hypothetical. In other words, for the Court to be able to decide the case through a declaratory judgment, a

---

[54] Gray, Judicial Remedies in International Law, 101.
[55] Gray, Judicial Remedies in International Law, 101.
[56] McIntyre, 'Declaratory Judgments' 121.
[57] McIntyre, 'Declaratory Judgments' 122.
[58] McIntyre, 'Declaratory Judgments' 122.
[59] Gray, Judicial Remedies in International Law, 101.
[60] Gray, Judicial Remedies in International Law, 103.
[61] Gray, Judicial Remedies in International Law, 103.

32   3 *Declaratory Judgments*

concrete dispute must be in existence, as provided by Article 36 paragraph 2 of its Statute. Therefore, a question raised could be abstract but still connected to the dispute and, hence, capable of being resolved through a declaratory judgment. This issue is directly connected with the fact that the declaratory judgment is binding and, consequently, has a res judicata effect, while the advisory opinion is not binding and does not have the same character.[62]

3.3 PRACTICAL PERSPECTIVES

3.3.1 *Types of Declaratory Judgments*

3.3.1.1 Declarations of Rights

The declaration of rights implies a request that the Court determines whether a right or a title exists or not. In this situation, the Court is not requested to determine whether a certain right has been breached or whether reparation is due for that breach. Here, the Court *'becomes an instrument not merely of curative but also of preventive justice'.*[63] A boundary delimitation case is a typical example, where the Court's mandate is to determine the correct boundary, even if a breach of a particular obligation has not yet occurred. Several cases have involved requests for declarations of rights before the Permanent Court of International Justice and before the International Court, which gave judgment regarding the legal entitlement of the parties.[64]

The Court has exercised its jurisdiction to issue declaratory judgments of rights in territorial and maritime delimitation disputes, and, further, in disputes regarding sovereignty rights over a certain territory. Illustratively, in the Aegean Sea Continental Shelf, Greece requested the Court to determine that certain islands are entitled to a portion of continental shelf, to determine what the course of the boundary between these portions is and to decide that Greece is entitled to exercise its sovereignty over its continental shelf.[65]

Further, in the Maritime Dispute between Peru and Chile, the applicant requested the Court to determine the course of the boundary between the

---

[62] Wellens, Negotiations in the Case Law of the ICJ, 288.
[63] Wellens, Negotiations in the Case Law of the ICJ, 288.
[64] Ian Brownlie, 'International Law at the Fiftieth Anniversary of the United Nations. General Course on Public International Law (Volume 255)' in *Collected Courses of the Hague Academy of International Law* (Martinus Nijhoff Publishers 1995) 136.
[65] *Aegean Sea Continental Shelf* (*Greece v Turkey*) [1976] ICJ Pleadings, Application instituting Proceedings, 11.

maritime zones of the two states in accordance with international law and to declare that the applicant is entitled to exercise its sovereign rights in the maritime area.[66] Similarly, in the Maritime Delimitation in the Black Sea dispute, the applicant requested the Court to '*draw*' a single maritime boundary between the continental shelf and the exclusive economic zones of the two states appearing before the Court.[67] Another relevant example is the Territorial and Maritime Dispute between Nicaragua and Colombia, in which the applicant requested a judgment in almost identical terms.[68]

The declaratory judgments that were requested in the above-mentioned cases involved claims related to the existence of a right of a certain state. The above submissions reveal that in the majority of cases that contained requests for declaratory judgments of rights, no breaches of international obligations occurred. This circumstance should not lead to the conclusion that in these cases the Court did not issue a judgment involving remedies of international law, inasmuch as through the said judgment the Court finally decided a dispute with a binding character.

Often, subsequent requests for more coercive remedies follow the requests for declaratory judgments. A relevant example in this respect is the Case concerning the Temple of Preah Vihear in which the application also involved a claim for specific performance and restitution in kind, in addition to a declaration of rights, because the respondent had breached its obligation to respect the right of the applicant over the territory. Thus, the applicant requested the Court to conclude that the responding state should withdraw its armed forces from the territory in dispute.[69] Similarly in the Right of Passage over Indian Territory, the applicant requested that the Court should provide a judgment, through which it would recognise and declare that the applicant was the holder of a right of passage and, following this finding, should order that the respondent should end the effects of the internationally wrongful act, through a judgment ordering cessation.[70] Another relevant example is the Passage through the Great Belt Case, in which the applicant requested the Court to conclude that it has a right of free passage and, following this finding,

---

[66] *Maritime Dispute (Peru v Chile)* [2008] ICJ Pleadings, Application instituting Proceedings, 6.

[67] *Maritime Delimitation in the Black Sea (Romania v Ukraine)* [2004] ICJ Pleadings, Application instituting Proceedings, 5–6.

[68] *Territorial and Maritime Dispute (Nicaragua v Colombia)* [2001] ICJ Pleadings, Application instituting Proceedings, 8.

[69] *Case concerning the Temple of Preah Vihear (Cambodia v Thailand)* [1959] ICJ Pleadings, Application instituting Proceedings, 15.

[70] *Case concerning Right of Passage over Indian Territory (Portugal v India)* [1955] ICJ Pleadings, Application instituting Proceedings, 6–7.

to order that the parties commence negotiations in order to reach specific performance.[71]

The circumstance that the above-mentioned requests contained other remedies, in addition to the declaration of the Court, should not determine the conclusion that the applicant sought one or the other. A more accurate conclusion would be that such requests include both a declaratory remedy and a coercive one. The ILC Articles seem to confirm this conclusion inasmuch as they do not contain any provision mentioning that the application of certain remedies excludes the application of others, the only exception in this respect being the priority given to restitution in kind, which is itself debatable.

3.3.1.2 Declarations of Applicable Law

A request for the declaration of applicable law implies that states request the Court to determine the applicable law to their dispute, which is relevant for a particular legal relationship. This type of declaratory judgment has been described as *'allowing the parties to learn authoritatively how they are to govern themselves in the future'*.[72] An example of such a case is the recent dispute regarding the Question of the Delimitation of the Continental Shelf between Nicaragua and Colombia beyond 200 nautical miles from the Nicaraguan Coast, in which Nicaragua requested the Court to adjudge and declare the following:

> First: The precise course of the maritime boundary between Nicaragua and Colombia in the areas of the continental shelf which appertain to each of them beyond the boundaries determined by the Court in its Judgment of 19 November 2012.
>
> Second: The principles and rules of international law that determine the rights and duties of the two States in relation to the area of overlapping continental shelf claims and the use of its resources, pending the delimitation of the maritime boundary between them beyond 200 nautical miles from Nicaragua's coast.[73]

---

[71] *Passage through the Great Belt (Finland v Denmark)* [1991] ICJ Pleadings, Application instituting Proceedings, 16.

[72] Borchard, 'Declaratory Judgment' 121.

[73] *Question of the Delimitation of the Continental Shelf between Nicaragua and Colombia beyond 200 nautical miles from the Nicaraguan Coast (Nicaragua v Colombia)* [2013] ICJ Pleadings, Application instituting Proceedings, 8.

Such a request includes two remedies that would resolve the dispute. First it includes a declaratory judgment of rights and, second, a declaratory judgment of applicable law. If the legal dispute exists with respect to the applicable legal principles or with respect to the applicable law regarding a certain relationship between states, a judgment of the Court that would decide the applicable law is not different from other remedies, as long as through this judgment the dispute is decided. Concluding otherwise would mean to assimilate the judgments of the Court, in such instances, with an advisory opinion, a circumstance that would undermine the requests of the parties in this respect.

3.3.1.3 Declarations of Responsibility

A declaration of responsibility implies that the Court determines if a breach of an international obligation occurred, and if responding states are responsible for such breaches. This type of declaration raises the question of whether it is sufficient to resolve the dispute. A restrictive perspective would lead to the conclusion that this type of declaration would suffice for the resolution of a dispute, and that, as a consequence, there is no duty upon the Court to provide another applicable remedy of a more coercive character. A more extensive perspective could consider that a declaration of responsibility would necessarily imply a duty upon the Court to further determine a subsequent coercive remedy, which would rest on such a declaration. The answer regarding the application of this type of declaration is included in the requests of states before the Court. Illustratively, in the Application of the Convention of 1902 governing the Guardianship of Infants Case, the applicant requested the Court to conclude that the measures undertaken were not in conformity with its international obligations.[74] Further, in the Lockerbie Case, the applicant state submitted the following request:

> That the United Kingdom has breached, and is continuing to breach, its legal obligations to Libya under Articles 5 (2), 5 (3), 7, 8 (2) and 11 of the Montreal Convention; and
> That the United Kingdom is under a legal obligation immediately to cease and desist from such breaches and from the use of any and all force or threats against Libya.[75]

---

[74] *Application of the Convention of 1902 regarding the Guardianship of Infants* (*Netherlands v Sweden*) [1957] ICJ Pleadings, Application instituting Proceedings, 10–11.

[75] *Questions of Interpretation and Application of the 1971 Montreal Convention Arising out of the Aerial Incident at Lockerbie* (*Libyan Arab Jamahiriya v United Kingdom*) [1992] ICJ Pleadings, Application instituting Proceedings, 4–5.

The two mentioned requests seem to confirm both perspectives described above. Thus, if the applicant considers that a declaration of responsibility is sufficient for the final resolution of the dispute, the Court is mandated to provide such a judgment, the application of another remedy being excluded by the principle of non ultra petita. Further, if the applicant considers that a declaration of responsibility should be followed by a more coercive remedy, such as cessation, the Court is mandated to provide both remedies. A relevant observation in this respect is that the declaration of responsibility can be an exclusive remedy before the International Court, the only limitation of the jurisdiction of the Court in this respect being the requests of states.

The requests in the above-mentioned cases confirm the views that the declaratory judgment is an appropriate remedy of international law because *'it strikes a balance between third party settlement and the sovereignty of states'*,[76] and that *'the declaratory judgment has the further advantage that it is undoubtedly available as a remedy for injury to the state'*.[77] In these cases, the post-adjudication role of the declaratory judgment is perhaps most apparent. Therefore, once the Court has delivered its judgment declaring that a state bears responsibility in a given relationship with another state, the process of negotiation, after the judgment is given, shall commence in a more concrete manner, both parties being aware of the objective assessment regarding their situation.

3.3.2 *Declaratory Relief and the Subject Matter of the Dispute*

The subject matter of the dispute seems to influence the manner in which the Court grants declaratory judgments. The main focus of this section is on the requests for remedies that are sought by states in i) disputes related to state sovereignty and ii) territorial disputes.

3.3.2.1 The Sovereignty Disputes

Certain authors argue that the law of state responsibility 'has hardly found application in cases of territorial and boundary disputes'.[78] However, relevant conclusions can be drawn from the requests for remedies in the territorial

---

[76] Gray, Judicial Remedies in International Law, 98.
[77] Gray, Judicial Remedies in International Law, 99.
[78] Enrico Milano and Irini Papanicolopulu, 'Territorial Disputes and State Responsibility on Land and at Sea' (paper presented at 20th anniversary conference of the International Boundaries Research Unit (IBRU) 'The State of Sovereignty', Durham University, 1–3 April 2009), p. 2, available at https://boa.unimib.it/retrieve/handle/10281/7845/8485/milano_papanicolopulu_paper.pdf.

3.3 *Practical Perspectives*

disputes that were submitted before the Court through notifications of special agreements as certain trends are discernible from the requests for relief sought by states in sovereignty disputes. Thus, the disputes regarding sovereignty rights involved determinations of title over a disputed area of land. Commentators concluded in this sense that the usual approach of states is to request the Court whether 'sovereignty over [a named territory] belongs to A or B'.[79]

Illustratively, in the Minquiers and Ecrehos Case,[80] the United Kingdom and France submitted the dispute before the Court through a special agreement. Thus, because of certain differences regarding the sovereignty over the islets and rocks in the Minquiers and Ecrehos groups, the parties requested the Court, through the notification of a special agreement, to determine whether the islets and rocks belonged to the United Kingdom or to the French Republic.[81] In the Case concerning Sovereignty over Certain Frontier Land,[82] the Netherlands and Belgium submitted the dispute regarding the sovereignty over certain parcels of land that had arisen between them, before the Court. Through the special agreement, the two states requested the Court to determine whether the sovereignty over certain parcels of land belonged to the Kingdom of Belgium or the Kingdom of the Netherlands.[83] Similarly, in the Case concerning Sovereignty over Pedra Branca, Pulau Batu Puteh, Middle Rocks and South Ledge,[84] Malaysia and Singapore submitted a dispute that had arisen between them regarding the sovereignty over certain territorial landmarks, through a special agreement. In this submission, they requested the Court to determine whether the sovereignty over these landmarks belongs to Malaysia or the Republic of Singapore. In the Case concerning the Frontier Dispute,[85] which entailed a dispute that had arisen between Burkina Faso and Mali regarding the frontier between the two states, a special agreement was concluded through which the Court was requested to determine the frontier between the two states. In the Case concerning the Sovereignty over Pulau Ligitan and Pulau Sipadan, the parties requested the judicial body to determine whether the sovereignty over Pulau Litigan and Pulau Sipadan belongs to the Republic of Indonesia or to Malaysia.[86]

---

[79] Tomka, 'The Special Agreement' 561.
[80] *Minquiers and Ecrehos (France v United Kingdom)* (Judgment), 47.
[81] *Minquiers and Ecrehos (France v United Kingdom)* (Judgment), 47.
[82] *Certain Frontier Land (Belgium v the Netherlands)* (Judgment), 209.
[83] *Certain Frontier Land (Belgium v the Netherlands)* (Judgment), 209.
[84] *Pedra Branca/Pulau Batu Puteh, Middle Rocks and South Ledge (Malaysia/Singapore)* (Judgment), 12.
[85] *Frontier Dispute* (Burkina Faso/Republic of Mali) (Judgment).
[86] *Pulau Ligitan and Pulau Sipadan (Indonesia v Malaysia)* (Judgment), 575.

An analysis of the above-mentioned cases, which revolved around the issue of territorial sovereignty, reveals that states used almost identical wording to request declaratory judgments from the Court. In all of the above cases, it was mandated to determine whether the sovereignty over the territorial landmarks that were in dispute belonged to one state or to the other.

It is important to note, at this juncture, that the Court was not requested to order any duties through an injunctive decision which could have imposed that they act in a specific manner. As such, the mechanisms for the implementation of the judgment were left for the parties to decide through a special agreement. Authors have concluded, in this sense, that the judgments of the Court which do not contain any orders for specific action confirm the fact that states benefit from the judicial pronouncement because it is a basis of subsequent negotiations held for the establishment of a new legal framework that would govern their relationship.[87]

The Case concerning the Temple of Preah Vihear is exceptional in this sense, because the declaratory relief was followed by clear indications regarding the actions that Thailand should have performed.[88] Nevertheless, the sovereignty disputes did not need such an order for restitution, and, thus, a declaration of rights was sufficient for the final resolution of the dispute. One element that influenced this approach of the Court was, thus, the manner in which the questions that were resolved by the Court were framed.

Another reasoning for which declarations of rights were suitable for these disputes was that in the majority of these cases no state had breached an international obligation by invading the territory in dispute, in the manner in which Thailand had done in the mentioned case. Therefore, a claim for a coercive remedy in such a situation would have been redundant, except for pecuniary satisfaction.

3.3.2.2 The Territorial Delimitation Disputes

Similarities are also discernible in requests that involved territorial delimitation issues. Commentators have concluded that in the delimitation cases states either requested a judgment regarding the applicable rules of international law or a judgment through which the Court would delimit the boundary or frontier.[89]

---

[87] Hersch Lauterpacht, *The Function of Law in the International Community* (Oxford University Press 1933) 340.

[88] *Temple of Preah Vihear (Cambodia v Thailand)* (Merits), 35.

[89] Tomka, 'The Special Agreement' 691.

3.3 *Practical Perspectives* 39

Illustratively, in the North Sea Continental Shelf Cases, involving a dispute with respect to the delimitation of the continental shelf in the North Sea, the parties concluded a special agreement through which they requested the Court to determine the rules of international law, applicable to the delimitation that was in dispute.[90] In the Case concerning the Continental Shelf, between Tunisia and Libyan Arab Jamahiriya, a similar request was submitted.[91] In the Case concerning Kasikili/Sedudu Island, the Court was requested to determine the boundary between them.[92]

Most cases regarding territorial delimitation involved claims which originated either from a lack of proper demarcation or from differing views with respect to the interpretation of existing boundaries. Thus, unable to resolve such disputes by diplomatic means, states submitted them before the Court through a special agreement. The requests of states in territorial delimitation disputes are broader in scope than the ones regarding sovereignty. Instead of requesting the Court to decide which state had the right over a determined portion of land, the parties sought a decision on the principles and rules that should be applied in the determination of certain territorial limits from the Court. It is relevant that the Court was not requested to *apply* the rules and principles to the dispute, but to declare these rules and principles, which would be subsequently applied by states.

It could be argued that the international law of territory and the law of state responsibility operate in different spheres. Authors such as Milano describe the interaction between the law of territory and the law of state responsibility as hardly interacting.[93] This alleged lack of interaction could be used to argue against the conclusion that requests for declaratory judgments are influenced by the fact that the parties signed a special agreement. Some authors therefore consider that the reason for which the cases that were submitted before the Court through a special agreement contained requests for declaratory judgments was that these disputes were territorial in nature.[94]

As such, it might be concluded that no other remedies would have been appropriate in these cases but for declaratory judgments, as remedies such as restitution in kind or compensation are generally not feasible for territorial disputes. This conclusion does not find support from the Court's practice, as

[90] *North Sea Continental Shelf (Germany/Netherlands and Germany/Denmark)* (Judgment), 3.
[91] *Continental Shelf (Tunisia/Libyan Arab Jamahiriya)* (Judgment), 18.
[92] *Kasikili/Sedudu Island* (Judgment), 1045.
[93] Enrico Milano and Irini Papanicolopulu, 'State Responsibility in Disputed Areas on Land and at Sea' (2011) 71 Houston Journal of International Law 587, 588.
[94] Milano and Papanicolopulu, 'State Responsibility in Disputed Areas' 587, 588.

the Court has had cases on its docket that involved territorial disputes that were submitted by unilateral application through which the applicant state requested compensation. The Land and Maritime Boundary Dispute[95] between Cameroon and Nigeria, in which Cameroon requested the Court to determine that Nigeria had incurred state responsibility and had an obligation to provide reparation for the injury caused (including monetary compensation), is such an example.[96]

This case entailed more than a mere request for a declaratory judgment regarding the sovereignty of a state over a certain portion of land. The dispute involved heads of claim related to the use of force and circumstances which contributed to material and non-material damages. However, the claim of Cameroon also involved the sovereignty over the Bakassi peninsula, and this was the central element of the dispute, i.e. the fact that sovereignty rights were breached. In this case, while the Court decided on the issues of sovereignty, it unanimously considered that the submissions of Cameroon with respect to reparation should be dismissed. It is therefore relevant to note that the Court concluded that a declaratory judgment would suffice and would represent the proper remedy in this case. In other territorial disputes, states reserved the right to claim compensation or restitution, through their application. An example of such a case is the Territorial and Maritime Dispute between Nicaragua and Colombia,[97] in which Nicaragua reserved the right to claim compensation through its application.[98] Similarly, in the Legal Status of the South-Eastern Territory of Greenland,[99] the applicant also reserved its right to claim reparation through the application instituting proceedings.

One reasoning for this approach could be that, often, states use the declaratory judgments and, further, the said reservations to claim other more coercive remedies, as a post-adjudication negotiation tool. There is, therefore, a tendency of states to request remedies other than the declaratory judgment in sovereignty and territorial delimitation disputes, and the Court has not rejected these pleas as inadmissible. However, the Court indeed appears to be more inclined towards issuing declaratory judgments in cases of this nature.

---

[95] *Land and Maritime Boundary between Cameroon and Nigeria (Cameroon v Nigeria: Equatorial Guinea intervening)* (Merits) [2002] ICJ Rep 303.

[96] *Land and Maritime Boundary between Cameroon and Nigeria (Cameroon v Nigeria: Equatorial Guinea intervening)* (Merits) [2002] ICJ Rep 316.

[97] *Territorial and Maritime Dispute (Nicaragua v Colombia)* (Merits) [2012] ICJ Rep 624.

[98] *Territorial and Maritime Dispute (Nicaragua v Colombia)* (Merits) [2012] ICJ Rep 624, 633.

[99] *Legal Status of the South Eastern Territory of Greenland (Norway v Denmark)* (Order Interim Measures of Protection) [1932] PCIJ Rep Series A/B No. 48.

3.3.3 Declaratory Relief and the Manner in which the Court Is Seized

Out of all the cases brought before the Court, relatively few have been initiated through the notification of a special agreement. A study of the impact of the manner in which the Court is seized is relevant at this juncture, for a determination of potential links between special agreements, unilateral applications and declaratory judgments.

3.3.3.1 The Effects of the Special Agreement

The special agreement is the classic method to refer a dispute before the International Court.[100] Its origins lie in international arbitration practice, where an agreement is the normal method of invoking arbitral proceedings.[101] The cases that were brought before the Court through this method have the most recognisable profile,[102] as the dispute is defined by states through this instrument, and the jurisdiction of the Court is established from the outset.

However, the exceptional character of the special agreement as a mechanism to refer a dispute before the Court[103] is justified by the fact that states rarely agree on the identification and definition of the dispute and also due to a certain reluctance of states to refer their disputes to the International Court when the factual framework of the case is favourable to them and less favourable to the opposing state. Nevertheless, even if rarely used, when states agree that the notification of the special agreement is the appropriate means of seizing the Court, it produces effects both from a substantive perspective and from a procedural one.

A relevant conclusion regarding the influence of the special agreement, from a substantive perspective, is that states cooperate throughout the existence of the dispute.[104] As such, the signing of a special agreement regarding the referral of the dispute before the Court also influences the manner in which states frame their submissions.[105]

The determination of the characteristics of the dispute also influences the requests for remedies that are available for that particular case. Usually, the

---

[100] Rosenne, The Law and Practice of the International Court, vol 1, 643.

[101] Rosenne, The Law and Practice of the International Court, vol. 1, 643.

[102] Kolb, The International Court of Justice, 535.

[103] AP Llamzon, 'Jurisdiction and Compliance in Recent Decisions of the International Court of Justice' (2005) 18:5 European Journal of International Law 818.

[104] Kolb, The International Court of Justice, 536.

[105] Serena Forlati, The International Court of Justice: An Arbitral Tribunal or a Judicial Body? (Springer 2014) 113.

preamble of the special agreement identifies the dispute, and, after this identification, states request the Court to resolve the dispute by delivering a judgment. Often, remedies such as restitution or compensation are abandoned in favour of the declaratory judgment through their special agreement. Therefore, the initiation of the dispute through the special agreement and the request for remedies, as part of the question that is brought before the Court, influence one another.

The disputes that were referred to the Court through the notification of a special agreement are considered by certain scholars as being not as politically sensitive[106] as the ones that were referred to the Court through a unilateral application. It has been observed in this sense that *'none of the great political conflicts'*[107] were referred to the Court through a special agreement. Other commentators conclude that the majority of the disputes that were referred to the Court through the notification of a special agreement were territorial in nature, and that such disputes are, in fact, factually and legally complex, especially in situations in which contradictory approaches are involved.[108] This latter conclusion is more apposite in this context.

If it can be considered that none of the territorial disputes were politically sensitive, it could also be concluded that the parties' agreement with respect to the definition of their dispute is a relevant factor which justifies, to a certain degree, that the cases described within this section contained requests for declaratory judgments. While political sensitivity might be considered as an element that further influences the requests for remedies, a conclusion that has merit in this sense is that this circumstance is not as relevant an element as the prior agreement of states through which they defined their dispute.

Procedurally, *'a special agreement gives the parties the greatest possible influence over the Court, so it approaches the case in line with their wishes'*.[109] The positive impact of a special agreement on the procedural side of the disputes submitted before the International Court arises from the fact that states also determine the framework of the proceedings of the case through their special agreement. Illustratively, the involved states agree upon issues such as the timeline related to the written and oral proceedings or the evidentiary stage. For example, in the Minquiers and Ecrehos Case, Article

---

[106] Kolb, The International Court of Justice, 535.

[107] Christian Tomuschat, 'Article 36' in Andreas Zimmerman, Christian Tomuschat, Karin Oellers-Frahm and Christian J Tams (eds), *The Statute of the International Court of Justice – A Commentary* (Oxford University Press 2012) 662.

[108] Rongxing Guo, *Territorial Disputes and Conflict Management: The Art of Avoiding War* (Routledge 2012) 9.

[109] Kolb, The International Court of Justice, 535.

2 of the special agreement provided that the parties shall submit a memorial, a counter-memorial and a reply.[110]

It is also important to note that in a number of cases, states agreed through the special agreement that they shall reach a subsequent agreement with respect to the Court's decision, once delivered. Thus, in the North Sea Continental Shelf Case between Germany and Denmark, Article 1 of the special agreement contained provisions through which the parties requested the Court to determine the rules and principles of international law that are applicable to the delimitation in question and, following this finding, the states agreed that they will delimit the continental shelf in pursuance of the Court's decision.[111]

This approach was pursued in other cases, such as the Case concerning the Continental Shelf between Tunisia and Libya[112] and in the Case concerning the Continental Shelf between Libya and Malta.[113] In the latter, the parties requested the Court to determine the rules and principles that were applicable to the delimitation of the area in dispute and a separate Article of the special agreement provided that they will enter into negotiations to determine the area of their continental shelves.[114]

The manner in which states referred the questions before the Court, and the fact that they agreed that the judgment of the Court shall be implemented by means of negotiations and subsequent agreement, supports the view that states are comfortable with remedies such as declaratory judgments rather than restitution or compensation, in cases that were referred to the Court by special agreements. It is relevant to point out, at this juncture, that there is no case that was brought before the Court in which states agreed that compensation should be paid or that restitution in kind should be applicable.

3.3.3.2 The Effects of Unilateral Applications

The possibility of seizing the Court through the submission of a unilateral application can be included in a treaty, through two types of clauses: i) the first may expressly provide in the treaty that either of them can seize the Court through a unilateral application or ii) the second may seize the Court through unilateral application if such mode was not expressly provided for, but was not expressly excluded through the treaty. It has been observed, in this regard, that

---

[110] *The Minquiers and Ecrehos Case (France v United Kingdom)* [1951] ICJ Pleadings, Special Agreement, 9.
[111] *North Sea Continental Shelf (Germany/Netherlands and Germany/Denmark)* (Judgment), 6.
[112] *Continental Shelf (Tunisia/Libyan Arab Jamahiriya)* (Judgment).
[113] *Continental Shelf (Libyan Arab Jamahiriya v Malta)* (Judgment).
[114] *Continental Shelf (Libyan Arab Jamahiriya v Malta)* (Judgment), 16.

an express provision regarding the possibility of unilaterally seizing the Court '*is the most common type, and it's the best way to ensure that the Court will have jurisdiction, without any obstacle'*.[115]

The unilateral application is the most used mechanism through which states seize the Court: out of all the submitted cases before the Court, the majority commenced through the notification of unilateral applications. This circumstance has influenced the Court's jurisprudence regarding the remedies requested by the applicant states.

The reason for which the cases in which unilateral applications were submitted before the Court have a bearing on the requests for remedies is that in this situation states do not cooperate for a common definition of their dispute. In these cases, the applicant state defines its own claims through the unilateral application, as opposed to the notification of the special agreement in which states jointly define the dispute. As a consequence, the parties of the disputes that commenced with unilateral applications have tended to show a more aggressive approach than the ones in disputes commenced through the notification of a special agreement, because the relationship is hostile from the outset of the pre-dispute negotiation process.

In this sense, the claims submitted before the Court through a unilateral application contain requests for remedies such as compensation and restitution in kind more often than the disputes referred through the notification of a special agreement, which almost exclusively contain requests for declaratory relief. This is not to say, however, that declaratory judgments are not requested through unilateral applications. On the contrary, the claims for compensation and restitution are also exceptional remedies in cases initiated through unilateral application.

Another significant feature of the submission of a unilateral application is that applicant states often include a multitude of remedies within the prayer for relief, and do not substantiate the specific manner in which the injury should be repaired. What this translates to, in the practice of the Court, is that states end up providing no specific lists of items regarding restitution, do not submit quantum claims regarding compensation, and sometimes omit to specify the means through which satisfaction would be achieved. While the majority of these claims involve requests that the Court determine the appropriate reparation either at the merits stage of the case, or at a subsequent stage, several other issues also arise regarding these types of submissions.

The submission of a dispute by unilateral application has procedural ramifications on the grant of remedies as well. The cases that are referred to

---

[115] Kolb, The International Court of Justice, 755.

the Court through the submission of a unilateral application involve a more complicated procedure than the ones that are initiated through a special agreement. In these cases, jurisdictional or admissibility objections are commonly formulated:[116] *'nearly half of the disputes submitted to the Court required separate hearings on jurisdictional issues'.*[117] The preliminary objections are often upheld by the Court and the Court does not end up analysing the remedies sought by the applicant state, since the dispute is dismissed for lack of jurisdiction or on the basis of inadmissibility. However, even in these cases, the requests of applicant states are useful to analyse in order to better understand the interpretation of remedies before the Court.

3.4 CONCLUSION

There is no contemporary reason for which to consider that the declaratory judgment is not an independent and flexible remedy, through which the International Court can tackle various issues of international law, with a binding character and without providing the parties with an explicit mechanism through which its decision shall apply. As such, the declaratory judgment, as a remedy of international law, does not depend upon, nor does it necessarily imply, subsequent findings regarding coercive remedies, such as restitution in kind, specific performance or compensation. It can be further concluded that the declaratory judgment, given its versatile character, even if subject to a degree of abuse by the parties, represents the remedy that states are most comfortable with, the reason being that it represents a perfect compromise between the resolution of the dispute by a third party, while still retaining an important role for the exercise of state sovereignty. Nevertheless, the versatility and flexibility of this remedy should be carefully considered by the International Court when deciding the instances in which the declaratory judgment has the potential to replace other remedies, such as satisfaction.

The wide scope of declaratory judgments and their interaction with other forms of relief should not lead to the conclusion that the declaratory judgment renders other remedies inapplicable. As such, this remedy is also characterised by its capacity to supplement the others, by establishing a certain foundation of illegality, that contributes to the final resolution of interstate disputes.

---

[116] Tomka, 'The Special Agreement' 259.
[117] Vanda Lamn, *Compulsory Jurisdiction in International Law* (Edward Elgar Publishing 2014) 244.

4

Specific Performance

4.1 INTRODUCTION

Specific performance as a remedy before the Court has a particular nature, and as such, its interaction with other concepts related to remedies such as cessation and restitution in kind is of interest. Further, some uncertainty exists regarding the availability of specific performance in the proceedings of the Court. The reason for which there is an apparent concern with regard to the power of the Court to grant this remedy is that specific performance is understood as taking the form of an order that has an inherent mandatory effect,[1] through which the Court concludes that states must carry out a certain conduct in order to fulfil their obligations.[2] It is generally accepted that specific performance means that a state has to fulfil its obligations, without having the possibility to replace performance with monetary relief. The distinct nature of specific performance, similar to declaratory judgments, is related to the fact that Article 36 of the Statute of the Court does not contain an express provision related to the applicability of this remedy.[3] This being the case, the Court has to determine certain procedural mechanisms in order to deliver a judgment through which it grants specific performance, if it considers this to be the appropriate manner in which the injured state would receive reparation. However, even if rarely referred to as such, specific performance has been ordered by the Court in several cases.[4]

The manner in which the Court grants specific performance ranges from determining the power of the Court to order specific performance to determining the relationship between specific performance and other remedies,

---

[1] Crawford, State Responsibility, 468.
[2] Crawford, 'Flexibility in the Award of Reparation' 696.
[3] Brownlie, 'Remedies in the International Court of Justice' 558.
[4] These cases shall be provided in the following sections of this chapter.

4.1 Introduction

such as cessation and restitution in kind. Commentators have expressed certain doubts in relation to the competence of the Court to order specific performance.[5] Others opine to the contrary, that the Court has the power to give injunctive orders in different forms, including specific performance.[6] The fact that specific performance, as a remedy, is not concretely defined in public international law further complicates[7] the interpretation of this remedy, in the sense that it could be confused with other remedies. A reason for which such confusion has arisen could be that the Court does not use the terminology of specific performance.[8] Thus, the issue of language appears relevant in defining the scope of the jurisdiction of the Court regarding specific performance. However, a linguistic analysis in an isolated manner, without considering the substance of the terminology used, might prove to be a superficial approach.[9]

Specific performance is a remedy that has never been addressed, as such, by the Court. The ILC Articles, however, consider it as being a natural consequence of an unlawful act. Thus, Article 29 of the ILC Articles provides that *'the legal consequences of an internationally wrongful act under this Part do not affect the continued duty of the responsible State to perform the obligation breached'*.

Certain disputes submitted before the Permanent Court involved specific performance as a remedy, but the Court did not clarify the particulars of specific performance in the same manner in which, for instance, it analysed issues related to restitution in kind. Generally, the Court issued judgments through which this remedy was implied, either by mentioning that a certain treaty has been duly entered into[10] or by ordering the parties to perform the particular obligations that were agreed upon in the said treaty.[11] One, rather exceptional, case of the International Court that dealt directly with this remedy was the Gabčíkovo–Nagymaros Case, which involved the effects of not performing the obligations contained in a treaty.

There are various opinions regarding the characteristics of specific performance as a remedy of international law. Illustratively, while Sornarajah considers that specific performance is illusory[12] due to the impossibility of

---

[5] Gray, *Judicial Remedies in International Law*, 99.
[6] Quintana, *Litigation at the International Court*, 1157.
[7] Gray, *Judicial Remedies in International Law*, 413.
[8] Crawford, *State Responsibility*, 468.
[9] Chittharanjan Felix Amerasinghe, *Jurisdiction of Specific International Tribunals* (Martinus Nijhoff 2009) 177.
[10] *The Société Commerciale Belgique Case* (*Belgium v Greece*) [1939] PCIJ Rep Series A/B 78.
[11] *Lighthouses Case* (*France v Greece*) (Judgment).
[12] M Sornarajah, *The Pursuit of Nationalized Property* (Martinus Nijhoff Publishers 1986) 298.

48   4 *Specific Performance*

enforcing a judgment that provides for it, other authors consider that specific performance is an important remedy that contributes to the re-establishment of the status quo ante, being the first effect of a breach.[13] Crawford further describes the conceptual framework of specific performance and concludes that even if its terminology is not necessarily used before the Court, the judicial organ has the power to order it and it has done so.[14] Even if the doctrine is slightly controversial with respect to specific performance as a remedy, the case-law of the International Court lacks controversy, as it provides arguments regarding the interpretation and clarification of this remedy.[15]

This chapter identifies the main elements that define specific performance, as a remedy before the Court, and clarifies the controversies that have arisen with regard to specific performance as a potential remedy, starting with the power of the Court to order it and concluding with the ways in which specific performance interacts with other similar remedies.

4.2 THEORETICAL PERSPECTIVES

4.2.1 *The Definition and Function of Specific Performance*

Specific performance as a remedy of international law has been defined as being '*a mechanism through which a party may require the other party to meet its obligations*'.[16] The terminology used for this remedy is, at times, misleading, as the wording of the notion of '*specific performance*' might lead to the conclusion that the Court has the possibility of ordering the parties to perform their obligations in a specific manner. As a consequence, this notion should be interpreted widely, by guaranteeing the right of election regarding the manner in which the said obligations should be performed. Thus, the term '*specific*' is not necessarily related to the means through which the parties choose to perform their obligations, but to the fact that the obligations should be performed as agreed in the treaty.

Consequently, the function of specific performance is to ensure that the provisions agreed by the states through treaties remain applicable in the post-adjudication phase of the proceedings before the Court. As such, this remedy is designed to restore the status quo ante in a rather abstract manner, meaning

---

[13] Crawford, State Responsibility, 277.
[14] Crawford, State Responsibility, 468.
[15] *Diplomatic and Consular Staff in Tehran* (USA v Iran) (Judgment); *Avena* (Mexico v USA) (Judgment).
[16] Farshad Rahimi Dizgovin, 'Foundations of Specific Performance in Investor-State Dispute Settlements: Is It Possible and Desirable?' (2016) 28:1 Florida Journal of International Law 28.

4.2 Theoretical Perspectives

that, usually, the responding state should fulfil its obligations in the manner in which it should have fulfilled them before the dispute has arisen.

4.2.2 The Availability of Specific Performance

Several opinions have been expressed regarding the power of the Court to order specific performance. One such argument revolves around *'the idea that sometimes is expressed that the Court cannot make orders which equate to orders of specific performance against states'*.[17] The reasoning behind this conclusion appears to stem from a conflation of specific performance with injunctions,[18] and, since injunctions cannot be issued[19] by the Court, the argument goes: nor can specific performance.

This argument has its origins in the submission that unless expressly provided through a provision in a treaty, specific performance should not be granted, as this remedy would be similar in scope to an injunction,[20] which is sometimes considered to be outside the scope of the judicial function of the Court. This view is contextualised through the decision of the Court in the Haya de la Torre Case.[21] In this instance, the parties requested the Court to decide the manner in which its decision in the Asylum Case[22] should have been implemented. It could be considered that, in this case, the Court was requested to make an order of specific performance, or, in the words of the Court, to *'make a choice amongst the various courses by which the asylum must be terminated'*.[23] The Court refused to make such a determination and concluded that it is for the parties to appreciate the mechanisms through which its judgments should be implemented, as such a determination would be outside the judicial function of the Court.[24]

The Haya de la Torre Case is rather peculiar, as the Court has in fact, made orders for specific performance throughout its case-law, without necessarily indicating the manner in which states should implement its judgments.[25]

---

[17] Crawford, State Responsibility, 468.

[18] Gray, Judicial Remedies in International Law, 95.

[19] Christoph Schreuer, 'Non-pecuniary Remedies in ICSID Arbitration' (2004) 20:4 Arbitration International 325, 326: *'The International Court of Justice has ordered relief in the form of judgments for specific performance in numerous cases.'*

[20] Gray, Judicial Remedies in International Law, 95, 96.

[21] *Haya de la Torre (Colombia v Peru)* (Judgment), 71.

[22] *Colombian–Peruvian Asylum (Colombia v Peru)* (Judgment).

[23] *Haya de la Torre (Colombia v Peru)* (Judgment), 79.

[24] *Haya de la Torre (Colombia v Peru)* (Judgment), 79.

[25] *Arrest Warrant of 11 April 2000 (Democratic Republic of Congo v Belgium)* (Judgment) [2002] ICJ Rep 3.

Therefore, while the Court has required a certain outcome in mandatory terms, it has also simultaneously allowed the parties to choose the manner in which such outcome should be achieved.[26]

The findings of the Permanent Court in the Chorzów Factory Case[27] are relevant for the determination as to whether specific performance falls within the Court's judicial function. Contrary to the determination in the Haya de la Torre Case, which could be considered the locus classicus for declining specific performance, the judgment of the Court in the Chorzów Factory Case has been considered the foundation of orders for specific performance, issued by the Court.[28] The Permanent Court, in adjudicating the Chorzów Factory Case, has concluded that it has the power to grant a remedy, even if there was no such reference in the treaty granting jurisdiction, since a breach of international law involves an obligation to provide reparation adequately.[29]

The question that arises in this context is whether specific performance could be considered as an 'adequate form' of reparation, according to the determination of the Court in the Chorzów Factory Case. Should the conclusion be in the affirmative, its inclusion within the agreement would prove unnecessary. If specific performance may not be ordered by the Court, in circumstances in which the parties did not include it within their agreement, then the consequence of such an argument would be that specific performance is, de facto, not a remedy before the Court and that, therefore, the Court does not have inherent jurisdiction to order it. Should it be considered that specific performance might be considered a remedy, it could also be argued, in this circumstance, that the Court has the inherent jurisdiction to grant it. Thus, the question that needs answer is whether specific performance is an available remedy of international law before the Court.

To determine whether specific performance is a remedy before the Court, a closer look at the case-law in which the Court has determined that specific performance should be ordered is warranted, as it seems that, even if not explicitly, the Court has granted, but not ordered, specific performance.

The judgment of the Court in the Haya de la Torre Case and the judgment in the Chorzów Factory Case represent two ends of the same spectrum regarding the power of the Court to order specific performance: the former considering that the Court does not have the judicial power to order specific performance, while the latter implies that specific performance could be

---

[26] Crawford, 'Flexibility in the Award of Reparation' 699.
[27] *Factory at Chorzów (Germany v Poland)* (Merits).
[28] Schreuer, 'Non-pecuniary Remedies' 326.
[29] *Factory at Chorzów (Germany v Poland)* (Merits), 21.

considered as an appropriate means of restoring the status quo ante. However, these are not the only judgments of the Court that considered specific performance. The Court has issued several other judgments, which seem to confirm that specific performance falls within its judicial function.[30] Illustratively, in the Iranian Hostages Case, the Court found that Iran should act in a manner that would lead to the fulfilment of its international obligations.[31]

It is arguable whether this solution is a veritable order or it is a declaratory judgment. The opinion that *'this was a case in which, although the word "ordered" was not used, the Court decided that the respondent should act in a certain way which is in effect an order for specific performance'*[32] has merit, as *'finding the Iranian government's inaction during the Iranian hostage situation to constitute a violation of international law, the ICJ ordered Iran to redress its unlawful omission by specific performance of its legal obligations'.*[33]

This conclusion seems reasonable, as the general idea expressed by the Court through the dispositif of its judgment was indeed that Iran should perform its international obligations. Thus, the view that the substance of the remedy supersedes its linguistic designation seems to be a reasonable approach when determining the scope of a decision of the Court. The Iranian Hostages Case is not an isolated one in its determination that specific performance is the appropriate form of reparation. In the Serbian Loans Case, the Court decided that the respondent state should specifically perform its obligations as provided by the agreement between the state parties, even if the Court did not use the word *'order'*.[34]

As such, the fact that the Court found the applicant entitled to the amounts that were included within the agreement is a clear determination that the said obligations should be specifically performed. The Court had the same approach in the Lighthouses Case, where it decided that the parties have duly entered into a contract and that it is operative.[35]

---

[30] Anne van Aaken, 'Primary and Secondary Remedies in International Investment Law and National State Liability: A Functional and Comparative View' in Stephen W Schill (ed), *International Investment Law and Comparative Public Law* (Oxford University Press 2010) 722, 731.

[31] *Diplomatic and Consular Staff in Tehran (United States v Iran)* (Judgment), 45.

[32] Amerasinghe, Jurisdiction of Specific International Tribunals, 175.

[33] Francisco Forrest Martin, Stephen J Schnably, Richard Wilson, Jonathan Simon and Mark Tushnet, *International Human Rights and Humanitarian Law: Treaties Cases and Analysis* (Cambridge University Press 2006) 302.

[34] *Serbian Loans (France v Serbia)* (Judgment), 48–49.

[35] *Lighthouses Case (France v Greece)* (Judgment), 29.

In these two above-mentioned cases, the Court considered that the obligations of the responding state should be respected and ordered the specific performance of the said obligations, albeit implicitly. It cannot be validly argued that the Court did not order specific performance but issued mere declarations. Another instance where the Court indicated that specific performance of the legal obligations should be carried out by the responding state is the Case concerning Military and Paramilitary Activities in Nicaragua[36] where the International Court concluded that the responding state should refrain from any acts that could constitute breaches of its international obligations.[37] This finding of the Court could be interpreted as ordering cessation, as the responsible state was ordered to refrain from certain acts. However, it being an order for cessation does not exclude it from also being an order for specific performance. It has been argued that *'these examples (Case Concerning Military and Paramilitary Activities in Nicaragua included) clearly demonstrate the ICJ's power to order specific performance against states'.*[38]

It becomes clear that the views that the Court lacks the power to order specific performance are rather exceptional. As such, the Court has the inherent jurisdiction to order specific performance in the same manner in which it does with respect to other remedies of international law. This view is substantiated by the case-law of the Court, where it has concluded that specific performance should be implemented by the respondent state. In other words, if the judgment of the Court is clear enough to determine its scope, the language in which the remedy is granted becomes secondary, if not irrelevant.

4.2.3 *Specific Performance and Other Remedies*

4.2.3.1 Specific Performance and Injunctive Relief

Views have been expressed in the sense that specific performance cannot be ordered by the Court, as this type of remedy is similar to injunctions, which are a procedural mechanism that is not available before the Court.[39] Even if the previous subsection has endeavoured to clarify the issue of the inherent powers of the Court to grant specific performance, the issue of the similarities between specific performance and injunctions remains.

---

[36] *Military and Paramilitary Activities in and against Nicaragua (Nicaragua v USA)* (Merits).
[37] *Military and Paramilitary Activities in and against Nicaragua (Nicaragua v USA)* (Merits), 149.
[38] Schreuer, 'Non-pecuniary Remedies' 327.
[39] Gray, Judicial Remedies in International Law, 96.

The arguments that injunctive relief might not be a proper remedy before the Court are based upon the consideration that the Court may not issue mandatory orders in the same manner as a regular municipal court often does.[40] One example that seems to support this conclusion is that the Court '*deliberately chose not to go into this problem*'[41] when it addressed the issues in the Iranian Hostages Case. However, the fact that the Court did not explicitly answer the question related to specific performance does not necessarily entail that it considered that this remedy was outside its judicial powers, or that it assimilated this remedy with injunctive relief.

The views that the Court does not have the power to issue injunctions have been contested. One argument in this sense is that restitution, considered the primary remedy of international law, is a form of injunctive relief.[42] This understanding is predicated on the dominant view that restitution and cessation are injunctive forms of relief, as these concepts often merge with one another,[43] and that the Court has made injunctive orders, amounting to both restitution and cessation.[44]

The opinions that conclude that specific performance should not be ordered, due to an alleged danger regarding a potential lack of compliance with the judgments of the Court, which grant this remedy, do not seem to observe the case-law of the Court. Practical arguments are relevant for the determination as to whether specific performance should or should not be ordered. In numerous cases, the Court presumed compliance[45] and did not consider the possibility of non-compliance, which might prove difficult to reverse once a state decides that it will not follow the judgment of the Court. More so, the Court has a generally satisfactory compliance record for its judgments.[46] Significantly, arguments of a practical nature should not supersede legal arguments, as the case-law of the Court proves that '*it may well be that the cases in which compensation is adequate are more numerous or that states prefer to agree upon the payment of compensation but this experience does not permit a legal principle to be inferred*'.[47] Further, even if it is seldom

---

[40] W Michael Reisman, 'The Enforcement of International Judgments and Awards' (1969) 63 American Journal of International Law 1, 2.
[41] Gray, Judicial Remedies in International Law, 95.
[42] Martin, Schnably, Wilson, Simon and Tushnet, International Human Rights, 302.
[43] Quintana, Litigation at the International Court, 1164.
[44] Crawford, 'Flexibility in the Award of Reparation' 697.
[45] Reisman, 'The Enforcement of International Judgments and Awards' 2.
[46] Llamzon, 'Jurisdiction and Compliance in Recent Decisions of the ICJ' 815, 825.
[47] Fritz A Mann, *Further Studies in International Law* (Oxford University Press 1990) 128.

54 4 *Specific Performance*

requested, the Court has rarely awarded compensation.[48] Thus, the arguments that substantiate the views that specific performance would be inappropriate before the Court prove to be of a rather superficial character.

The controversy regarding the availability of specific performance and injunctive relief before the Court also stems from the fundamental differences between the common law and civil law system regarding the prioritisation of one remedy over another. In the common law system, compensation has priority over specific performance, which is an exceptional remedy, while in the civil law system the priority of remedies is reversed, specific performance being the remedy which has priority over compensation.[49]

As such, in the Anglo-American system, the granting of specific performance as a remedy is limited, as it can be ordered only in situations in which compensation is inadequate.[50] It is therefore understandable that common law–trained lawyers and scholars could be supporting the view that specific performance should be awarded by the Court in limited instances, it being the exceptional remedy while compensation is the rule.

On the other hand, in civil law systems, such as France or Germany, the right to request specific performance is an established principle that originates in the sacrosanct character of contracts.[51] A distinction should also be made between the German and the French legal systems, at this juncture. Under German law there is no norm with respect to the priority of a certain remedy, the rule being that the parties have to elect and the Courts must grant a specific relief. However, in France specific performance is the norm.[52]

Even if under most municipal systems there is a predetermined priority regarding the remedies awarded by national courts, it seems that this strict prioritisation of remedies falls short of much consideration by the Court. The general approach in this respect is that the parties have the inherent right of electing and determining the appropriate and suitable remedy for their cause.[53] In other words, states that submit disputes before the Court have the right to choose any remedy they consider applicable to their dispute. For

---

[48] Stephen M Schwebel, *Justice in International Law: Selected Writings of Judge Stephen M. Schwebel* (Cambridge University Press 1994) 419.

[49] Robert Bejesky, 'The Evolution in and International Convergence of the Doctrine of Specific Performance in Three Types of States' (2003) 13:2 Indiana International and Comparative Law Review 353, 362.

[50] Schwebel, Justice in International Law, 418.

[51] Schwebel, Justice in International Law, 418.

[52] Thomas D Musgrave, 'Comparative Contractual Remedies' (2009) 34:2 University of Wollongong Australia, Law Review 300, 309, 327.

[53] Crawford, State Responsibility, 508.

example, the applicant state has the option to choose specific performance as a remedy, without considering restitution in kind even if the latter might be applicable for the said dispute. The alleged primacy of restitution in kind would not render its claim for specific performance invalid, in such a situation. In fact, the jurisprudence of the Court confirms that specific performance or mere findings of illegality represent the normal type of relief, while orders for compensation are rather exceptional.[54]

It is thus clear, at this stage, that there is no indication that injunctive forms of relief are unusual or not proper before the Court and, as a consequence, it also becomes clear that there is no evident general rule in this respect. This approach seems similar to the German municipal approach towards specific performance. Therefore, the question whether specific performance is an appropriate relief is to be answered by the Court when analysing the factual matrix of each case, as *'basically, the Court has as wide an inherent jurisdiction in regard to remedies as is appropriate to its judicial functions as international tribunals'.*[55]

It could, therefore, be concluded that states should not be restricted in their determination of the appropriate remedy that would properly restore the status quo ante, as the Statute and the Rules of the Court do not contain any restrictions as to the manner in which states should request reparation, specific performance included.

4.2.3.2 Specific Performance, Cessation and Restitution in Kind

Examples of cases where these notions interact are numerous before the International Court, Avena,[56] LaGrand[57] and Arrest Warrant[58] being the disputes in which certain related confusions are perhaps most apparent.

Cessation and restitution in kind are well-established remedies before the Court, their availability being clearer than that of specific performance. Specific performance could also be inferred through a declaratory judgment, as the relationship before these two remedies is one of cause and effect: the declaration being the cause, while specific performance is the effect.

The relationship between specific performance, cessation and restitution in kind is of the same causal nature as the relationship between declaratory judgments and specific performance, but turns that relationship on its head.

---

[54] Crawford, State Responsibility, 367.
[55] Amerasinghe, Jurisdiction of Specific International Tribunals, 177.
[56] *Case concerning Avena and Other Mexican Nationals (Mexico v USA)* (Judgment) [2004] ICJ Rep 12.
[57] *LaGrand (Germany v USA)* (Judgment).
[58] *Arrest Warrant (Democratic Republic of the Congo v Belgium)* (Judgment).

Thus, an order for specific performance is one consequence of the issuance of a declaratory judgment. In other words, specific performance could be the practical consequence of a finding of illegality.[59] The scope of specific performance would, therefore, extend from its declaratory nature to an injunctive one – of a positive nature in the case of restitution in kind and of a negative one in the case of cessation. Considering that specific performance means the implementation of a certain international obligation, it can be concluded that the structure of a judgment issued by the Court in this respect, would be framed, generally, as such:

i) The responsible state has breached a norm of international law (the declaratory judgment);
ii) The responsible state should specifically perform the said obligation (the cause – specific performance);
iii) The responsible state should cease violating the rights of the injured state (the negative effect – cessation);
iv) The responsible state should resituate any property or rights that it has infringed (the positive effect – restitution in kind).

Potential confusions between these remedies stem from the fact that the Court does not always refer to the above structure and seldom explicitly indicates these elements within its declaratory judgment. This approach of the Court allows the parties to infer that cessation and restitution are means through which states implement its declaratory judgments. One example in which the Court has respected the above-mentioned framework is the Case concerning the Temple of Preah Vihear[60] in which the dispositif of the judgment had a similar structure to the one provided above.[61] The first part of the dispositif of the Court represents the declaration regarding the location of the object in dispute, *i.e.* the temple. This declaration is the cause that generated the conclusion of the Court that the responsible state must specifically perform its obligations. Further, this finding generated both the negative effect that the responsible state must withdraw its forces (cessation) and the positive effect that the responsible state must restore certain objects to the injured state (restitution in kind). It has been argued in this respect, and rightly so, that *'the substance of the matter is that a Judgment is binding and the performance required is the consequence of the decision on entitlement'.*[62]

---

[59] Quintana, Litigation at the International Court, 1164.
[60] *Temple of Preah Vihear (Cambodia v Thailand)* (Merits), 34.
[61] *Temple of Preah Vihear (Cambodia v Thailand)* (Merits), 36–37.
[62] Brownlie, 'Remedies in the International Court of Justice' 129.

This is not the only case where the Court has in fact respected the above-mentioned framework. One such example, in which the Court issued a declaratory award upon which an order for specific performance was issued, is the Arrest Warrant Case where the Court decided that Belgium, by means of its own choosing, should take all necessary steps to cancel the warrant in question.[63]

4.3 PRACTICAL PERSPECTIVES

4.3.1 *The Availability of Specific Performance*

4.3.1.1 The Gabčíkovo–Nagymaros Case

In 1977, Hungary and Czechoslovakia signed a treaty that provided for the construction and operation of a barrage system on the river Danube, which constituted their common border. The parties began the construction of the said project in 1978. The project was not finalised because political and economic turmoil influenced its development. The main element of the dispute submitted before the Court was that Hungary first suspended its part of the construction of the project in 1989 and later abandoned it. In response, Czechoslovakia started construction works in 1991 regarding a new version of the initial plan.

Following the separation of Czechoslovakia in 1993, Hungary and Slovakia jointly submitted a dispute before the Court. Through a special agreement the two states requested the Court to determine, on the basis of international law, whether Hungary was entitled to suspend and then abandon its part of the performance of the Danube project.[64] The International Court was, therefore, faced with issues regarding the performance of the treaty. Even if the Court did not refer to specific performance as such, this judgment represents one of the very few in which the Court provided certain conclusions leading to a better understanding of specific performance as a remedy of international law.

Before analysing the judgment of the Court in the Gabčíkovo–Nagymaros Case, it is relevant to note that the state parties referred to this remedy in their

[63] *'The Court accordingly considers that Belgium must, by means of its own choosing, cancel the warrant in question and so inform the authorities to whom it was circulated ... The Court sees no need for any further remedy.' Arrest Warrant (Democratic Republic of the Congo v Belgium)* (Judgment), 32.

[64] *Gabčíkovo–Nagymaros Project (Hungary/Slovakia)* (Judgment), 11.

pleadings, and thus asserted that specific performance is not only an obligation which should be observed throughout the life of the treaty, but also a remedy that the Court has the power to order, in case of a breach.[65] Even though the Slovak Republic referred to performance expressly, the Republic of Hungary submitted arguments in this respect, without referring to specific performance directly, but by requesting the Court to conclude that it had the right to 'suspend and subsequently abandon the works on the Nagymaros Project'.[66] However, irrespective of the terminology used by the parties, their claims and arguments represent veritable requests regarding the specific performance of the treaty.[67]

Although the judgment did not fully address the concept of specific performance, as such, the Court analysed and interpreted the requests of the parties. The judgment contains important findings that contribute to the interpretation of specific performance. The judicial body concluded that the obligations contained in the treaty must be performed, without mentioning an explicit mechanism in this respect. Thus, the Court referred to the obligation to 'ensure'[68] that the objectives of the treaty are fulfilled, through good faith negotiations.

This finding of the Court regarding the manner in which specific performance could be achieved is confirmed by a previous paragraph of the same judgment. The Court therein concluded that due to the general scope of the obligations, the performance of the treaty should be achieved by the parties and should not be ordered by the Court.[69] The Court provided further elements through which specific performance is achieved: it stressed that in agreeing upon the manner in which specific performance should be achieved, the treaty should not be disregarded, especially because both states were involved in the operation regime regarding the construction of the Gabčíkovo–Nagymaros project.[70]

The wording that the Court included in its finding is sufficient for concluding that specific performance was provided. Thus, the fact that the Court mentioned that the parties must act in accordance with the Treaty of 1977 implies that they should specifically perform the international obligations contained therein. The second paragraph of the dispositif further substantiates

---

[65] *Gabčíkovo–Nagymaros Project (Hungary/Slovakia)* (Judgment), 16.
[66] *Gabčíkovo–Nagymaros Project (Hungary/Slovakia)* (Judgment), 11.
[67] Crawford, State Responsibility, 260.
[68] *Gabčíkovo–Nagymaros Project (Hungary/Slovakia)* (Judgment), 83.
[69] Crawford, State Responsibility, 68.
[70] *Gabčíkovo–Nagymaros Project (Hungary /Slovakia)* (Judgment), 82–84.

the conclusion that the remedy of specific performance was ordered by the Court, as it referred to an effective implementation of the provision of the treaty in dispute.

The Court, in the Avena Interpretation Judgment, further confirmed the fact that a judgment for specific performance should not provide the mechanism through which the remedy is implemented in the post-adjudication stage, and that the mechanism through which such an order would be complied with is for the parties to agree upon, not for the Court to impose,[71] especially because the Statute of the Court provides no guidance in this respect.[72]

4.4 CONCLUSION

The main controversies regarding specific performance are related to its availability as a remedy of international law before the Court and its interaction with other remedies. The outcome that can be drawn from the above analysis has been aptly formulated by Quintana as such:

> It is suggested that it cannot be seriously put in doubt that the Court has the power to grant the remedy of consequential orders, whether in the form of mandatory orders, orders for specific performance or negative injunctions.[73]

Even if the Court concluded, throughout its jurisprudence, that an obligation of performance exists, and to a certain degree ordered the parties to comply with this obligation, the Court could have pursued a more detailed analysis of specific performance as a remedy of international law, as its application is presently determined implicitly. The vague approach of the Court with respect to this remedy might be justified, because this remedy is sensitive due to its coercive nature. Nevertheless, it can also be concluded that, in the future, the Court might endeavour to better clarify and interpret the manner in which specific performance applies when a dispute in this respect is submitted before it. Without a proper analysis of specific performance by the Court, its case-law regarding this remedy remains rather uncertain. More so, the Court could refer to specific performance as such, in its future

---

[71] *Request for Interpretation of the Judgment of 31 March 2004 in the Case concerning Avena and Other Mexican Nationals (Mexico v USA)* (Order for Provisional Measures) [2008] ICJ Rep 331, 326.

[72] Brownlie, 'Remedies in the International Court of Justice' 558.

[73] Quintana, Litigation at the International Court, 1161.

practice, in order to clarify that it is available before it and that state parties have the possibility of requesting it, if the case so requires. Thus, although specific performance is not sufficiently clarified, its availability, as a remedy before the International Court, is currently established in the sense that it has the potential to restore the status quo ante.

5

Cessation, Assurances and Guarantees of Non-repetition

5.1 INTRODUCTION

Cessation, assurances and guarantees of non-repetition represent a special category of remedies, and they differ fundamentally from other types of remedies, such as restitution, compensation, specific performance and satisfaction. The doctrine and case-law of the Court places cessation and assurances in a different category of remedies – forward-looking ones – in contrast with the other types that look to the past.[1] The complexity of these remedies led authors like Stern to observe that international responsibility has reached a high degree of complexity.[2] As opposed to other remedies that are available before the Court, cessation, assurances and guarantees of non-repetition generally imply a negative action or an abstention, respectively.[3]

Due to this difference, these remedies were difficult to classify, in the past. For example, certain authors considered that cessation could be perceived *'simply as a form of satisfaction'*[4] while others argued that this remedy is but a form of restitution.[5] These conclusions seem to contradict the time-related difference regarding the scope of cessation and assurances and guarantees of non-repetition. What is certain is that *'learned opinion is not unanimous regarding the nature of cessation'*.[6]

---

[1] Julio Barboza, 'Legal Injury: The Tip of the Iceberg in International Responsibility' in Maurizio Ragazzi (ed), *International Responsibility Today: Essays in Memory of Oscar Schachter* (Brill/Nijhoff 2005) 12.
[2] Brigitte Stern, 'A Plea for Reconstruction of International Responsibility Based on the Notion of Legal Injury' in Ragazzi (ed), International Responsibility Today, 98.
[3] Crawford, State Responsibility, 459.
[4] Quintana, Litigation at the International Court, 1153.
[5] Philippe Couvreur, *The International Court of Justice and the Effectiveness of International Law* (Brill/Nijhoff 2017) 233.
[6] Barboza, 'Legal Injury' 105.

62 · 5 *Cessation, Assurances, Guarantees of Non-repetition*

Questions have also been raised as to the availability of cessation as a veritable remedy of international law, it being considered as a form of injunctive relief, which is not a remedy before the Court.[7] Certain concerns have also been expressed with respect to requests for cessation by states that have not suffered an injury, because in the absence of an injury the basic mechanisms of state responsibility are not applicable.[8]

Assurances and guarantees of non-repetition have encountered hostility as well, occasionally being considered less powerful in comparison with other remedies. Commentators opined in this sense that there is risk regarding the potential lack of consequences of a failure to comply with a judgment that provides for these remedies.[9]

Cessation, assurances and guarantees of non-repetition represent the remedies of international law through which the Court decides that states must discontinue a breach of an international obligation and must promise that the same breach will not occur in the future. However, unlike judgments providing for specific performance, although rare, the judgments of the Court on the remedies described in this chapter provide a clearer picture.

The most relevant cases in this regard are the Avena Case,[10] the Case concerning Military and Paramilitary Activities in and against Nicaragua[11] and the LaGrand Case,[12] which entailed cessation and assurances and guarantees of non-repetition. The joinder of these remedies often occurs because they sometimes work together towards the restoration of the status quo ante. The commentary to the ILC Articles indicates that these remedies are both aspects of the restoration of the legal relationship between states.[13]

However, this conclusion should not be interpreted in the sense that there are no situations in which only one of the remedies may be requested. In other words, there is no general obligation for a state to request both remedies as means of reparation; states have the discretion to choose either one of them, or both. The Court has rarely granted cessation as a remedy, even though it has been requested by the parties in the disputes that were submitted before it. However, certain conclusions can be drawn from these proceedings, that establish the fact that cessation is an available remedy.

---

[7] Gray, Judicial Remedies in International Law, 98.

[8] Stern, 'A Plea for Reconstruction of International Responsibility' 105.

[9] Crawford, State Responsibility, 475.

[10] *Avena (Mexico v USA)* (Judgment).

[11] *Military and Paramilitary Activities in and against Nicaragua (Nicaragua v USA)* (Merits).

[12] *LaGrand (Germany v USA)* (Judgment).

[13] ILC Draft Articles with Commentaries, 88.

5.2 Theoretical Perspectives

This chapter endeavours to demonstrate that they are veritable and autonomous remedies and that they apply with the same force as restitution, compensation or satisfaction. Therefore, cessation and assurances and guarantees of non-repetition should not be confused or assimilated with other remedies. Further, cessation and guarantees and assurances of non-repetition contribute, substantially, to the elimination of the consequences of a wrongful act leading to a breach of an international obligation.

5.2 THEORETICAL PERSPECTIVES

5.2.1 *Cessation*

Cessation has often been ignored in the doctrine, because of its special characteristics related to the manner in which the effects of this remedy are manifested.[14] Cessation is an autonomous remedy and its analysis should not be restricted to its interaction with other remedies. Certain authors agree with this individual characterisation of cessation, and consider cessation as being the normal type of relief.[15] Others conclude that, in practice, cessation is the primary remedy of international law.[16] These opinions lend further credence to the claim that the primacy of restitution in kind as a remedy before the Court is often an exaggeration.

The interaction of cessation with restitution and satisfaction also deserves attention. This issue is central to the interpretation and clarification of the notion of cessation, as several opinions seem to underestimate cessation as a remedy before the Court. In this sense, it has been argued that, at times, cessation corresponds to a form of restitution.[17] Nevertheless, the ILC has concluded that cessation is an independent remedy, and commentators have labelled the inclusion of cessation on the list of consequences of internationally wrongful acts as fortunate.[18] As such, the conclusion that '*both cessation of the violation and guarantees of non-repetition are appropriate remedies under international law*'[19] must be considered by state parties and the Court when faced with disputes of international law.

---

[14] Gaetano Arangio-Ruiz, 'Preliminary Report on State Responsibility' UN Doc A/CN.4/416, 13.
[15] Crawford, State Responsibility, 461–464.
[16] Gideon Boas, *Public International Law: Contemporary Principles and Perspectives* (Edward Elgar Publishing 2012) 296.
[17] Couvreur, 'The Effectiveness of International Law' 233.
[18] Quintana, Litigation at the International Court, 1153.
[19] Adrienne M Tranel, 'The Ruling of the International Court of Justice in Avena and Other Mexican Nationals: Enforcing the Right to Consular Assistance in U.S. Jurisprudence' (2005) 20:2 American University International Law Review 403, 450.

5.2.1.1 The Definition and Function of Cessation

The Commentary of the Articles on State Responsibility does not define cessation.[20] This might have occurred because the drafters of the Articles intended to leave the means of interpreting this notion to the state parties to the dispute or to the International Courts and Tribunals faced with adjudicating upon this remedy.

Even so, there is less to no controversy with respect to the definition of cessation. Thus, the conclusion that *'cessation consists in what Special Rapporteur Riphagen called "an obligation to stop the breach"'*[21] seems reasonable, and it has not provoked special analysis, or further arguments. Several definitions of cessation have been provided by the doctrine and by the Court. The conclusion of Judge Tomka in his Separate Opinion from the Avena Case is relevant from the perspective of the definition of cessation, linking this remedy with the continuing nature of the obligation.[22] Commentators have confirmed this perspective, and argued that the case law of the Court confirms that cessation is the applicable remedy where continuous breaches of international law occur.[23] Thus, the main feature of cessation is that it is focused on obligations that are of a continuing nature. This has been aptly summarised by commentators who conclude that cessation is focused on breaches of a continuing nature, meaning that the breach persists on the date on which the judgment of the Court is delivered.[24] As such, should the responsible state cease the illegal act during the proceedings, the claim for cessation would become moot.

The ILC Articles contain provisions related to cessation and guarantees of non-repetition within Article 30, which contains corroborated provisions regarding the two remedies. This provision clarifies that cessation and assurances and guarantees of non-repetition are available remedies depending upon the nature of the illegal act, *i.e.* whether the act is of a continuing nature or whether the act has stopped. The Court has determined that cessation represents a remedy in the Dispute related to Navigational and Related Rights case, in which it concluded that *'the cessation of a violation*

---

[20] ILC, 'Draft Articles on Responsibility of States for Internationally Wrongful Acts with Commentaries' (2001) YBILC vol 2, Part Two, 88–91.

[21] Quintana, Litigation at the International Court, 1150.

[22] *Case concerning Avena and Other Mexican Nationals (Mexico v USA)* [2004] (Separate Opinion of Judge Tomka), 90.

[23] Crawford, State Responsibility, 265.

[24] Quintana, Litigation at the International Court, 1150.

of a continuing character and the consequent restoration of the legal situation constitute a form of reparation for the injured State'.[25]

The Commentary to the ILC Articles further mentions that the obligation to cease the continuous breach of an international obligation is the first requirement for eliminating the consequences of that breach. Thus, the ILC Articles implicitly confirm that cessation represents an autonomous remedy of international law, since it contributes to the restoration of the status quo ante, cessation being *'the first requirement in eliminating the consequences of wrongful conduct'.*[26] The Commentary of the ILC describes the function of cessation as a remedy of international law as putting an end to *'a violation of international law and to safeguard the continuing validity and effectiveness of the underlying primary rule'.*[27] Therefore, the Court can order cessation only in a situation in which the breach is contemporaneous with the delivery of the judgment. Consequently, the responding state can prevent such an award by ceasing the act during the proceedings. To sum up, the establishment of the secondary obligation to cease the act depends upon the continuing nature of the violation of an international obligation.[28]

5.2.1.2 Cessation and Other Remedies

The interaction between cessation and reparation, in general, and with other remedies in particular, is probably the most controversial issue with respect to this remedy. Certain scholars have gone so far as to conclude that cessation is not reparation at all.[29] Also, as mentioned above, the interaction of cessation with particular remedies such as restitution, satisfaction and specific performance is of relevance, as different opinions have been expressed that the above remedies encompass, to a certain degree, or imply the cessation of the wrongful act.

5.2.1.3 Cessation and Restitution

The relationship between cessation and other remedies such as restitution in kind has constantly been under the scrutiny of the doctrine. Illustratively,

---

[25] *Dispute regarding Navigational and Related Rights (Costa Rica v Nicaragua)* (Judgment) [2009] ICJ Rep 213, 267.

[26] ILC Draft Articles with Commentaries, 89.

[27] ILC Draft Articles with Commentaries, 89.

[28] ILC Draft Articles with Commentaries, 89.

[29] ME Schneider, 'Selected Other Cases' in ME Schneider and J Knoll (eds), *Performance As a Remedy: Non-onetary Relief in International Arbitration*, ASA Special Series No. 30 (JurisNet 2011) 201.

66   5 Cessation, Assurances, Guarantees of Non-repetition

Crawford considers that cessation and restitution are similar with respect to their final scope and argues that *'often, the result of restitution will be indistinguishable from that of cessation'*.[30] Julio Barboza is harsher in his characterisation of the relationship between cessation and restitution, and considers that *'cessation is but a form of restitution'*.[31] Gideon Boas further concludes that, in certain situations, cessation and restitution are identical, implying that a request for one would imply the other *'especially where the wrongful conduct is an omission'*.[32]

It could be argued that the first conclusion, provided by Crawford, related to the scope of these remedies, has merit, as the opinions of Barboza and Boas seem too drastic and overarching, in their implication that cessation is not a remedy of international law, as it has identical characteristics with restitution. Nevertheless, the conclusion should not imply that cessation and restitution in kind should be confused.[33]

If the wrongful act is an omission, a request for restitution would be redundant, and at times even moot, as the responding state would not have anything material or legal to restore. A claim for restitution would therefore be without a precise object. Further, should the act be an omission, the request for cessation would also seem moot as the responding state would not have to stop any legal action, but would have to perform a certain action. Therefore, when the illegal act is an omission, the appropriate cause of action should be specific performance and not cessation or restitution.[34]

In this sense, Gray understandably argues that in the sense that there is some uncertainty as to the relationship between restitution, specific performance and cessation.[35] It is undeniable that a relationship between cessation and restitution exists. The judgment of the Tribunal in the Rainbow Warrior arbitration might have contributed to the contemporary misinterpretation of cessation and to the confusion between cessation and restitution. Gray confirms this view, and concludes that the Rainbow Warrior Tribunal misinterpreted the requests of the parties, which applied for restitution and specific performance while the Tribunal granted cessation.[36] In the Wall Advisory Opinion, cessation was also addressed by the Court. The Court concluded

---

[30] Crawford, State Responsibility, 465.
[31] Barboza, 'Legal Injury' 9.
[32] Boas, Public International Law, 296.
[33] Catherine Deman, 'Cessation de l'Acte Illicite' (1990) 23:2 Belgian Review of International Law 486.
[34] Barboza, 'Legal Injury' 14.
[35] Gray, Judicial Remedies in International Law, 61.
[36] Gray, 'The Choice between Restitution and Compensation' 420.

that Israel should demolish the Wall, and that, should it fail to do so, the international obligation would be continuingly breached. In this vein, one very relevant issue with respect to the difference between cessation and restitution is that the first cannot be avoided by the responding party due to material impossibility.[37]

Cessation, therefore, can repair in certain cases what restitution is not able to, which goes to reaffirm the conclusion that the better view is to understand cessation as a stand-alone, autonomous remedy.

5.2.1.4 Cessation and Specific Performance

Cessation and specific performance are both facets of the general principle of pacta sunt servanda.[38] Thus, it could be, indeed, considered that a duty of specific performance implies a duty to cease the breach of an obligation, should it occur. However, this is not always the case. Crawford refers to the Commentary to the ILC Draft Articles on State Responsibility, and concludes that there exist justifications for interpreting cessation as a function of the continuous duty to comply with an international obligation.[39] This conclusion has merit, as long as specific performance, i.e. the duty to fulfil an international obligation, and cessation are not treated as identical remedies. The distinction between cessation and specific performance is demonstrated by Article 48(1) b of the ILC Articles, which gives a state the possibility of choosing between these two remedies.

As mentioned at the beginning of this section, both cessation and specific performance are part of the general principle of pacta sunt servanda. However, the manner in which this principle manifests itself differs for each of these two remedies. The statement that concludes that *a wrongful act does not affect the state's continued duty to perform its obligation*'[40] confirms the view that cessation and specific performance apply differently. The first is conditioned upon the existence of a breach, while the second overarches the behaviour of the parties throughout the performance of the treaty whether a breach exists or not. This conclusion is substantiated by Article 29 of the Articles on State Responsibility which provides that *the legal consequences of an internationally wrongful act under this Part do not affect the continued duty of the responsible*

---

[37] Pierre d'Argent, 'Compliance, Cessation, Reparation and Restitution in the Wall Advisory Opinion' in Pierre-Marie Dupuy et al (eds), *Common Values in International Law: Essays in Honor of Christian Tomuschat* (Kehl, 2006) 463.

[38] Crawford, State Responsibility, 264.

[39] ILC Draft Articles with Commentaries, 89.

[40] Boas, Public International Law, 296.

68   5 *Cessation, Assurances, Guarantees of Non-repetition*

State to perform the obligation breached'.[41] It can, therefore, be concluded that, even if cessation and specific performance represent two different facets of the same coin, they are different in scope – one being conditioned upon a breach, while the other remains in force throughout the performance of a treaty.

5.2.1.5 Cessation and Satisfaction

The interpretation and characteristics of cessation have led certain commentators to conclude that under the Basic Principles and Guidelines on the Right to a Remedy and Reparation for Victims of Gross Violations of International Human Rights Law and Serious Violations of International Humanitarian Law, cessation is a form of satisfaction.[42] However, the ILC Articles contain a different understanding in this respect, in the sense that cessation is different from satisfaction. Satisfaction implies that the responding state presents apologies and acknowledges the breach of the international obligation; cessation implies that the responding state should act in a manner that would stop the continuous breach of the said obligation. Circumstances exist in which ceasing the act contains similarities with the remedy of satisfaction. For example, should the responding state cease the breach, it necessarily means that it would implicitly acknowledge the breach. Nevertheless, this circumstance should not lead to the conclusion that the two remedies are the same.

The characteristics of the breach are relevant for assessing the differences between cessation and satisfaction. While cessation applies solely to international breaches that have a continuous character, satisfaction is not limited as such. Further, the manner in which these remedies apply is also different. Perhaps the most relevant conclusion related to cessation is that not just any form of cessation means that this remedy is performed. Commentators have concluded in this sense that the conduct that replaces the continuous wrongful act should be conformant with international law,[43] implying that not any mechanism implementing cessation can be regarded as compliant with the implementation of this remedy.

5.2.2 *Assurances and Guarantees of Non-repetition*

Assurances and guarantees of non-repetition is the second remedy provided by Article 30 of the ILC Articles. In this framework, cessation represents the

---

[41] ILC Draft Articles with Commentaries, 89.
[42] C Schleker, 'Reparations' in DP Forsythe (ed), *Encyclopedia of Human Rights, Volume 1* (Oxford University Press 2009) 332.
[43] Barboza, 'Legal Injury' 13.

primary remedy if the breach of the obligation is of a continuing nature, and assurances and guarantees of non-repetition is rather secondary. It would apply to situations where the party has stopped the breach of the international obligation but the applicant state has reasons to believe that this breach might occur in the future. Nevertheless, this conclusion does not imply that assurances and guarantees of non-repetition cannot be independently granted by the Court, even in situations in which cessation is not necessary.

This remedy is also controversial, as the legal opinion is not necessarily unanimous regarding its interpretation.[44] This section aims to provide certain clarifications with respect to assurances and guarantees of non-repetition.

5.2.3.1 The Definition and Function of Assurances and Guarantees of Non-repetition

This remedy entails two distinct notions: assurances of non-repetition and guarantees of non-repetition. A common characteristic of these concepts relates to the agreement, and official expression in this sense, of the responding state not to breach a certain international obligation in the future.[45] However, the manner in which this effect is manifested differs between the two, as they imply different degrees of formality through which they are implemented by the responding state, even if the final scope of the two is the same.

Assurances of non-repetition are the more familiar means of providing the injured state with a promise that the breach shall not occur in the future, while guarantees of non-repetition imply a stronger obligation. As such, the first remedy is usually given verbally, while the second involves additional acts such as taking potential preventive measures.[46]

Although guarantees of non-repetition are, arguably, a more formal remedy, the manner in which they apply is not yet established before the Court, because the mechanisms through which guarantees of non-repetition are requested is not necessarily coherent.[47] A relevant example regarding the incertitude with respect to the mechanisms through which this remedy should be performed is the LaGrand Case, in which the applicant submitted a very

---

[44] Barboza, 'Legal Injury' 16.
[45] James Crawford, 'The International Court of Justice and the Law of State Responsibility' in CJ Tams and J Sloan (eds), *The Development of International Law by the International Court of Justice* (Oxford University Press 2013) 82.
[46] Crawford, State Responsibility, 476.
[47] Pronto and Wood, The International Law Commission, 255.

70   5 *Cessation, Assurances, Guarantees of Non-repetition*

broad request in this respect.[48] This is not the only case in which applicants have formulated vague requests with respect to assurances and guarantees of non-repetition. Similarly, in the Dispute regarding Navigational and Related Rights, Costa Rica requested the Court *'to give appropriate assurances and guarantees that it shall not repeat its unlawful conduct, in such form as the Court may order'.*[49]

This remedy entails either a promise or a more formal declaration, followed by certain acts, on behalf of the responding state. The scope of assurances and guarantees of non-repetition is that of the restoration of trust between states,[50] which is often requested when the injured state has concerns that an order of cessation would not suffice.[51] Thus, should the injured state consider that certain circumstances exist, in which there is a possibility that the responding state would breach the obligations in the future, it has the right to request the Court to provide that the latter offers sufficient guarantees that it shall not breach its obligations.

5.2.3.2 The Availability of Assurances and Guarantees of Non-repetition

Even though the ILC Articles include these remedies within its framework, the doctrine of international law seems rather inconsistent with respect to the availability of assurances and guarantees of non-repetition. Some authors consider that assurances and guarantees of non-repetition are not remedies and that the Court has not confirmed their availability,[52] nor has it granted, as such, through its judgments. Nevertheless, this argument should not lead to the conclusion that the Court did not confirm the existence of this remedy in international law. Commentators have concluded in this sense that this approach of the Court, *i.e.* to confirm the existence of the remedy but not to grant it per se, is justified by the fact that the Court avoids the need to supervise whether their implementation is performed or not.[53]

However, the Court does not have the duty to verify whether states respect, or implement, its judgments.[54] This procedural effect of giving a judgment is

---

[48] *LaGrand Case (Germany v USA)* [1999] ICJ Pleadings, Application instituting Proceedings, 6.
[49] *Navigational and Related Rights (Costa Rica v Nicaragua)* (Judgment), 223.
[50] ILC Draft Articles with Commentaries, 89.
[51] ILC Draft Articles with Commentaries, 89.
[52] Christian J Tams, 'Recognizing Assurance and Guarantees of Non Repetition: LaGrand and the Law of State Responsibility' (2002) 27:2 Yale Journal of International Law 441.
[53] Tams, 'Recognizing Assurance and Guarantees of Non Repetition' 443.
[54] B Ajibola, 'Compliance with Judgments of the International Court of Justice' in M Bulterman and M Kuijer (eds), *Compliance with Judgments of International Courts* (Martinus Nijhoff Publishers 1996) 12.

justified, because a verification of the implementation of any remedy would be difficult to address by the Court, irrespective of its character. More so, the Court has accepted that guarantees of non-repetition exist as a remedy of international law. As such, the details regarding its supervision or scope do not influence the finding that it is, in fact, a remedy of international law. Ajibola concludes that this remedy is rather different from the traditional forms of reparation as it is concerned with reparation for future breaches.[55] As such, cessation and guarantees of non-repetition should not be disregarded as remedies of international law, as long as their scope converges with that of the classic remedies of international law.

Furthermore, guarantees of non-repetition, as a remedy, produce certain effects with respect to the continuing diplomatic relationship between the states in question.[56] Therefore, in the same manner in which satisfaction as a remedy contributes to the re-establishment of a fair relationship between states, assurances and guarantees of non-repetition play the same role, which cannot discredit them as remedies under international law. Crawford rightfully points out that it is clear that *'the Court at least considers that it has the power to order assurances and guarantees of non-repetition'*.[57]

This remedy has been described as being far-reaching with respect to both the obligation that it imposes and to the entities that have the right to claim it before the Court.[58] However, this conclusion rather drifts away from the scope of the remedy of protecting the injured state from future breaches of the same obligations that has triggered the dispute before the Court. The opinion of Brigitte Stern is preferable in this respect, when she concludes that the obligation of assuring and guaranteeing non-repetition participates in the re-establishment of the breached legal order for the future.[59] It is also relevant to point out, at this juncture, that Article 48 of the ILC Articles further contextualises this remedy, by providing that the state entitled to invoke assurances and guarantees can do so, along with cessation.

However, it bears emphasis that the Court has never applied this Article, and the Commentary to the ILC Articles mentions, with respect to assurances and guarantees of non-repetition, that this measure is one of progressive development.[60]

---

[55] Ajibola, 'Compliance with Judgments of the International Court of Justice' 12.
[56] Crawford, 'The ICJ and the Law of State Responsibility' 82.
[57] Crawford, State Responsibility, 473.
[58] Stern, 'A Plea for Reconstruction of International Responsibility' 98.
[59] Stern, 'A Plea for Reconstruction of International Responsibility' 104.
[60] ILC Draft Articles with Commentaries, 90.

5.2.3.3 Implementing Assurances and Guarantees of Non-repetition

Once it is accepted that assurances and guarantees of non-repetition are veritable remedies under international law, the question as to how these remedies would be implemented by a state which has to fulfil the obligation imposed by the Court deserves attention. The Commentary of the ILC Articles further provides that the Court confirmed that the obligation of giving assurances and guarantees of non-repetition can be performed by states.[61]

The Court has not yet rendered a judgment clarifying the means through which assurances and guarantees of non-repetition would be implemented. It therefore appears, from the case-law of the Court, that the party which must comply with its judgment has the discretion to choose the mechanism through which it should provide assurances or guarantees of non-repetition in such a manner that the applicant state is satisfied. Crawford considers that the Court is inclined to give judgments regarding points of international law, rather than to give judgments with respect to the mechanism through which assurances and guarantees of non-repetition are implemented by the responding state, because *'the Court is a discrete settlement mechanism and it is keen to show that the main point in its judgments is given effect'.*[62] He further argues that a judgment that would simply declare that assurances and guarantees of non-repetition are due would contribute to the re-establishment of diplomatic relations between the states involved. Such a declaration would not prevent the resolution of international disputes, but would rather contribute to the settlement thereof.[63]

5.3 PRACTICAL PERSPECTIVES

5.3.1 *Cessation as a Form of Reparation*

In the Dispute Related to Navigational Rights, Costa Rica requested the Court to order cessation, and further substantiated its request by stating the following:

> *Costa Rica seeks the cessation of this Nicaraguan conduct which prevents the free and full exercise and enjoyment of the rights that Costa Rica possesses on the San Juan River, and which also prevents Costa Rica from fulfilling its responsibilities under Article II of the 1956 Agreement and otherwise. In the event that Nicaragua imposes the economic sanctions referred to above, or any other unlawful sanctions, or otherwise takes steps to aggravate and extend the*

---

[61] ILC Draft Articles with Commentaries, 90.
[62] Crawford, 'The ICJ and the Law of State Responsibility' 82.
[63] Crawford, State Responsibility, 474.

present dispute, Costa Rica further seeks the cessation of such conduct and full reparation for losses suffered.[64]

The Court delivered important findings with respect to the origin of the obligation to cease, and concluded that in situations in which the conduct of the respondent persists on the date of its judgment, it has the duty to cease the wrongful act immediately, in accordance with the general obligations of states to respect international law.[65] Further, the Court concluded that cessation is a veritable form of reparation, when it stated that *'the cessation of a violation of a continuing character and the consequent restoration of the legal situation constitute a form of reparation for the injured State'.*[66] As such, the Court did not consider that this remedy is devoid of scope. As such, cessation is a form of reparation that is capable of contributing to the restoration of the status quo ante, either independently, or in conjunction with other remedies of international law, it being the underlying principle of pacta sunt servanda.[67]

5.3.2 *The Obligation to Cease*

The Case concerning Military and Paramilitary Activities in and against Nicaragua entailed a dispute in which the applicant requested cessation and the Court granted it. This case is rather exceptional because the Court did not shy away from determining that an obligation of cessation exists on behalf of the United States and that this obligation should be complied with.

On 9ᵗ April 1984, Nicaragua submitted this dispute before the Court regarding the responsibility of the United States for certain military and paramilitary activities in and against Nicaragua. On 10 May 1984, the Court issued its order, through which it indicated provisional measures. One of these measures required the United States immediately to cease and refrain from any action restricting access to Nicaraguan ports, and, in particular, the laying of mines. Nicaragua requested the Court to order the following:

> *That, in view of its breaches of the foregoing legal obligations, the United States is under a particular duty to cease and desist immediately: from all use of force – whether direct or indirect, overt or covert – against Nicaragua, and from all threats of force against Nicaragua.*[68]

---

[64] *Navigational and Related Rights (Costa Rica v Nicaragua) (Judgment)* 222.

[65] *Navigational and Related Rights (Costa Rica v Nicaragua) (Judgment)* 222.

[66] *Navigational and Related Rights (Costa Rica v Nicaragua) (Judgment)* 267.

[67] Boas, Public International Law, 296.

[68] *Military and Paramilitary Activities in and against Nicaragua (Nicaragua v USA)* [1984] ICJ Pleadings, Application Instituting Proceedings, 16.

74   5 *Cessation, Assurances, Guarantees of Non-repetition*

Owing to the United States' failure to comply with the above-mentioned order, Nicaragua submitted the following request in its memorial:

> *Nicaragua's Application asserts that the United States has breached and continues to breach specific legal obligations under existing multilateral and bilateral treaties as well as general and customary international law. On this basis, Nicaragua seeks a judgment from the Court declaring that the United States is under a particular legal duty to cease its unlawful conduct and make reparation to Nicaragua for injuries suffered as a result of such conduct.*[69]

It could be argued that Nicaragua used the request it submitted at the provisional measures stage to further demonstrate through its memorial that the obligation was continuously breached by the responding state. The Court decided to follow the argumentation provided by the applicant state. Taking note of Nicaragua's arguments, the Court ruled that Nicaragua is under a duty to immediately cease all acts that could constitute breaches of international obligations.[70]

This case is probably the most straightforward circumstance in which the Court expressly ordered cessation. In fact, this case is also relevant from the perspective of the object of the obligation of cessation. The Court remained general in its approach and did not order the USA to refrain from certain specific acts, but ordered a rather general obligation of cessation with respect to any act, which might amount to a breach of the international obligations of the United States. Whether this approach is advisable, because it enforces the idea that the parties of a treaty should perform their obligations as agreed upon, or unwise, because it could be used as a justification for the continuance of the breach, due to its vagueness, is debatable. It could be considered that, given the factual framework of the case at hand (involving violations of human rights), and the particularities of the obligations that were breached (substantial violations of the fundamental principles of international law), the International Court could have provided Nicaragua with a more contextualised dispositif. This manner of approaching cessation by leaving the specific mechanism in the hands of the state is in line with the general approach of the Court regarding all coercive remedies.

5.3.3 *Cessation, Guarantees of Non-repetition and Restitutio in Integrum*

The Case concerning Avena and Other Mexican Nationals clarified the manner in which cessation can be considered as a fundamental element of

---

[69] *Military and Paramilitary Activities in and against Nicaragua (Nicaragua v USA)* [1984] ICJ Pleadings, Memorial of Nicaragua, 423.
[70] *Military and Paramilitary Activities in and against Nicaragua (Nicaragua v USA)* (Merits), 149.

5.3 *Practical Perspectives* 75

restitutio in integrum. As such, even if, generally, cessation is rather protective in scope, it would appear that this is a general rule, which entails certain specific exceptions.

On 9 January 2003 this case was submitted before the International Court by Mexico for alleged breaches of the VCCR by the USA. Mexico requested the Court to find that the USA committed breaches of Article 5 and Article 36 of the said treaty, because its nationals were sentenced to death without being provided with the right to consular assistance. Therefore, Mexico requested the Court to decide that it is entitled to restitutio in integrum and that the respondent must apply the procedural default to preclude the exercise of certain rights.[71] Following the above-mentioned prayer for relief, Mexico also submitted arguments on cessation as a remedy concluding that without this remedy, the status quo ante would not be fully restored. As such, Mexico concluded that it seeks only the remedies that are essential for the protection of its rights, and included cessation in its request for reparation.[72] Mexico concluded that cessation represents a *'fundamental concern for compliance with international obligations'*[73] and requested that the Court should order guarantees of non-repetition, in order to prevent violations of the same kind in the future.[74]

In the same manner in which the Court was provided with a well-structured argumentation regarding the mechanisms through which guarantees of non-repetition should be performed in the LaGrand Case, Mexico also requested the Court to determine that an informal or formal apology would not suffice regarding the order for assurances of non-repetition and submitted that the United States should take specific actions in order to provide these remedies.[75]

The above-mentioned arguments regarding reparations for violations of the Vienna Convention show that the Court was seized with a number of important issues relevant for the interpretation and clarification of the said remedies. Firstly, and perhaps most importantly, the Court was provided with arguments which described the manner in which assurances and guarantees

---

[71] *Avena and Other Mexican Nationals (Mexico v USA* [2003] ICJ Pleadings, Application of Mexico, 44.

[72] *Avena and Other Mexican Nationals (Mexico v USA)* [2003] ICJ Pleadings, Memorial of Mexico, 5.

[73] *Avena and Other Mexican Nationals (Mexico v USA)* [2003] ICJ Pleadings, Memorial of Mexico, 169.

[74] *Avena and Other Mexican Nationals (Mexico v USA)* [2003] ICJ Pleadings, Memorial of Mexico, 170.

[75] *Avena and Other Mexican Nationals (Mexico v USA)* [2003] ICJ Pleadings, Memorial of Mexico, 171.

of non-repetition can be delimited, as being either i) apologies or ii) formal mechanisms. Secondly, the Court was provided with the possibility to interpret the function of cessation, *i.e.* that it has the potential to resolve a fundamental concern of compliance with international obligations. The Court could have determined the intricacies of these remedies through a finding of principle, which could have clarified and interpreted both notions.

Nevertheless, the Court was rather reluctant to clarify the details regarding cessation, assurances and guarantees of non-repetition. The Court delivered its judgment with respect to cessation rather bluntly, without addressing the arguments raised by the applicant with respect to assurances and guarantees of non-repetition and concluded that Mexico did not establish a continuing nature of the violations of international obligations.[76]

As such, the Court merely stated that cessation could not be granted because the fundamental condition of a continuing breach of an international obligation was not met. The Court pursued a similar approach towards guarantees and assurances of non-repetition. Its finding is not necessarily a contribution to the interpretation of this remedy. The Court seemed to consider that, because the United States demonstrated that it undertook certain efforts to prevent further breaches of the Vienna Convention, assurances and guarantees of non-repetition were no longer appropriate, observing the good faith efforts of the United States to implement its obligations.[77]

The Court therefore concluded that the factual circumstances of the case indicated that the responding state was making its best efforts to respect its obligations and that, therefore, an order for guarantees of non-repetition would have been redundant. However, the fact that the Court did not provide sufficient details regarding the interpretation of the requested remedies still remains an issue that should be resolved by the judicial body in the future.

5.3.4 *The Meaning of Guarantees of Non-repetition*

The LaGrand Case represents the locus classicus for assurances of non-repetition. This case was also referred to by the Court when it received requests for cessation and for assurances of non-repetition in other cases.[78] The LaGrand Case is the only one that the Commentary of the ILC Articles refers to regarding these remedies. The reason for this might be that the

---

[76] *Avena (Mexico v USA)* (Judgment), 68.
[77] *Avena (Mexico v USA)* (Judgment), 68.
[78] *Avena (Mexico v USA)* (Judgment), 12, 59.

5.3 *Practical Perspectives* 77

applicant state requested both remedies for the breaches of international law performed by the responding state.

On 2 March 1999, Germany submitted the dispute before the Court. In its application, Germany argued that the United States failed to comply with Articles 5 and 36 of the Vienna Convention on Consular Relations. This breach occurred because the USA had detained, tried and sentenced to death two German nationals without granting their right of consular protection. Thus, Germany submitted the following request before the Court, inter alia, that the Court should declare that the responding state is under an obligation of specific performance and that the responding state should provide a guarantee of non-repetition of the illegal acts.[79]

Germany did not substantiate its claims regarding cessation and guarantees of non-repetition included in the above-mentioned application. However, through its memorial it submitted that the remedy of guarantees of non-repetition represents one of the minimum requirements to ensure that breaches of international obligations do not occur.[80] Thus, even if initially Germany sought compensation through its application, it later amended its claims by requesting solely a declaration of wrongfulness and guarantees of non-repetition.[81]

The arguments of Germany with respect to the mechanism through which the requested remedies would be complied with is one of the few instances in which guarantees of non-repetition were interpreted and clarified, albeit by a state and not by the Court. Thus, Germany indicated that the requested guarantees must be formally delivered, and further, that specific measures should be undertaken by the responding state through which it would make sure that the international obligations would not be breached in the future:

> *State practice knows two kinds of demands for guarantees: (1) demands for safeguards against the repetition of the wrongful act without any specification, and (2) demands for specific measures to secure that the future conduct of the wrongdoing State will be in compliance with international law.*
>
> *In precise terms, Germany demands formal assurances that the United States will bring its practice in conformity with the requirements of international law, without laying out in detail whether these modifications are to be brought about by formal changes in its domestic law or simply by changing the practical application of its respective legislation. Nevertheless, Germany wishes to emphasise that the result of the endeavour must be complete*

---

[79] *LaGrand (Germany v USA)* (Application), 6.

[80] *LaGrand (Germany v USA)* (Memorial of Germany), para 1.11.

[81] *LaGrand (Germany v USA)* (Memorial of Germany), para 6.25.

conformity of United States conduct with Art. 36 of the Vienna Convention on Consular Relations.[82]

The arguments of the applicant show that these remedies are complex, particularly assurances and guarantees of non-repetition. Germany interpreted guarantees of non-repetition as a formal mechanism, not just a unilateral declaration that the breach of an obligation shall not occur in the future. In Germany's perspective, the meaning of guarantees of non-repetition implies a specific change in the national legislation of the responding state, or a change in state practice. It can be concluded that Germany provided sufficient elements for the Court to interpret the meaning of guarantees of non-repetition. Nevertheless, although the Court was seized with issues that could have been clarified at length, such as the manner in which guarantees of non-repetition apply, whether formally or informally, and the circumstances which would fall in one category or the other, the Court merely *'took note*'[83] of the commitment undertaken by the United States in this respect.

Further, it is important to note that the Court did not distinguish between assurances and guarantees of non-repetition. It seems that the Court interpreted Germany's request for guarantees of non-repetition, a remedy which implies a certain degree of formality, as being a request for assurances of non-repetition, a remedy which is informal in nature, and can take the form of a unilateral declaration.

As such, whether this represents a veritable judgment for guarantees of non-repetition is highly debatable. Similarly to its declaratory judgment in the Corfu Channel Case, the Court considered that the promise of the responding state during the course of the proceedings represents appropriate satisfaction.[84] The fact that the Court considered guarantees of non-repetition as a remedy of international law can be read implicitly from its judgment. Nevertheless, the delivery of a judgment in which the claim of the applicant regarding guarantees of non-repetition is granted by referring to certain documentary evidence submitted by the respondent during the proceedings is not sufficient for reaching the conclusion that this remedy has been granted. The wording of the Court with respect to this remedy, included in the dispositif of the judgment, cannot necessarily be considered as an order for complying with a certain remedy. This approach contributes to the opinions that guarantees of non-repetition cannot be deemed a veritable remedy of international

---

[82] *LaGrand (Germany v USA)* (Memorial of Germany), para 6.71.
[83] *LaGrand (Germany v USA)* (Judgment), 513.
[84] *Corfu Channel Case (Great Britain v Albania)* (Merits), 36.

law before the Court because it cannot be enforced and, further, its implementation by the responding state is not necessarily an obligation.

The Memorial of Germany is clear in the sense that it sought an order from the Court through which it would request the United States to take certain formal measures, for the future, to prevent further breaches of the Vienna Convention on Consular Relations.[85] Thus, even if LaGrand might have been the case where the clarification and interpretation of assurances could have been discussed at length by the Court, it decided to ignore the possibility of clarifying the characteristics of these remedies. However, the fact that the Court considered this remedy as being available before it and that it applied it as such is relevant for its future practice.

5.4 CONCLUSION

It can be considered that cessation is a veritable remedy of international law, and that the effects of this remedy are capable of bringing a dispute before the International Court to an end. Brigitte Stern confirms this opinion by concluding that cessation is capable of repairing injuries, by asking the following question: *'If cessation is thus a form of reparation, what does it rectify, if not what I call legal injury?'*[86] Further, assurances and guarantees of non-repetition share the same fate as cessation. Even if contested at times as being remedies of international law, these remedies contribute to the restoration of the status quo ante.[87] The Court's approach towards these remedies, in the sense that it does not usually prescribe the means of their implementation, is beneficial to the final resolution of the dispute because it does not over-formalise the mechanisms through which cessation and assurances and guarantees of non-repetition are complied with, in the post-adjudication phase.

The Court demonstrated a reluctance to interpret the remedies that have been described in this section. The reason for this approach might be that these remedies have similar characteristics to injunctive relief, which is rarely granted by the Court.[88] Another reason could be that the Court considers that an order through which it would specifically provide for these types of remedies would not be complied with. Moreover, the Court might consider that negotiations and diplomatic relations would be preserved and encouraged by approaching these remedies in the manner that it does.

---

[85] *LaGrand (Germany v USA)* (Memorial of Germany), para 1.11.
[86] Stern, 'A Plea for Reconstruction of International Responsibility' 104.
[87] Barboza, 'Legal Injury' 16.
[88] Gray, Judicial Remedies in International Law, 95.

However, even if certain arguments could have merit, it can be concluded that an interpretational attitude towards a better clarification of these remedies would be advisable for the future case-law of the Court, as nothing would prevent the Court from providing certain general principles that would apply, even in situations in which it decides not to grant these remedies, such as the Case concerning Avena and Other Mexican Nationals.

6

Restitution in Kind

6.1 INTRODUCTION

Restitution in kind has not yet received a proper and detailed interpretation or clarification by the Court. Few cases can be identified in which this remedy has been granted[1] or in which the Court laid out principles with respect to it. The finding of principle provided by the Permanent Court regarding the primacy of restitution in kind[2] has never been contradicted throughout its case-law, the judgment in the Chorzów Factory Case being mostly relied upon when interpreting this remedy. The principle identified by the Court refers mainly to the general applicability of restitution in kind and its interaction with other remedies such as compensation.

Nevertheless, even though the Permanent Court established certain applicable principles related to restitution in kind, its analysis of this remedy is not necessarily substantial. As restitution has not received much consideration from the Court, its clarification was substantiated by doctrine. For example, some commentators do not consider the arguments which support the view of the Permanent Court with respect to the primacy of restitution to be very convincing,[3] and others consider that restitution in kind is the primary remedy in international law.[4] Authors have considered that certain cases, such as Paraguay v USA, *'highlight dramatically the fundamental uncertainties as to the availability of restitution in international law'.*[5] Other views have also been expressed to the contrary effect, that restitution in kind is the usual kind of relief before the International Court.[6]

---

[1]   *Temple of Preah Vihear (Cambodia v Thailand)* (Merits).
[2]   *Factory at Chorzów (Germany v Poland)* (Merits), 47.
[3]   Gray, Judicial Remedies in International Law, 96.
[4]   Alina Kaczorowska, *Public International Law* (Routledge 2010) 483.
[5]   Gray, 'The Choice between Restitution and Compensation' 413.
[6]   Crawford, State Responsibility, 509.

82   6 *Restitution in Kind*

As such, contradictory views exist regarding the multitude of issues that have arisen with respect to the interpretation of this remedy, which include the competence of the Court to analyse restitution in kind and the limitations that the parties must take into account when requesting it. This chapter endeavours to clarify certain interpretational uncertainties related to restitution in kind.

States do not frequently seek restitution in kind. Even though the Chorzów Factory Case[7] represents the locus classicus for the interpretation of restitution in kind, this remedy is rather exceptional, as states have invoked it in relatively few cases. Initial requests for restitution in kind are included in prayers for relief, but they are replaced by requests for compensation or declaratory relief through subsequent pleadings, such as memorials or through final oral arguments.[8] The Chorzów Factory Case is such an example,[9] within which the applicant first requested restitution in kind, but later considered that compensation is more appropriate. Despite the exceptional nature of this remedy, the applications of states seeking restitution in kind have contributed to the contemporary interpretation of this remedy. Issues such as the primacy of restitution over compensation, types of restitution and the manner in which restitution in kind can be utilised as a valuation tool have been addressed throughout the case-law of the Court.

The most relevant case that established the principles applicable to restitution in kind was the Chorzów Factory Case.[10] Even though the Permanent Court did not grant restitution in kind in this case, its findings are relevant for the interpretation of restitution in kind and its obiter dictum has been cited in several other cases that were resolved by the Court. The Case concerning the Temple of Preah Vihear[11] is another relevant dispute for the interpretation of restitution in kind. In this case, although the Court's judgment did not substantiate the reasoning for which it granted restitution in kind, it is one of the few instances in which the Court granted the remedy. The Wall Advisory Opinion[12] is also relevant for determining the applicability of restitution in kind as a remedy, where the Court delivered an advisory opinion rather than a judgment. Yet, this case is often cited with respect to the interpretation of restitution in kind and its interaction with compensation, when the former

---

[7] *Factory at Chorzów (Germany v Poland)* (Jurisdiction).
[8] *LaGrand Case (Germany v USA)* [1999] ICJ Pleadings, Memorial of the Federal Republic of Germany.
[9] *Factory at Chorzów (Germany v Poland)* (Jurisdiction).
[10] *Factory at Chorzów (Germany v Poland)* (Merits).
[11] *Temple of Preah Vihear (Cambodia v Thailand)* (Merits), 37.
[12] *Legal Consequences of the Construction of a Wall in the Occupied Palestinian Territory* (Advisory Opinion) [2004] ICJ Rep 136.

proves to be materially impossible. The mentioned cases are fundamental in understanding the manner in which restitution in kind applies before the Court. This jurisprudence of the Court shall be critically analysed below in order to arrive at certain relevant conclusions for the interpretation of restitution in kind as a remedy before the Court.

6.2 THEORETICAL PERSPECTIVES

6.2.1 *The Definition and Function of Restitution in Kind*

The main controversy related to the definition of restitution in kind in international law is its confusion with restitutio in integrum. The analysis of the case-law of the Court highlights that states often request restitutio in integrum with the meaning of restitution in kind, and vice versa. This confusion is confirmed, and perhaps generated, by the ILC Articles, which do not mention the concept of restitution in kind as such, but they refer to restitution with the more general meaning of restitutio in integrum. As such, Article 35 of the ILC Articles contains the following provision:

> A *State responsible for an internationally wrongful act is under an obligation to make restitution, that is, to re-establish the situation which existed before the wrongful act was committed.*

A plain reading of Article 35 establishes that the notion of restitution embodied in the ILC Articles is the one of restitutio in integrum, and not restitution in kind. Nevertheless, it is essential to mention, at this juncture, that the two concepts are not identical. The main difference between restitutio in integrum and restitution in kind is that while the former requires that the injured party be restored to the situation as it existed before the international obligation was breached, the latter implies that the injuries should be restored in their material form. Consequently, restitutio in integrum is not a remedy of international law, strictly speaking, but a mechanism that would encompass all the remedies of international law which would contribute to the restoration of the status quo ante. As such, restitution in kind is but an element that, either alone, or in conjunction with other remedies, such as compensation or declaratory judgments, is used to reach restitutio in integrum.

6.2.2 *Types of Restitution in Kind*

There is less controversy when classifying restitution in kind. Authors have stated that the Court is flexible, as it gives the state parties the '*freedom to*

84 6 *Restitution in Kind*

determine the specific modality for effecting restitution',[13] and that '*it is generally recognized that it is the injured state which has the choice as to the form of reparation, and, in particular, as to whether to request restitution*'.[14] The vast majority of the claims of states can be included, up to a certain degree, into one of the two categories of restitution in kind: material restitution and juridical restitution.[15] For the sake of clarity, it is worth mentioning that certain scholars refer to juridical restitution as legal restitution.[16]

Material restitution may include '*return of territory, persons or property, or the reversal of some juridical act, or a combination of them*'.[17] Juridical restitution often implies the modification of a legal situation.[18] This modification could be implemented through '*a declaration that an offending treaty or act of the executive judiciary or legislature is invalid*'.[19]

6.2.3 *The Primacy of Restitution in Kind*

Certain authors have interpreted the findings of the Court in the Chorzów Factory Case as clearly establishing the principles that suggest that restitution in kind is the primary remedy in international law.[20] Others argue that restitution is the primary remedy in international law because it has the potential to eliminate all the consequences of an unlawful act, as opposed to other remedies such as compensation.[21] Further arguments have been raised in the sense that this remedy is a form of reparation which best contributes to the restoration of the status quo ante.[22]

It is, thus, generally argued that the framework of remedies before the International Court implies a hierarchy of remedies, based on their

---

[13] Crawford, State Responsibility, 515.
[14] Christine Gray, 'The Different Forms of Reparation: Restitution' in James Crawford, Alain Pellet and Simon Olleson (eds), *The Law of International Responsibility* (Oxford University Press 2010) 593; Kaczorowska, Public International Law, 483.
[15] Crawford, State Responsibility, 511; Eric De Brabandere, *Investment Treaty Arbitration as Public International Law: Procedural Aspects and Implications* (Cambridge University Press 2014) 180.
[16] Gray, 'The Different Forms of Reparation: Restitution' 590.
[17] Gray, Judicial Remedies in International Law, 99.
[18] Crawford, State Responsibility, 512.
[19] Kaczorowska, Public International Law, 483.
[20] Scott Leckie and Chris Huggins, *Conflict and Housing, Land and Property Rights: A Handbook on Issues, Frameworks, and Solutions* (Cambridge University Press 2011) 133.
[21] Borzu Sabahi, *Compensation and Restitution in Investor-State Arbitration: Principles and Practice* (Oxford University Press 2011) 61.
[22] Crawford, State Responsibility, 509.

importance,[23] The Chorzów Factory Case is the usual cornerstone upon which this conclusion rests.[24] The relevance of this case is that there exist few other international judgments that interpreted the application of remedies in international law in a similar, in-depth, manner,[25] and the prevalent opinion is that this finding of the Court confirms the view that restitution in kind is the primary remedy in international law. In this view, compensation would be a secondary remedy, in the sense that it should be granted only if restitution in kind is impossible. Thus, restitution in kind would be at the top of the hierarchy, followed by specific performance, and then compensation, which are followed by satisfaction and, finally, by declaratory judgment.

The fact that restitution in kind is considered the primary remedy in international law is further confirmed by its inclusion, as such, in the ILC Articles, reflecting the approach of the Permanent Court in the Chorzów Factory Case. Thus, Article 34 of the ILC Articles provides that full reparation is achieved by restitution, compensation and satisfaction either singly or in combination. Further, Article 35 of the ILC Articles provides that a state that is responsible for an internationally wrongful act is under an obligation to make restitution.

Nevertheless, the main issue regarding this conclusion is not reflected in the practice of the Court, as states rarely request restitution in kind, and the Court rarely grants it. Certain cases that the Court has resolved *'highlight dramatically the uncertainties as to the availability of restitution in international law'.*[26] Nevertheless, to argue that restitution in kind is not available to states might be an overreaching conclusion. Referring to the obiter dictum of the Chorzów Factory Case,[27] authors have argued that restitution in kind is available before the Court. Some go even further, by stating that *'the Permanent Court of International Justice implied that restitution is the normal form of reparation and that indemnity could only take its place if restitution is not available'.*[28] Restitution in kind has been referred to as being *'the ideal*

---

[23] Amerasinghe, Jurisdiction of Specific International Tribunals, 178.

[24] Takele Soboka Bulto, *The Extraterritorial Application of the Human Rights to Water in Africa* (Cambridge University Press 2014) 229.

[25] Dinah Shelton, 'Righting Wrongs: Reparations in the Articles on State Responsibility' (2002) 96 American Journal of International Law, 833, 836.

[26] Gray, 'The Choice between Restitution and Compensation' 413.

[27] *Factory at Chorzów (Germany v Poland)* (Merits), 27–28.

[28] Eduardo Jiménez de Aréchaga and Attila Massimiliano Tanzi, 'International State Responsibility' in Mohammed Bedjaoui (ed), *International Law: Achievements and Prospects* (Martinus Nijhoff Publishers 1991) 369.

form of reparation,[29] being the sole manner in which the status quo ante could be fully restored.

This dichotomy between theory and practice, related to the availability, primacy and scope of restitution in kind as a remedy before the International Court, represents an interesting compromise: in theory, nothing appears to prohibit restitution in kind, while in practice several hurdles appear. More so, a strict interpretation of the Chorzów Factory Case dictum might lead to an infringement of the right of a state to elect the manner in which reparation should be granted. In this vein, if the Chorzów Factory Case dictum is interpreted restrictively, it could be concluded that a state may request compensation only after requesting restitution in kind. A wider interpretation would confirm the conclusion that states have the right to elect the remedies which they consider suitable for the dispute without any restrictions regarding the primacy, or lack thereof, of certain remedies of international law. Even so, this right is not absolute or unlimited. Before the Court, the parties have a right of election[30] as long as the choice is not abusive.[31] The ILC Articles confirm that states have a right of election concerning the means of reparation through Article 43(2) (b) which provides that the injured state may specify in particular the form of reparation, which it seeks through its claim.

Thus, if a state demonstrates the suitability of its request for reparation, which would subsequently be decided by the Court, its choice should be respected. It is relevant to point out, at this juncture, that in the Chorzów Factory Case the German Government had abandoned its original claim for restitution, its reasoning being that the original state of the factory no longer corresponded to its state at the time of the proceedings before the Court.[32] This justification of the German Government was sufficient for the Court to accept its choice.

Thus, a systemic analysis of the Chorzów Factory Case dictum would lead to a more complex interpretation than may appear at first glance, and to important conclusions about the manner in which the judgment of the Permanent Court influences the application of this remedy in other cases. As a consequence, even if it has been argued that the reasons for which the Chorzów Factory Case dictum is cited oversimplifies a complex dispute,[33] it is

---

[29] René Lefeber, *Transboundary Environmental Interference and the Origin of State Liability* (Kluwer Law International 1996) 133.

[30] Crawford, State Responsibility, 508.

[31] Crawford, State Responsibility, 508.

[32] *Factory at Chorzów (Germany v Poland)* (Jurisdiction), 17.

[33] Panos Merkouris, 'The Advisory Jurisdiction of the Permanent Court of International Justice in Practice: A Tale of Two Scopes' in Malgosia Fitzmaurice and Christian Tams (eds), *Lasting Legacies of the Permanent Court of International Justice* (Martinus Nijhoff 2013) 72.

mostly recognised that restitution in kind is the primary remedy in international law.[34] However, issues of practicality still remain, as restitution in kind might not be the proper remedy in certain circumstances.

Even if the judgment in the Chorzów Factory Case established that restitution in kind is the primary remedy in international law, the restoration of the status quo ante, as such, is in most cases impossible,[35] and *'one of the problems in establishing the primacy of restitution is the large gap between practice and theory'*.[36] Thus, the principles stated in the Chorzów Factory Case appear, at times, abandoned.[37]

The interpretation of the obiter dictum in the Chorzów Factory Case has been questioned, as authors have cynically noted that *'Chorzów Factory is the one that has survived to be cited with great frequency, often by people who would appear never to have read it'*.[38] It has also been argued that restitution is not necessarily appropriate in cases other than the ones that involve territory or durable items.[39] These views appear to be justified at times.

6.3 PRACTICAL PERSPECTIVES

6.3.1 *The Availability of Restitution in Kind*

Even if states have the right to elect their preferred remedy, which, in their view, is the suitable form of reparation, the Court has the power to censor the requests with respect to restitution in kind. In this sense, restitution in kind might be objectively unavailable in certain cases. In these circumstances, the Court can decline to award restitution in kind, not because it does not have jurisdiction to do so, but because its jurisdiction extends to analysing the merits of the request for restitution. In other words, the Court has the power to verify the availability of restitution in kind, on a case-by-case basis.

In analysing claims for restitution, the Court generally considers two hypotheses: whether this remedy is materially impossible and whether the weight of the burden imposed by restitution on the responsible state would be disproportionate. These elements do not touch upon the power of the Court to award restitution in kind, but influence the availability of this remedy.

---

[34] Kaczorowska, Public International Law, 483.
[35] Kaczorowska, Public International Law, 483.
[36] Gray, Judicial Remedies in International Law, 416.
[37] Crawford, State Responsibility, 598.
[38] Merkouris, 'The Advisory Jurisdiction of the PCIJ' 72.
[39] Michael J Matheson, *International Tribunals and Armed Conflict* (Martinus Nijhoff Publishers 2012), 224.

6.3.1.1 Material Impossibility

The doctrine is not unanimous regarding the manner in which restitution in kind operates in disputes before the Court. Some authors have concluded that the case of material impossibility is clear and without controversy,[40] while others have argued that the limits of claims for restitution are not at all clear.[41]

The condition of material impossibility implies that the responsible state would be prepared to respect a judgment of the Court through which restitution in kind is ordered but, for objective reasons, such an order would be moot because its performance would be materially impossible. In such a scenario, it would be in the interest of the injured state to seek compensation and not restitution in kind, so that the judgment of the Court is not otiose.

There are few examples where either the Court or the parties have argued that restitution in kind was unavailable because it would have been materially impossible to perform a potential judgment of the Court, in this respect.[42] One case in which reference has been made to material impossibility is the Chorzów Factory Case, where the Permanent Court stated that reparation could be achieved through:

> *Restitution in kind, or, if this is not possible, payment of a sum corresponding to the value which a restitution in kind would bear.*[43]

Material impossibility was implicitly referred to by the International Court, in the Corfu Channel Case[44] where Great Britain submitted that a ship exactly like the 'Saumarez' could not have been restored to it.[45] This submission referred to the Chorzów Factory Case to argue that restitution in kind should be the measure through which compensation is assessed. However, Great Britain also requested the Court to determine that the object of the dispute had ceased to exist and, therefore, it would have been impossible for the respondent to restore the status quo ante by rebuilding a ship. Another contentious case in which the Court has analysed the issue of material

---

[40] Sotirios-Ioannis Lekkas and Antonios Tzanakopoulos, 'Pacta sunt servanda versus flexibility in the suspension and termination of treaties' in Christian J Tams, Antonios Tzanakopoulos and Andreas Zimmermann (eds), *Research Handbook on the Law of Treaties* (Edward Elgar Publishing 2014) 312, 329.

[41] Giuseppe Sperduti, 'Restitution' in Linda J Pike (ed), *Encyclopedia of Disputes Installment 10* (Elsevier 2014) 377.

[42] Crawford, State Responsibility, 513.

[43] *Case concerning Factory at Chorzów (Germany v Poland)* (Merits), 47.

[44] *Corfu Channel Case (Great Britain v Albania)* (Oral Proceedings Second Part).

[45] *Corfu Channel Case (Great Britain v Albania)* (Oral Proceedings Second Part), 709.

impossibility, in passing, was the Bosnian Genocide Case, in which the applicant recognised that restitution in kind was not appropriate.[46] In this case, where the source of the dispute was the application of the Convention on the Prevention and Punishment of the Crime of Genocide, restitution in kind was considered as being impossible of being performed because a fundamental right was breached and, further, that this right could not have been objectively restored. Commentators confirm that certain injuries, of a high degree of complexity, cannot be fully repaired, one such example being situations in which force is used.[47] Therefore, the only manner in which reparation could have been achieved in this situation was by means of compensation. Furthermore, in the Gabčíkovo–Nagymaros Case, the Court concluded that the practical possibilities and impossibilities should be observed when assessing the potential orders for future conduct.[48]

Thus, the Court observes the factual circumstances of each case when determining whether restitution in kind is possible or impossible to achieve. In cases such as the Gabčíkovo–Nagymaros, where environmental harm had been caused, the Court concluded that it could not disregard the manner in which the parties had acted.[49] The Court also assessed material impossibility in its Advisory Opinion regarding the Wall Case,[50] and concluded that Israel should return certain lands and immovable property, but should such restitution prove materially impossible that compensation would be the applicable remedy.[51]

The determination that the Court made in the Wall Case was formulated as part of an advisory opinion, which lacks the binding force of a judgment. Nevertheless, the advisory opinions of the Court should be addressed accordingly, when assessing the interpretation of the concepts of international law, state responsibility included.[52] Thus, the fact that the determination of the Court was a part of an advisory opinion should not diminish the scope of its finding, *i.e.* that material impossibility is an observed criterion when granting restitution in kind. Even if not in the same terminology as the one used by the

---

[46] *Application of the Convention on the Prevention and Punishment of the Crime of Genocide (Bosnia and Herzegovina v Serbia and Montenegro)* (Judgment).

[47] Jean-Claude Tcheuwa, 'Communauté internationale, guerre et responsabilité: réflexion autour de la responsabilité internationale des états' (2005) 58:1 Revue Hellénique de Droit International 106.

[48] *Gabčíkovo–Nagymaros Project (Hungary/Slovakia)* (Judgment), 76.

[49] *Gabčíkovo–Nagymaros Project (Hungary/Slovakia)* (Judgment), 76.

[50] *Construction of a Wall in the Occupied Palestinian Territory* (Advisory Opinion).

[51] *Construction of a Wall in the Occupied Palestinian Territory* (Advisory Opinion), 66.

[52] *Construction of a Wall in the Occupied Palestinian Territory* (Advisory Opinion), 66.

Permanent Court in the Chorzów Factory Case, it appears that, in the Wall Case, the Court suggested that restitution in kind is the adequate primary form of reparation, but should material impossibility occur, compensation would be the appropriate remedy. This consideration seems to allow the responsible state to determine whether it would be materially possible to respect the Court's decision with respect to restitution in kind.

As such, it could be concluded that there is a tendency of states to argue that restitution in kind cannot be granted by the Court, a perspective which demonstrates the reason for which this remedy is not necessarily the norm, before the Court. As epitomised in the case-law of the Court, discussed above, examples of such material impossibility are various and they include cases where the caused environmental harm could not be restored by means of clean-up or where the object of the dispute had seized to exist, or where fundamental rights had been breached. There also have been instances where the object of the dispute had been transferred to a bona fide third party and, as a consequence, the applicant had considered that restitution in kind was no longer possible.[53]

These perspectives, which include the various manners in which material impossibility manifests itself, are reflected in Article 35 of the ILC Articles which does not contain an exhaustive list in which this criterion displays its effects. It can, therefore, be considered that the condition regarding material impossibility remains clear and logical, as it protects the interests of the injured state in seeking and obtaining reparation for wrongful acts committed against it, while safeguarding the responsible state from performing an impossible task. However, that is not necessarily the case for the second criterion, discussed in the following subsection.

6.3.1.2 The Weight of the Burden Imposed on the Responsible State

Few references regarding the condition of a proportionate burden upon the responsible state exist in the case-law of the Court. Even if the ILC Articles refer to this condition within Article 35 (b), the Commentary of the ILC Articles does not refer to any case that was decided by the Court in this respect.[54]

The finding of the Permanent Court in the Chorzów Factory Case might imply the conclusion that restitution in kind should not be awarded if the

---

[53] *Case concerning Barcelona Traction Light and Power Co Ltd* (*Belgium v Spain*) (Judgment) [1970] ICJ Rep 1, 3.

[54] ILC Draft Articles with Commentaries, 98.

burden of such granting would be *'out of all proportion'*. This reasoning could stem from the interpretation given to the following conclusion:

> *Reparation must, as far as possible, wipe out all the consequences of the illegal act and re-establish the situation which would, in all probability, have existed if that act had not been committed.*[55]

However, to interpret the wording of the Court in such a manner where *'as far as possible'* would mean that the Court referred to a burden *'out of all proportion'* might amount to an exaggeration, as the Court did not provide any indication to this end. Further, this wording would rather refer to the material possibility standard rather than anything else. While material impossibility is an objective standard, the burden out of proportion is a more subjective one. Thus, what is materially impossible for a state would be the same for any other state while a burden might prove to have a certain weight for a state and a different weight for another state, depending on several factors such as economic, political or social ones. Such an interpretation is in accordance with the Commentary to the ILC Articles, which mentions that the application of Article 35 (b) is based on considerations of equity and reasonableness.[56] Authors have confirmed this view when concluding that establishing the weight of the burden is a subjective act, because proportionality should be respected when awarding restitution in kind.[57] Factually, a question that has been answered in the affirmative when interpreting the burden *'out of all proportion'* standard was whether a state would have to re-inhabit a region which was contaminated by a nuclear accident.[58] The affirmative answer to the above quoted question seems reasonable. However, if it can be considered that the responsible state should have foreseen the consequences of rendering the region uninhabitable that was contaminated due to its fault, the answer is no longer clear, inasmuch as the case-law of the Court leads to the conclusion that states often foresee the consequences of their actions upon the environment.

---

[55] *Interpretation of Judgments nos. 7 and 8 concerning the Case of the Factory at Chorzów* (Judgment), 47.

[56] ILC Draft Articles with Commentaries, 98.

[57] *'In cases of restitution, not involving the return of persons, property, or territory to the injured State the notion of reverting the status quo ante has to be applied having regard to the respective rights and competences of the States concerned. This may be the case, for example, where what is involved is a procedural obligation conditioning the exercise of the substantive powers of the state.'* Crawford, State Responsibility, 515.

[58] Christian Tomuschat, 'International Crimes by States: An Endangered Species?' in Karel Wellens (ed), *International Law: Theory and Practice: Essays in Honour of Eric Suy* (Martinus Nijhoff Publishers 1998) 254–256.

92   6 *Restitution in Kind*

Nevertheless, conclusions are yet to be drawn about the condition regarding the proportionality of the burden imposed on the responsible state, as this condition has not yet occurred in practice.

6.3.2 *The Locus Classicus of Restitution in Kind*

The contemporary interpretation of restitution in kind is closely connected to the Chorzów Factory Case,[59] one of the first cases that were submitted before the Permanent Court, because its findings represent the locus classicus for determining the interpretation of this remedy.

In this case, Germany filed an application before the Permanent Court, through which it requested it to determine that Poland was responsible for illegal liquidation and was, thus, liable under international law. The judgments of the Permanent Court in the Chorzów Factory Case have influenced the manner in which reparation, generally, and restitution in kind, specifically, are interpreted, as it has analysed a multitude of issues with respect to its power to adjudge claims for reparation and to the place that restitution in kind takes in the hierarchy of remedies. These issues will be assessed in the following subsections.

6.3.2.1 The Primacy of Restitution in Kind

The Permanent Court analysed the manner in which the injury caused could be repaired by Poland. Even though the parties agreed that restitution in kind was no longer possible, the Permanent Court seemed to consider that it was worth establishing what would amount to reparation in this case. The Court concluded the following in this respect:

> *Restitution in kind, or, if this is not possible, payment of a sum corresponding to the value which a restitution in kind would bear; the award, if need be, of damages for loss sustained which would not be covered by restitution in kind or payment in place of it – such are the principles which should serve to determine the amount of compensation due for an act contrary to international law.*
>
> *This conclusion particularly applies as regards the Geneva Convention, the object of which is to provide for the maintenance of economic life in Upper Silesia on the basis of respect for the status quo.*[60]

---

[59] *Factory at Chorzów (Germany v Poland)* (Jurisdiction).
[60] *Factory at Chorzów (Germany v Poland)* (Merits), 47.

The first paragraph of the *dispositif* could lead to the general conclusion that should a breach of an international obligation occur, restitution in kind would be the primary remedy of international law, irrespective of the nature of the obligations breached. This conclusion is sometimes isolated from the second paragraph, which provides that the first applies *'particularly'* with respect to the Geneva Convention. As such, the second paragraph necessarily implies that restitution in kind should not be considered as the primary remedy of international law generally, but in certain disputes that contain specific elements related to the breached international obligations. What is also important to note is that, in the Chorzów Factory Case, the parties agreed that the undertaking in dispute could not be restored. In other words, the applicant abandoned any claims with respect to restitution in kind and maintained the ones related to compensation[61] and this could have been one justification for which the Court rendered a judgment through which it established certain principles related to reparation in general, and to restitution in kind and compensation in particular. The finding of the Permanent Court, regarding the manner in which reparation manifests its effects, is the *obiter dictum* that is most often quoted when referring to restitution in kind as a remedy of international law. The Permanent Court concluded as follows:

> *The essential principle contained in the actual notion of an illegal act – a principle which seems to be established by international practice and in particular by the decisions of arbitral tribunals – is that reparation must, as far as possible, wipe out all the consequences of the illegal act and re-establish the situation which would, in all probability, have existed if that act had not been committed.*[62]

The first issue that the Permanent Court clarified is that the scope of reparation is to restore the situation that existed before the illegal act occurred, *i.e.* the status quo ante. Secondly, the Permanent Court determined the manner in which reparation could be reached, *i.e.* either through restitution in kind or, if restitution would be impossible, through monetary relief.

The primary character of restitution in kind was analysed through other cases as well. Thus, in the Nottebohm Case,[63] the subsidiary character of compensation was included in the request of the applicant, which sought a determination of the Court in the sense that restitution in kind is the appropriate remedy for illegal expropriation. Compensation was requested as a

---

[61] *Factory at Chorzów (Germany v Poland)* (Merits), 48.
[62] *Factory at Chorzów (Germany v Poland)* (Merits), 47.
[63] *Nottebohm Case (Liechtenstein v Guatemala)* (Judgment Second Phase) [1955] ICJ Rep 4.

replacement of restitution in kind, should the latter be impossible to perform.[64] This submission was further explained through the memorial that was submitted by Liechtenstein, which requested the Court to find that Guatemala should restore the illegally seized properties and, alternatively, that Guatemala should pay compensation.[65] In the Certain Phosphate Lands Case, the primary character of restitution and, consequently, the subsidiary character of other remedies was emphasised through the application of Nauru, which requested the Court to decide that restitution should be granted or another appropriate reparation.[66]

The primacy of restitution in kind was ignored in cases that entailed different heads of claim. Thus, in the Armed Activities on the Territory of the Congo, restitution in kind was treated at par with compensation,[67] as the request of the applicant state included both remedies. The Memorial on Compensation submitted by Nicaragua in the Military and Paramilitary Activities in and against Nicaragua case is also relevant from the perspective of the availability of compensation in cases in which the remedy of restitution in kind is unavailable, once again highlighting their nature as alternatives to each other. In this case, Nicaragua submitted it decided to request compensation because *'any other form of reparation would be unsuitable in the present case'*.[68]

The reason for which the International Court has refrained from giving judgment on the request for compensation submitted by Nicaragua is relevant for understanding the view of the Court with respect to the impact of a judgment providing for this remedy. The Court concluded that it should refrain from acts that would not be necessary for a potential negotiated settlement between the parties in dispute.[69] As such, the Court therefore considered that a declaration is preferable to a judgment granting a coercive remedy, the latter being capable of further amplifying the dispute, rather than resolving it. It is relevant to note, at this juncture, that the Court is mindful of the post-adjudication phase of the disputes submitted before it.

---

[64] *Nottebohm Case (Liechtenstein v Guatemala)* [1951] ICJ Pleadings, Application instituting Proceedings, 15.

[65] *Nottebohm Case (Liechtenstein v Guatemala)* [1952] ICJ Pleadings, Memorial Submitted by the Government of the Principality of Liechtenstein, 70.

[66] *Certain Phosphate Lands in Nauru (Nauru v Australia)* [1989] ICJ Pleadings, Application instituting Proceedings, 30, 32.

[67] *Case concerning Armed Activities on the Territory of the Congo (Democratic Republic of the Congo v Uganda)* [2005] ICJ Rep 168.

[68] *Military and Paramilitary Activities in and against Nicaragua (Nicaragua v USA)*, Memorial of Nicaragua, 287.

[69] *Military and Paramilitary Activities in and against Nicaragua (Nicaragua v USA)* (Merits), 143.

6.3 Practical Perspectives

Even if arguments exist in the case law of the International Court, for considering restitution as the primary remedy, they remain rather exceptional. In the majority of the cases that were submitted before the Court, compensation has been requested in lieu of restitution in kind. Thus, even though the ILC Articles give primacy to restitution in kind when assessing the responsibility of states for illegal acts, the conclusion that a discrepancy exists between theory and practice with respect to the primacy of restitution in kind has merit.[70]

6.3.2.2 Assessing Compensation

The value of the Chorzów Factory Case does not solely reside in the interpretation provided with respect to restitution in kind, as it contained relevant findings regarding compensation as a remedy of international law and its interaction with restitution in kind. In this sense, the obiter dictum of the Permanent Court does not only refer to the alleged primacy of restitution in kind in international law but also to the manner in which the Court determines amounts of compensation. Due regard should be given to the reasoning of the Permanent Court in this respect, by observing the relevant passages of its judgments. The paragraph before the dictum of the Chorzów Factory Case refers to compensation in the following terms:

> It follows that the compensation due to the German Government is not necessarily limited to the value of the undertaking at the moment of dispossession, plus interest to the day of payment. This limitation would only be admissible if the Polish Government had had the right to expropriate, and if its wrongful act consisted merely in not having paid to the two Companies the just price of what was expropriated.[71]

The paragraph after the dictum also refers to the manner in which compensation would be assessed:

> The impossibility, on which the Parties are agreed, of restoring the Chorzów Factory could therefore have no other effect but that of substituting payment of the value of the undertaking for restitution; it would not be in conformity either with the principles of law or with the wish of the Parties to infer from that agreement that the question of compensation must henceforth be dealt with as though an expropriation properly so called was involved.[72]

---

[70] Gray, 'The Different Forms of Reparation: Restitution' 589.
[71] *Factory at Chorzów (Germany v Poland)* (Merits), 47.
[72] *Factory at Chorzów (Germany v Poland)* (Merits), 47.

96   6 *Restitution in Kind*

The interpretation of the dictum, in its context, leads to the conclusion that the finding of the Permanent Court in the Chorzów Factory Case also refers to the substitution of restitution in kind with compensation. Thus, the finding of the Permanent Court is not only a declaration of principle, but also a justification for the calculation of damages.[73] Therefore, where restitution in kind is not materially possible, the Court has the possibility to use this remedy as a valuation tool, restitution in kind being the only remedy of international law with this secondary function. The Court confirmed this finding throughout its jurisprudence. In the Anglo-Iranian Oil Co Case compensation was requested as a primary remedy and restitution in kind was relied upon as a valuation method.[74] Another case that considered restitution in kind as the valuation tool for compensation was the Nottebohm Case, in which the applicant requested that the amounts requested represented the market value of the seized property calculated as if it would have maintained its original condition.[75] However, this calculation does necessarily imply that compensation is limited to the value of restitution in kind, at the moment of dispossession.[76]

The phrasing of the requests in the above-mentioned cases, regarding the use of restitution in kind as a valuation tool for the determination of compensation, is similar to the one used by the Permanent Court in the Chorzów Factory Case dictum. This reliance also confirms the legacy of the obiter dictum and its relevance in the practice of the Court, which is manifest when assessing the distinction between lawful and unlawful expropriation.

6.3.2.3 Lawful and Unlawful Expropriation

The principles expressed by the Permanent Court in the Chorzów Factory Case with respect to restitution in kind should be appreciated by examining the factual framework of each case. The Chorzów Factory obiter dictum should not be isolated from the subsequent findings of the Permanent Court, which influence its interpretation. It should be noted, at this juncture, that the Permanent Court made a further reference with respect to its dictum, in the sense that it particularly applies to the Geneva Convention.[77] The fact

---

[73] Lauterpacht, The Development of International Law, 316.

[74] *Anglo-Iranian Oil Co Case (United Kingdom v Iran)* [1951] ICJ Pleadings, Memorial Submitted by the Government of the United Kingdom of Great Britain and Northern Ireland, 125.

[75] *Nottebohm (Liechtenstein v Guatemala)* (Memorial of Liechtenstein), 69.

[76] *Nottebohm (Liechtenstein v Guatemala)* (Memorial of Liechtenstein), 68–69.

[77] *Factory at Chorzów (Germany v Poland)* (Merits), 47.

6.3 Practical Perspectives

that the finding of the Permanent Court with respect to restitution in kind in the Chorzów Factory Case involved illegal liquidation should not be ignored.

Thus, restitution in kind is appropriate in cases involving illegally nationalised property, this remedy being applicable upon a finding of a commission of a wrongful act.[78] To apply the same principles to legal nationalisation would be without merit because, in certain circumstances, states have the right to nationalise foreign property.[79] The Chorzów Factory Case involved the issue of expropriation, its illegality and consequences. The Court first analysed whether the source of the dispute was a lawful or an unlawful expropriation, so that its determination with respect to the applicable remedies would follow the effects of this dichotomy.

Commentators mention that the birthplace of the distinction between legal and illegal expropriation is the date on which the Court issued its judgment in the Chorzów Factory Case.[80] This conclusion is relevant because the Court did not expressly conclude that its findings with respect to restitution in kind should apply indiscriminately throughout its case-law. It further contextualised its finding by linking it with the notions of lawful and unlawful expropriation.

Unlawful expropriation has been characterised as occurring when states are prohibited from expropriating through a treaty or an international convention.[81] In other words, if states expropriate, in such circumstances, they perform an unlawful expropriation. Lawful expropriation occurs when states have the right to expropriate, but under the condition of fulfilling certain conditions, such as fair compensation. In such circumstance, if the state does not fulfil the conditions of the expropriation ante factum, its obligation is to fulfil those conditions post factum. For example, if a state does not pay a fair amount of compensation when expropriating, the Court can only order that state to provide adequate and fair compensation. However, if the state did not have the right to expropriate in the first place, the Court may choose to order restitution in kind, as a primary form of redress, or compensation, if restitution proves to be materially impossible.

The difference between lawful expropriation and unlawful expropriation under international law entails certain consequences that manifest with respect to restitution in kind and to compensation. However, at this juncture, it is relevant to discuss the manner in which this difference influences restitution in kind.

---

[78] Sornarajah, The Pursuit of Nationalized Property, 143.

[79] Sornarajah, The Pursuit of Nationalized Property, 143.

[80] ST Ratner, 'Compensation for Expropriation in a World of Investment Treaties: Beyond the Lawful/Unlawful Distinction' (2017) 111 American Journal of International Law 1, 4.

[81] Ratner, 'Compensation for Expropriation' 48.

The Permanent Court explained the difference between these two forms of expropriation through the Chorzów Factory Case. As the extract from the judgment below demonstrates, the Permanent Court did not expressly make the distinction between lawful and unlawful expropriation. The Court rather considered the latter as an unlawful act under international law, as such:

> *The action of Poland which the Court has judged to be contrary to the Geneva Convention is not an expropriation – to render which lawful only the payment of fair compensation would have been wanting; it is a seizure of property, rights and interests which could not be expropriated even against compensation, save under the exceptional conditions fixed by Article 7 of the said Convention.*[82]

Having established that the case involved a seizure of property, the Permanent Court further described the manner in which reparation for this breach would operate. The Permanent Court determined that the concept of expropriation implies that it is lawful, while seizure of property means what is presently understood as unlawful expropriation. Thus, the finding of the Permanent Court regarding the remedies available for the two different types of expropriation has merit and the fact that the action of Poland was what is today considered as unlawful expropriation is relevant.

It is worth mentioning at this point that, following the finding of the Permanent Court, the notion of expropriation was also further addressed by the United Nations, through Resolution 1803 of the General Assembly, which concluded the following in this respect:

> *Nationalization, expropriation or requisitioning shall be based on grounds or reasons of public utility, security or the national interest which are recognized as overriding purely individual or private interests, both domestic and foreign. In such cases the owner shall be paid appropriate compensation, in accordance with the rules in force in the State taking such measures in the exercise of its sovereignty and in accordance with international law.*[83]

It has been concluded in this sense that *'the right of expropriation, even in its widest sense, is recognised by international law irrespective of the patrimonial rights involved'*,[84] As a consequence, the expropriation is legal if it is grounded upon reasons of public utility, for example. Without a proper demonstration of

---

[82] *Factory at Chorzów (Germany v Poland)* (Jurisdiction), 21.

[83] United Nations General Assembly Resolution 1803 (XVII) on the 'Permanent Sovereignty over Natural Resources' (1962) (adopted by 87 votes in favour to 2 votes against; 12 abstentions), 2.

[84] FV García Amador, Louis Bruno Sohn and Richard R Baxter, *Recent Codification of the Law of State Responsibility for Injuries to Aliens* (Martinus Nijhoff Publishers 1974) 46.

6.3 Practical Perspectives

such legal grounds, the expropriation is unlawful and restitution in kind becomes applicable.

The conclusion that the Permanent Court reached in this case demonstrates that the consequence of lawful expropriation is the payment of fair compensation and that if unlawful expropriation occurs, a different set of remedies would be applicable. As such, in the situation of unlawful expropriation, remedies such as restitution in kind would not only be available, but rather primary.

6.3.3 Restitution in Kind and Restitutio in Integrum

Restitution in kind is often included within the more general notion of restitutio in integrum—thereby leading to the mistaken conflation of the two concepts. Illustratively, restitutio in integrum was requested in the Case concerning the Vienna Convention on Consular Relations. The unilateral application of Paraguay contained the following request:

> Paraguay is therefore entitled to restitutio in integrum;
>   The United States of America should restore the status quo ante, that is, re-establish the situation that existed before the detention of, proceedings against, and conviction and sentencing of Paraguay's national in violation of the United States of America's international legal obligations took place.[85]

At first blush, it seems that the meaning that Paraguay attributed to restitutio in integrum is different from the meaning of restitution in kind. However, its understanding can be further gleaned from the memorial submitted by Paraguay, which was delivered before the Court after the restoration of the status quo ante became impossible.[86] Thus, the remedies that were sought by Paraguay were considered restitutio in integrum in the sense of restorations of national legal frameworks and the consequences thereof, *i.e.* an invalidation of all national proceedings, so that the notification under the Vienna Convention for Consular Relations could be performed and the rights of the prosecuted could be respected. As such, even though it might seem that Paraguay requested restitutio in integrum, in this case it becomes clear that Paraguay requested legal restitution in kind.

Restitutio in integrum was also sought in the Avena Case and involved similar claims for legal restitution. The factual framework and the request for

---

[85] *Vienna Convention on Consular Relations (Paraguay v USA)* ICJ Pleadings, Application instituting Proceedings, 5.
[86] *Vienna Convention on Consular Relations (Paraguay v USA)* (Memorial of Paraguay), 6–7.

100   *6 Restitution in Kind*

remedies in the Avena Case is almost identical to the one in the Case concerning the Vienna Convention on Consular Relations.[87] Thus, in two of the three cases that involved requests for restitutio in integrum, this remedy had a wider interpretation than restitution in kind. The meaning attributed to restitutio in integrum in these cases contained the following elements: i) a restoration of the legal framework prior to the illegal act, through the invalidation of a law; ii) the invalidation of a judgment issued by a national court, through a new trial; iii) the re-establishment of a situation that existed before the illegal convictions. An example that included restitution in kind, and not restitutio in integrum, was the Temple of Preah Vihear Case, in which the applicant state requested the Court to order the return of certain material goods that were removed from the Temple.[88]

It is important to note, at this juncture, that restitutio in integrum can encompass restitution in kind, compensation, or any other remedy of international law. This is demonstrable by referring to the unilateral applications that were submitted before the Court. Even if the requests were not worded as such, the manner in which restitutio in integrum was sought indicated that the involved states were seeking the full restoration of the status quo ante. This is discernible from the request that was submitted by Nicaragua in the Case concerning the Construction of a Road in Costa Rica along the San Juan River. In this case, the applicant requested the Court to conclude that Nicaragua had invaded and occupied Costa Rican territory, and that it illegally constructed a channel on this territory. Thus, Costa Rica requested the Court to declare that Nicaragua should restore the status quo ante and that it should pay for the damages caused.[89] The same understanding of restitutio in integrum of applicant states appears from the Dispute regarding Navigational and Related Rights. Costa Rica considered that Nicaragua wrongfully denied the free exercise of certain rights of navigation regarding the San Juan River and requested a judgment from the Court in almost identical terms.[90]

The restoration of the status quo ante was also sought in the request of the applicant in the Barcelona Traction Case. This case represents the most accurate request for remedies with respect to the confusion between restitutio in integrum and restitution in kind, as the Court was requested the following:

---

[87] *Vienna Convention on Consular Relations (Paraguay v USA)* (Application).

[88] *Temple of Preah Vihear (Cambodia v Thailand)* (Merits), 6.

[89] *Construction of a Road in Costa Rica over the San Juan River (Nicaragua v Costa Rica)* [2011] ICJ Pleadings, Application instituting Proceedings, 30.

[90] *Dispute regarding Navigational and Related Rights (Costa Rica v Nicaragua)* [2005] ICJ Pleadings, Application instituting Proceedings.

6.3 Practical Perspectives

that the state of Spain is consequently liable to restore Barcelona Traction in the entirety of its properties, rights and interests, as they existed before the 12th February 1948, and, in addition, to ensure the compensation to this company for any prejudices resulting from the said bankruptcy and related procedures [...]

subsidiarily, to rule that in case that restitutio in integrum proves to be totally or partially impossible, by reason of constitutional obstacles, the State of Spain would be liable to pay to the State of Belgium an indemnity equivalent to the value of the properties, rights and interests of which Barcelona Traction has been deprived.[91]

The cases mentioned above demonstrate that even when not referred to as such, restitutio in integrum was requested together with compensation, as part of the same request for remedies. This manner of framing remedies demonstrates that the notion of restitutio in integrum is wider in scope than restitution in kind, and that the former could encompass a multitude of remedies in order to fully restore the status quo ante. This conclusion is also borne out from the request in the Avena Case, in which, once restitution in kind became impossible, the applicant mentioned that the full restoration of the status quo ante became impossible, compensation being the only remaining remedy available.

Following this analysis, it can be concluded that the legacy of the Chorzów Factory Case towards the interpretation of restitution in kind and its interaction with other remedies, is undeniable. Nevertheless, the Court has provided insights regarding this remedy throughout its case-law, in matters that were not necessarily related to the ones provided through the Chorzów Factory Case. These cases shall be assessed below.

6.3.4 *The Application of Restitution in Kind*

The impact of the judgment of the Permanent Court in the Chorzów Factory Case on the interpretation and clarification of restitution in kind is clear, at this juncture. The jurisprudence of the International Court further clarified certain issues regarding this remedy, such as the manner in which this remedy applies in disputes regarding sovereignty rights or individual rights. The following subsections shall briefly assess the case-law of the Court regarding these issues.

---

[91] *Case concerning Barcelona Traction Light and Power Co Ltd (Belgium v Spain)* [1958] ICJ Pleadings, Application instituting Proceedings, unofficial translation, 19.

6.3.4.1 Restitution in Kind in Sovereignty Disputes

The Temple of Preah Vihear Case illustrates the manner in which restitution in kind might be awarded in disputes related to sovereignty. The main issue in this case was the sovereignty over the region of the Preah Vihear Temple. In this sense, Cambodia considered that the Kingdom of Thailand had unlawfully occupied an area that appertained to the Cambodian State. As such, Cambodia requested the Court to find that it had sovereignty over the territory in question and further, to order Thailand to restore to Cambodia all the objects that were removed from the Temple of Preah Vihear. The Temple of Preah Vihear Case concerned a different subject matter than the Chorzów Factory Case. While the latter concerned questions related to the legality of expropriation, or the lack thereof, in the former the subject matter concerned issues of sovereignty over a certain determined portion of land. Thus, if the Court was to find that Thailand was responsible for breaching international law and, as a consequence, the Temple of Preah Vihear had been illegally occupied by Thailand, from the perspective of remedies the Temple could have been restored in its entirety, along with the religious objects that were included in it. The Court found in this respect that:

> Thailand is under an obligation to restore to Cambodia any objects of the kind specified in Cambodia's fifth Submission which may, since the date of the occupation of the Temple by Thailand in 1954, have been removed from the Temple or the Temple area by the Thai authorities.[92]

The Court did not provide any explanation regarding the acceptance of Cambodia's request with respect to the objects that were present in the Temple. One argument that could be inferred is that it chose to pursue this approach seemingly because it considered the restitution of the said artefacts as a natural consequence of the restoration of the status quo ante. This case represents one of the few cases in which the Court ordered restitution in kind. This is the reason why a majority of writers refer to this case when addressing the case-law of the court regarding this remedy.[93] This finding of the Court confirms the fact that restitution in kind could be applicable in cases involving sovereignty disputes, if the particularities of the case render it appropriate. In other words, the judgment of the International Court in the Case concerning the Temple of Preah Vihear further contributes to the idea that restitution in kind is available for disputes other than the ones involving unlawful

---

[92] *Temple of Preah Vihear (Cambodia v Thailand)* (Merits), 37.

[93] Crawford, State Responsibility, 511; Dinah Shelton, *Remedies in International Human Rights Law* (Oxford University Press 2015) 94; Kaczorowska, Public International Law, 483.

6.3 Practical Perspectives

expropriation and that its primacy regarding the latter does not imply that it is not available in disputes involving the former.

6.3.4.2 Restitution in Kind in Advisory Proceedings

The Wall advisory opinion demonstrates that the Court may provide advisory opinions through which it could determine that restitution in kind is applicable. In this case, the General Assembly of the United Nations adopted resolution ES – 10/14, through which the Court was requested to determine the legal consequences arising from the construction of a wall that was being built by Israel in the Occupied Palestinian Territory.[94] Restitution in kind was a remedy that was included in the pleadings. Thus, the League of Arab States concluded that Israel should make full reparation, which would prioritise restitution in kind.[95]

The Court noted in this respect that restitution in kind, as submitted, implied the demolition of certain portions of the wall and the annulment of the legal acts associated with its construction.[96] The Court opined that, because unlawful expropriation had occurred in this case, restitution in kind would necessarily be the primary remedy.[97] The Court, therefore, confirmed that the Permanent Court undertook in the Chorzów Factory Case and determined that restitution in kind is the primary remedy for unlawful expropriation and, should that prove to be materially impossible, that compensation is appropriate.[98] This case further demonstrates that the dictum of the Permanent Court in the Chorzów Factory Case manifests its effects on the Court's advisory opinions and that the finding of principle related to the application of restitution in kind as a remedy is, and will be, relevant for the practice of the International Court.

6.3.4.3 Restitution in Kind and Individuals

The Tehran Hostages Case demonstrates the manner in which the Court interprets restitution in kind in cases in which the rights of individuals are affected. On 4 November 1979, during the course of a demonstration, certain individuals attacked the Embassy of the USA. The fact that the Iranian

---

[94] *Construction of a Wall in the Occupied Palestinian Territory* (Advisory Opinion), 141.
[95] *Legal Consequences of the Construction of a Wall in the Occupied Palestinian Territory* [2004] ICJ Pleadings, Written Statement of the League of Arab States, 104.
[96] *Construction of a Wall in the Occupied Palestinian Territory* (Advisory Opinion), 196.
[97] *Construction of a Wall in the Occupied Palestinian Territory* (Advisory Opinion), 198.
[98] *Construction of a Wall in the Occupied Palestinian Territory* (Advisory Opinion), 198.

Government's security personnel performing their duty at the USA Embassy did not make any effort to deter or discourage the demonstrators from taking over the Embassy also contributed to the dispute.[99] Access to the compound and Chancery building was gained by cutting chains and removing bars from a Chancery basement window, and control of the first floor of the Chancery was rapidly seized. In the process, security officers were held hostage. A large group of Embassy personnel, including consular and non-American staff and visitors, took refuge on an upper floor of the Chancery.[100] Given these circumstances, the USA submitted an application before the Court, through which it requested the release of its nationals and to assure that such persons be allowed to leave Iran safely.[101]

The Court ordered restitution in kind in the Tehran Hostages Case, where it accepted the submissions of the United States and ordered Iran to terminate the unlawful detention of the diplomatic and consular staff, and the other nationals of the USA, that were held hostage.[102] Similarly to the Case concerning the Temple of Preah Vihear, the Tehran Hostages Case is another example in which the International Court ordered restitution in kind, this case being a demonstration that this remedy applies to individuals[103] as well.

6.3.4.4 Restitution in Kind under Customary International Law

The judgment of the Court in the Pulp Mills on the River Uruguay Case demonstrates that restitution in kind is a remedy of customary international law. This dispute concerned the alleged breach by Uruguay of certain obligations of the Statute of the River Uruguay, a treaty signed by Argentina and Uruguay at Salto (Uruguay) on 26 February 1975 and having entered into force on 18 September 1976. The treaty that was signed by the parties concerned the authorisation, construction and future commissioning of two pulp mills on the River Uruguay. Argentina submitted an application before the Court, through which it requested that the international responsibility of Uruguay should be engaged and, as a consequence, that Uruguay should provide reparation.[104]

---

[99] *Diplomatic and Consular Staff in Tehran* (USA v Iran) (Judgment).
[100] *Diplomatic and Consular Staff in Tehran* (USA v Iran) (Judgment).
[101] *United States Diplomatic and Consular Staff in Tehran* (USA v Iran) [1979] ICJ Pleadings, Application instituting Proceedings, 7.
[102] *Diplomatic and Consular Staff in Tehran* (USA v Iran) (Judgment), 44.
[103] Crawford, State Responsibility, 512.
[104] *Pulp Mills on the River Uruguay* (*Argentina v Uruguay*) [2006] ICJ Pleadings, Application instituting Proceedings, 19.

6.4 Conclusion

Even if the application did not contain any reference to restitution in kind, the applicant submitted several arguments with respect to this remedy through its Memorial. Thus, Argentina requested the Court to decide that restitution in kind was the appropriate remedy. Firstly, the annulment of authorisations[105] was requested (implying legal restitution) and further, the dismantling of the mills (implying material restitution).[106] The Court issued its judgment on 20 April 2010, through which it concluded that restitution represents a form of reparation for injury under customary international law. It stated the following in this sense:

> The Court recalls that customary international law provides for restitution as one form of reparation for injury, restitution being the re-establishment of the situation which existed before occurrence of the wrongful act.[107]

It is telling that the Court did not grant this remedy in this case. The Court further concluded that '*ordering the dismantling of the mill would not, in the view of the Court, constitute an appropriate remedy for the breach of procedural obligations*'.[108] This finding reaffirms the condition provided by Article 35 (b) of the ILC Articles which mentions that other remedies should be applicable if the burden is out of all proportion to the benefit implied by restitution. Further, the International Court followed the same approach as its predecessor, and concluded that restitution in kind is applicable in certain specific circumstances, and not in a general manner without a proper consideration of the particularities of the case at hand.

6.4 CONCLUSION

It appears that the inconsistencies in the interpretation of restitution in kind originate from a wide application of the findings and conclusions of the Permanent Court in the Chorzów Factory Case to disputes that do not contain similar circumstances. Such application of the judgment of the Permanent Court would rather complicate than resolve the controversies regarding the interpretation of restitution in kind as a remedy of international law. As such, the obiter dictum of the Permanent Court in the Chorzów Factory Case should be applied in cases involving illegal expropriation, where

---

[105] *Pulp Mills on the River Uruguay (Argentina v Uruguay)* [2007] ICJ Pleadings, Memorial of Argentina, 202.
[106] *Pulp Mills on the River Uruguay (Argentina v Uruguay)* [2007] ICJ Pleadings, Memorial of Argentina, 203.
[107] *Pulp Mills on the River Uruguay (Argentina v Uruguay)* [2010] (Judgment) ICR Rep 14, 93.
[108] *Pulp Mills on the River Uruguay (Argentina v Uruguay)* [2010] (Judgment) ICR Rep 14, 104.

restitution in kind could indeed be regarded as a primary remedy. Consequently, the dictum should not be applied generally, in any given dispute submitted before the Court.

Another relevant conclusion with respect to this remedy is that while the competence of the Court to grant restitution in kind is less disputed, other topics that refer to restitution in kind, such as its primacy or its limitations, remain to be further developed by the practice of the Court or by institutions such as the International Law Commission. Gray argues that the latter should not be *'unduly dogmatic or over ambitious in its quest for universal rules in its draft Articles'*.[109] Even if this conclusion might be too drastic, it can be reasonably concluded that the ILC Articles seem too rigid, at times, especially with respect to the general prioritisation of restitution in kind as a remedy of international law.

Referring to the obiter dictum of the Chorzów Factory Case,[110] it can be concluded that restitution in kind is available before the International Court, for a variety of disputes. Nevertheless, the reasons for which restitution in kind is rarely granted by the International Court are various. Firstly, it bears emphasis that this remedy is not often requested by applicant states, the Court being limited by the submissions of the parties when it gives its decisions. Thus, if the applicant state requests compensation, the Court cannot give a judgment through which it would provide for restitution in kind. Secondly, the particularities of the disputes submitted before the Court render restitution in kind either impossible to perform or inappropriate. In this context, it seems that restitution in kind is available in a rather limited range of disputes, such as the ones involving illegal expropriation.

Therefore, the conclusion that restitution in kind is the primary remedy in international law, without any contextualisation, seems rather divorced from the practice of the Court, as it does not provide any circumstantial qualifications. Thus, although it can be agreed that restitution in kind is the normal type of relief in cases in which unlawful expropriations or illegal dispositions of territory have occurred, in other circumstances restitution in kind becomes exceptional.

It can be said that the requests that the parties submit before the Court, with respect to restitution in kind, are at times confusing. The reliance on the Chorzow Factory Case is apparent in most of these pleadings, even if restitution in kind, restitutio in integrum or compensation is sought, further

---

[109] Gray, 'The Choice between Restitution and Compensation' 413.
[110] *Factory at Chorzów (Germany v Poland) (Merits)*, 27–28.

demonstrating that this historical case, resolved by the Permanent Court, influences the manner in which states frame their requests. The development of the practice of the Court in this respect would undeniably impact the requests of the state parties for restitution in kind as, presently, states do not seem to fully grasp the notion and legal consequences of this remedy.

7

Compensation

7.1 INTRODUCTION

The Court has the power to order compensation as a remedy of international law. This has been clarified and laid down, as a matter of principle, by the International Court in the Gabčíkovo–Nagymaros Case, as follows:

> it is a well-established rule of international law that an injured state is entitled to obtain compensation from the state which has committed an international wrong for the damage caused by it.[1]

Compensation is often considered as being the most frequent form of reparation,[2] and the Commentary to the ILC Articles further provides in this respect that this remedy is most frequently sought in international practice.[3] Even if the power of the Court to give judgment regarding compensation has been challenged in a few cases,[4] the general view is that the power of the Court to grant compensation remains unquestioned.[5]

The Court awarded compensation in relatively few judgments. Commentators have concluded in this respect that *'although pecuniary or monetary compensation is the most commonly sought form of remedy in international practice, it has not often featured before the ICJ, where it has made an appearance in a handful of cases'.*[6] Even so, although compensation was requested in approximately one-third of all the cases that were decided by

---

[1] *Gabčíkovo–Nagymaros Project (Hungary/Slovakia)* (Judgment), 81.
[2] Kaczorowska, Public International Law, 483.
[3] ILC Draft Articles with Commentaries, 99.
[4] *Factory at Chorzów (Germany v Poland)* (Jurisdiction); *Mavrommatis Jerusalem Concessions (Greece v United Kingdom)*; *Corfu Channel Case (United Kingdom v Albania)* (Judgment on Preliminary Objections), 17.
[5] Brownlie, 'Remedies in the International Court of Justice' 558.
[6] Quintana, Litigation at the International Court, 1135.

the Permanent Court,[7] it was awarded only once – in the 'Wimbledon' Case.[8] Further, only a handful of cases that were adjudicated by the International Court offer any guidance regarding the characteristics of compensation as a remedy: the Corfu Channel Case[9], the Diallo Case,[10] and the more recent Certain Activities Carried out by Nicaragua in the Border Area.[11]

That the Court has granted compensation in a very limited amount of its caseload demonstrates its reserved attitude towards this remedy. Significantly, the Diallo Case is the only case where the International Court has issued an award through which it determined the amount of compensation without the aid of expert opinions. On the other hand, in the Corfu Channel Case, the Court relied on expert opinions for the determination of compensation. This has led certain authors to conclude that the Court is reluctant to award compensation.[12]

It also appears that the Court does not necessarily have any clear methodology for analysing and assessing compensation claims, even though the Chorzów Factory Case obiter dictum has been interpreted as being the locus classicus for determining the amount of compensation due as the value that restitution in kind would bear. As such, one of the most difficult tasks[13] before the Court is assessing the amount of compensation due. However, certain clarifications regarding the definition of compensation need address from the outset.

The Permanent Court and the International Court have issued judgments interpreting and clarifying compensation as a remedy. The right of states to claim compensation is established and has never been contested in the Courts' recent practice. The Gabčíkovo–Nagymaros Case is one such example,[14] through which the Court confirmed that receiving compensation is a principle of international law. The most relevant details of this remedy, such as the burden of proof, the qualification of damages as being material or

---

7 Crawford, State Responsibility, 516.
8 S.S. 'Wimbledon' (Britain et al v Germany), 33.
9 Corfu Channel Case (Great Britain v Albania) (Compensation), 244.
10 Diallo (Republic of Guinea v Democratic Republic of the Congo) (Merits).
11 Certain Activities Carried Out by Nicaragua in the Border Area (Costa Rica v Nicaragua) (Compensation) [2018] ICJ Rep 15.
12 Crawford, State Responsibility, 518.
13 Stephan Wittich, 'Compensation' in Max Planck Encyclopaedia of Public International Law (2008) 47–48.
14 The Court issued judgments through which compensation was granted in other cases as well, such as: Corfu Channel Case (Great Britain v Albania) (Compensation); Diallo (Republic of Guinea v Democratic Republic of the Congo) (Merits).

moral, or the quantification of compensation, have been raised before and clarified by the Court.

As such, even though the number of judgments in which compensation was granted is scarce, the Permanent Court and the International Court have issued relevant findings which have contributed to the interpretation and clarification of compensation as a remedy of international law. In the Chorzów Factory Case, the Permanent Court laid out important principles with respect to the quantification of compensation; in the Corfu Channel Case the Court issued its first judgment with respect to the possibility of nominating experts for the quantification of damages, while in the Gabčíkovo–Nagymaros Case, the Court set out the principle that a state has a right to receive indemnity when it is damaged.

The terminology used by applicant states when requesting compensation is not necessarily consistent. '*Damages*', '*indemnity*' or even the more general notion of '*reparation*' have the meaning of compensation, in accordance with the pleadings of states. One such example is the Anglo-Iranian Oil Company Case, in which the applicant did not explicitly refer to compensation as such, but requested that indemnity should be paid.[15] Another example in which the applicant state referred to compensation differently, as the wider notion of reparation, is the more recent Certain Iranian Assets Case, in which the Court was requested to find that reparation is due and that its amount should be determined in a subsequent stage of the proceedings.[16] Both examples demonstrate that even if compensation is requested by using different terminology, this remedy of international law is generally defined as '*reparation for loss suffered; a judicially ascertained compensation for wrong*',[17] and it seems that the parties requested it with the same definition in mind.

The Corfu Channel Case[18] and the Diallo Case[19] are among the most referred to when analysing and interpreting compensation, and the cases are also relevant from the perspective of interpreting and categorising compensation, even though the Court did not reach a final decision and thus, did not give a judgment upon the remedies requested by the parties.

Requests for compensation are of various types, and its categories may be discerned from an analysis of the requests submitted before the Court. While in certain cases states include the amount due as compensation within their

---

[15] *Anglo-Iranian Oil Co Case (United Kingdom v Iran)* (Judgment) [1952] ICJ Rep 93, 96.

[16] *Certain Iranian Assets (Islamic Republic of Iran v USA)* [2016] ICJ Pleadings, Application instituting Proceedings, 17.

[17] *Opinion in the Lusitania Cases (United States/Germany)* (1923) RIAA vol 7, 39.

[18] *Corfu Channel Case (Great Britain v Albania)* (Compensation).

[19] *Diallo (Republic of Guinea v Democratic Republic of the Congo)* (Merits).

pleadings, in other cases states do not include the amount of compensation, but request the Court to determine it, either at the merits stage, or in a subsequent procedural stage. The former kind of compensation shall be referred to as *'determined compensation'*, and the latter as *'undetermined compensation'*. There is also a third manner of referring to compensation, as the more general notion of reparation.

7.2 THEORETICAL PERSPECTIVES

7.2.1 *The Definition and Function of Compensation*

The ILC Articles do not provide a definition of compensation. However, a combined reading of Article 31, Article 34 and Article 36 of the ILC Articles provides sufficient insight to determine the characteristics of compensation. The ILC Articles prescribe that compensation is a form of reparation,[20] it being included within the scope of Article 34, along with restitution and satisfaction. Further, Article 36 of the ILC Articles describes compensation as being the remedy that covers financially assessable damages,[21] for which restitution cannot be granted. Expressis verbis, the role of Article 36 appears to determine the scope rather than the definition of compensation. However, Article 31 further clarifies a potential definition of compensation when describing *'damages'* as part of the wider notion of *'reparation'*.[22]

The Permanent Court, through its judgment in the Chorzów Factory Case, held that damages represent a form of reparation for wrongs.[23] Further, compensation has been defined as being *'an appropriate and counterbalancing payment to somebody for some sort of loss or detriment'*.[24] Some authors refer to the ILC Articles, when defining compensation as being *'the offset of damage or material injury suffered by the state'*,[25] while others opine that *'we will be used to describe reparation in the narrow sense of the payment of money in the measure of the wrong done'*.[26] Interpreting the above-mentioned provisions, compensation could be succinctly defined as a form of reparation through which the injured state recovers the damages it suffered from the state that committed an international wrongful act. The above characteristics

---

[20] ILC Draft Articles, 95.
[21] ILC Draft Articles, 98.
[22] ILC Draft Articles, 91.
[23] *Factory at Chorzów (Germany v Poland)* (Merits), 47.
[24] Wittich, 'Compensation' 1.
[25] Quintana, Litigation at the International Court, 1147.
[26] Brownlie, 'Remedies in the International Court of Justice' 567.

112   7 *Compensation*

of compensation, provided by the Court and the doctrine, are accurate representations of this remedy. However, perhaps the definition that does most justice to the notion of compensation is the one provided by Wittich, in the following terms:

> *Compensation denotes a form of reparation in the law of State responsibility apart from restitution and satisfaction (Reparations). It means the payment of damages as a remedy for making good the damage caused by a previous violation of an international obligation (Remedies). In this sense, compensation is also called reparation by equivalent or indemnification.*[27]

7.2.2 *Compensation and Damages*

The differences between the notions of '*damages*', '*injury*' and '*compensation*' need clarification, as they interact with and influence one another, but are not synonyms.[28] Authors have concluded that, traditionally, damages were defined in international law as a duty to pay for certain consequences of an unlawful act.[29] As such, it might appear that for damages to be ordered, the existence of an illegal act that was contrary to international law is necessary. Nevertheless, in certain instances, compensation also rests upon a finding of '*a lawful exercise by state of their sovereign rights, especially the right to expropriate*'.[30] The International Law Commission might have eroded the distinction between the two notions.[31] Even so, damages usually imply a certain injury caused by an illegal act[32] while compensation is generally used when considering reparation for injuries caused by both legal and illegal acts. However, even if the two notions are often confused,[33] due to the fact that the definition of compensation is rather broad,[34] the Court has not adopted the same interpretation with respect to '*compensation*' and '*damages*', as they are not one and the same.

---

[27] Wittich, 'Compensation' 2.

[28] Clarisse Barthe-Gay, 'Réflexions sur la satisfaction en droit international' (2003) 49 Annuaire Français de Droit International 107.

[29] Sergey Ripinsky and Kevin Williams, *Damages in International Investment Law* (British Institute of International and Comparative Law 2008) 4.

[30] Ripinsky and Williams, Damages in International Investment Law, 4.

[31] Ripinsky and Williams, Damages in International Investment Law, 4.

[32] Brownlie, 'Remedies in the International Court of Justice' 567.

[33] Ripinsky and Williams, Damages in International Investment Law, 5.

[34] Wittich, 'Compensation' 1.

7.2.3 *The Function of Compensation*

The definition of compensation predicts the scope of this remedy, as reparatory and not punitive in function. This distinction is relevant because the term *'punitive'* implies a punishment *'for the defendant acting with recklessness, malice or deceit, or otherwise reprehensibly'.*[35] The conclusion that compensation does not have a punitive role before the Court is also derived from its case-law. The interpretation that the Permanent Court provided in the Chorzów Factory obiter dictum with respect to reparation supports this conclusion, and the circumstance that compensation has a reparatory nature[36] is further confirmed by the Commentary to the ILC Articles, which provides that compensation is *'not concerned to punish the responsible State, nor does compensation have an expressive or exemplary character'.*[37]

7.2.4 *Types of Compensation*

Compensation is among the broadest remedies under international law. Whether compensation falls within a certain category is relevant and, at the same time, difficult to determine. Brownlie illustrates the difficulty of confining compensation to a determined category when he writes that the task of delimiting compensation and pecuniary satisfaction is not easy.[38] The determination of the types of compensation is understood through both objective and subjective criteria. Article 31 of the ILC Articles provides that two types of damages exist in international law: i) material damages and ii) moral damages. Thus, the assessment and interpretation of compensation is two-pronged, *i.e.* i) compensation for material damages and ii) compensation for moral damages.

Another categorisation of compensation rests on the nature of the injury caused to the state. In this inquiry, there are two types of injuries that are caused to states: i) direct injury and ii) indirect injury. From this perspective, the assessment and interpretation of compensation depends on the kind of injury suffered, in addition to the analysis on material or moral damages. Authors have argued in this respect that *'in standard cases a state protects its*

---

[35] Crawford, State Responsibility, 523.
[36] Stephan Wittich, 'Punitive Damages' in James Crawford, Alain Pellet and Simon Olleson (eds), *The Law of International Responsibility* (Oxford University Press 2010) 671.
[37] ILC Draft Articles with Commentaries, 99.
[38] Ian Brownlie, *System of the Law of Nations – State Responsibility Part 1* (Oxford University Press 1983) 208.

114 7 Compensation

own legal interests in seeking reparation for damage – material or otherwise – suffered by itself or its citizens'.[39]

7.2.5 Assessing Compensation

Even if Article 36(2) of the Commentary to the ILC Articles provides that this remedy covers *'any financially assessable damage including loss of profits insofar as it is established'*, the Court has yet to determine a methodology of quantifying compensation. Given the limited case-load, the assessment of quantification of damages should take into consideration the findings of the Court in certain cases, by way of example.[40] When analysing assessment and quantification of damages, two main categories are relevant: i) liquidated damages and ii) unliquidated damages.

The first category represents a situation in which the parties to the dispute have foreseen and quantified the damages through the governing instrument of the dispute, *i.e.* before the breach occurred. In this situation, the Court does not need to perform any assessment but is just required to acknowledge the agreement with respect to the compensation. This type of remedy is specific to commercial international law rather than public international law.

The second category represents the circumstance in which the parties to the dispute did not quantify the damages through the governing instrument. This is more the case in interstate disputes. Authors have opined with respect to unliquidated damages that irrespective of the nature of the damages (be it material or moral), the process of quantifying damages involves three stages: i) an analysis of the heads of claim, ii) a consequential link between the damage and the illegal act and iii) the evaluation of quantum.[41] The notion of *'valuation'* implies the attribution of value to a certain concept. With respect to the valuation process, authors have concluded that:

> the attribution of values to the objects of the attribution and the constitution of axiomatic circumstances can be performed by reference to certain explicit or implicit principles or can be completely unprincipled. In the former case the attribution and predication of values or – to use an expression embracing

---

[39] James Crawford, *Brownlie's Principles of Public International Law* (8th edn, Oxford University Press 2012) 568.

[40] Crawford, State Responsibility, 519.

[41] Rutsel Silvestre J Martha, *The Financial Obligation in International Law* (Oxford University Press 2015) 421.

7.3 Practical Perspectives

both – valuation is axiomatically substantiated (or founded) while in the latter case it is axiomatically arbitrary.[42]

7.3 PRACTICAL PERSPECTIVES

7.3.1 *Determined Compensation*

Certain disputes that were submitted before the Court through a unilateral application involved requests for compensation in which the amount was determined by the applicant in its application. However, relatively few cases have contained such claims. Illustratively, determined compensation was requested in the following cases: Nottebohm,[43] Aerial Incident of 10 March 1953,[44] Aerial Incident of 7 October 1952,[45] Aerial Incident of 27 July 1955,[46] Aerial Incident of 4 September 1954,[47] and Diallo.[48]

These cases have some common features, and for ease of analysis, shall be divided into two categories, which shall be assessed below.

7.3.1.1 The Illegal Expropriation Disputes

Two unilateral applications involved determined compensation with respect to illegal expropriation disputes before the Court. These cases are similar with respect to their subject matter and the requested remedies as they both included submissions that harm was caused to individuals and their property by acts of alleged illegal expropriation. These cases are the Nottebohm Case and the Diallo Case.

In the Nottebohm Case, Liechtenstein claimed compensation for the measures that were undertaken by Guatemala against an individual –

---

[42] Ilmar Tammelo, *Justice and Doubt: An Essay on the Fundamentals of Justice* (Springer-Verlag 1959) 371.

[43] *Nottebohm Case (Liechtenstein v Guatemala)* (Judgment Second Phase).

[44] *Aerial Incident of 10 March 1953 (USA v Czechoslovakia)* [1955] ICJ Pleadings, Application instituting Proceedings.

[45] *Aerial Incident of 7 October 1952 (USA v Union of Soviet Socialist Republics)* [1955] ICJ Pleadings, Application instituting Proceedings.

[46] *Aerial Incident of 27 July 1955 (Israel v Bulgaria; USA v Bulgaria; United Kingdom of Great Britain and Northern Ireland v Bulgaria)* [1957] ICJ Pleadings, Application instituting Proceedings.

[47] *Aerial Incident of 4 September 1954 (USA v Union of Soviet Socialist Republics)* [1958] ICJ Pleadings, Application instituting Proceedings.

[48] *Diallo (Republic of Guinea v Democratic Republic of the Congo)* (Merits).

116   7 *Compensation*

Mr Nottebohm – and against his property. As a consequence, Liechtenstein requested the Court to find that the Government of Guatemala has acted in a manner that was contrary to international law and that international responsibility occurred, as a result.[49] Thus, along with requesting a declaration of wrongfulness, Liechtenstein requested determined compensation for the use of and for the profits resulted from the sequestrated properties.[50] This claim was further substantiated through the Memorial of Liechtenstein, and the amount claimed was increased.[51] Liechtenstein considered this case as a dispute involving illegal expropriation on the basis that Guatemala: i) provided no compensation and ii) acted in a discriminatory manner towards Mr Nottebohm. For these reasons, the unilateral application of Liechtenstein contained a request for declaratory relief regarding the responsibility of Guatemala, and a subsequent claim for restitution in kind, followed by a claim for compensation, in the alternative, should restitution in kind prove to be impossible.[52] In the Diallo Case, Guinea instituted proceedings against the Democratic Republic of the Congo claiming that certain measures taken by the Democratic Republic of the Congo were against the freedom and property of an individual – Mr Diallo. Guinea requested determined compensation through its unilateral application, for the financial loss caused.[53] Guinea sought compensation for illegal expropriation.

The difference between these two cases is that Guinea did not seek restitution from the Court for the breaches of international law committed by the Democratic Republic of the Congo. It is important to note that determined compensation was requested in these cases because a substantiation of the claim was relatively uncomplicated. The enumeration of the assets and the corresponding values for which Liechtenstein requested determined compensation were included in its unilateral application[54] through which the proceedings were instituted.

7.3.1.2 The Aerial Incident Disputes

The Aerial Incident Cases are almost identical, with respect to the facts and the requests for remedies contained in the unilateral applications of the

---

[49] *Nottebohm* (*Liechtenstein v Guatemala* (Application), 10.
[50] *Nottebohm* (*Liechtenstein v Guatemala* (Application), 15.
[51] *Nottebohm* (*Liechtenstein v Guatemala*) (Memorial of Liechtenstein), 70.
[52] *Nottebohm Case* (*Liechtenstein v Guatemala*) (Application), 9–10.
[53] *Ahmadou Sadio Diallo* (*Republic of Guinea v Democratic Republic of the Congo*) ICJ Pleadings, Application instituting Proceedings, 37.
[54] *Nottebohm Case* (*Liechtenstein v Guatemala*) (Application), 17–18.

applicant states. These cases involved claims for determined compensation regarding damages caused to certain aircraft and for injuries caused to individuals, *i.e.* the pilots and persons who were killed as a result. In the Case concerning the Aerial Incident of 10 March 1953 between the USA and Czechoslovakia, the applicant requested the Court to find that the Czechoslovak Government was liable for damages caused and that the responding state should pay a determined amount in this respect.[55]

The amounts framed as determined compensation, requested by the USA in this case consisted of i) the replacement value of an airplane and ii) the damages that were caused to individuals as a result of damaging the airplane. Similarly, in the Case concerning the Aerial Incident of 1952, the USA submitted that the Soviet Government is liable for the damages caused and that the Court should award damages in a determined amount.[56]

The determined compensation that was requested by the USA Government in this case consisted of i) the damages that were caused to the USA airplane and its contents, and ii) the damages that were caused to the families of the crew members who were killed in the incident. The USA also requested determined compensation in the case concerning the Aerial Incident of 27 July 1955.[57] The amount of determined compensation that was requested by the USA Government consisted of the damages that were caused to the descendants of the crew members who were killed in the incident.

It is important to note that restitution in kind was not included in any of the unilateral applications due to the fact that this remedy was no longer materially possible – the objects that were destroyed, as a consequence of the respondent's illegal acts, were impossible to restore. Furthermore, a claim regarding restitution in kind with respect to the loss of human life would have been redundant, compensation being the only suitable remedy in this circumstance.

The first conclusion that can be drawn after analysing the requests that were submitted by the applicant states in the above-mentioned cases is that the Court was not requested to provide the amounts of compensation due, but to accept the amounts that were presented by the applicant state through its unilateral application. The second conclusion is that the claims that determined the request for compensation were easily identifiable. Thus, in the Aerial Incidents Cases, the evidence regarding the fact that the airplanes were

---

[55] *Aerial Incident of 10 March 1953 (USA v Czechoslovakia)* (Application), 25–26.

[56] *Aerial Incident of 7 October 1952 (USA v Union of Soviet Socialist Republics)* (Application), 25.

[57] *Aerial Incident of 27 July 1955 (Israel v Bulgaria; USA v Bulgaria; United Kingdom of Great Britain and Northern Ireland v Bulgaria)* (Application), 23–24.

118   *7 Compensation*

destroyed or damaged could be provided by the applicant. Also, the physical injuries and costs thereof for the individuals who were involved in the relevant incidents were easily identifiable.

However, in other disputes that involved loss of human life, the quantification of compensation was more difficult to assess. One such example is the Memorial on Compensation submitted by Nicaragua in the case concerning Military and Paramilitary Activities in Nicaragua,[58] which aptly noted that the complexity of the dispute has certain effects over assessing amounts of compensation due, making them incalculable.[59] The cases in which determined compensation was requested did not deal with such complex issues as the impact of a certain illegal activity on the entire economy of a state, or with several breaches of fundamental rights.

The third conclusion is that the cases in which requests for determined compensation were made included, mainly, disputes in which material damage had been caused. The Diallo Case is an exception to this, inasmuch as the claim for determined compensation also sought moral damages.[60]

7.3.2 *Undetermined Compensation*

States seem more comfortable with requesting the Court to determine the amount of compensation, instead of taking on the task of assessing the amounts on their own. Thus, out of all the cases that were brought before the Court, the requests for undetermined compensation represent the majority. It is important to note that in the cases that involved this type of compensation, the Court was requested either to:

i)   determine the amount of compensation due,

or to

ii)   declare that compensation is due, without any further request regarding its determination.

As such, states use two procedural mechanisms for requesting undetermined compensation: i) the determination of compensation is made by the Court through its judgment or ii) a more general claim is submitted in which the

---

[58] *Military and Paramilitary Activities in and against Nicaragua (Nicaragua v USA)* (Memorial of Nicaragua).

[59] *Military and Paramilitary Activities in and against Nicaragua (Nicaragua v USA)* (Memorial of Nicaragua), 246.

[60] *Diallo (Republic of Guinea v Democratic Republic of the Congo)* (Merits), 333.

7.3 Practical Perspectives

Court is not requested to determine compensation and which renders it as undetermined throughout the proceedings.

The claims that fall within the first category are represented by cases such as the Case concerning Elettronica Sicula in which the applicant requested the Court to decide that the respondent is liable to pay compensation 'in an amount to be determined by the Court'.[61] A similar request was submitted by the USA in the Diplomatic and Consular Staff in Tehran, where the Court was requested to determine the sum that should be provided by the Government of Iran.[62] Although the claim of the USA in this case cannot be construed as being a request for a declaration of responsibility, the fact that compensation was not determined by the applicant state remains, even if the Court was requested to endeavour to determine its quantum. Finally, another example is the Certain Property Case, in which Liechtenstein requested the Court to determine that Germany is responsible for its wrongful acts and, should the parties fail to agree on the amounts of compensation, that the Court determines them, in a separate stage of the proceedings.[63]

This request is not singular throughout the practice of the International Court. In the Certain Iranian Assets Case, the applicant also requested amounts of reparation.[64] Also, in the more recent case of Immunities and Criminal Proceedings, Guinea submitted a similar claim.[65] However, merely because the applicant state included within its application a request that the Court determine the amount of compensation did not absolve it from the responsibility of substantiating its claim for compensation. Failing to do so entailed that the Court would refuse to grant this remedy. An example that confirms this approach is the Diallo Case in which, even though the applicant included three heads of claim related to compensation for material and moral damage, it failed to substantiate. For this reason, the Court rejected most of Guinea's claims. An exception to this approach was the moral damages sought by the applicant state, for which the Court considered that no substantiation was required.

---

[61] Case concerning Elettronica Sicula SpA (ELSI) (USA v Italy) [1987] ICJ Pleadings, Application instituting Proceedings, 7.

[62] Case concerning United States Diplomatic and Consular Staff in Tehran (USA v Iran), ICJ Pleadings, Application instituting Proceedings, 8.

[63] Certain Property (Liechtenstein v Germany) [2001] ICJ Pleadings, Application Instituting Proceedings, 18.

[64] Certain Iranian Assets (Islamic Republic of Iran v USA) (Application), 17.

[65] Immunities and Criminal Proceedings (Equatorial Guinea v France) [2016] ICJ Pleadings, Application instituting Proceedings, 9.

120　　　　　　　　　　　　　　　　*7 Compensation*

Thus, it is not sufficient for a state to request that the Court determines that compensation is due for the Court to grant a specific amount; the applicant state must also submit relevant details and evidence substantiating its claim. Illustratively, in the Elettronica Sicula Case, the applicant amended its initial submission and requested the Court to find that the respondent state *'should pay to the United States of America the amount of US$12,679,000, plus interest, computed as described above'*,[66] and also filed detailed calculations related to the requested amount. In the Case concerning the Electricité de Beyrouth Company, the applicant requested the Court to declare that compensation is due, without issuing a subsequent judgment on quantum.[67] Other such examples include the Case concerning Armed Activities on the Territory of the Congo, in which the applicant requested the Court to find that it is entitled to compensation *'in respect of all acts of looting, destruction, removal of property and persons and other unlawful acts attributable to Burundi'*.[68]

This argument is further supported by the judgments of the Court and the subsequent pleadings of the applicant states in this respect. Thus, for example, in the LaGrand Case, the applicant requested through the application that compensation is due without substantiating the amounts,[69] but it later submitted its Memorial requesting declarations of illegality and assurances of non-repetition for the future.[70] This change within the pleadings of the applicant further demonstrates that requests for undetermined compensation can be assimilated, in certain circumstances, to declaratory judgments. In the Fisheries Case, the Court's power to determine the amount of compensation was implied through the application, in which the Court was requested to *'award damages to the Government of the United Kingdom in respect of all interferences by the Norwegian authorities with British fishing vessels'*.[71] In the Franco-Egyptian Case, France requested the Court to conclude that *'compensation for the damage suffered by the French Government in the person of the victims of the said measures is due by the Government of Egypt'*.[72]

---

[66] *Case concerning Elettronica Sicula SpA (ELSI) (USA v Italy)* [1987] ICJ Pleadings, Memorial of the USA, 116.

[67] *Électricité de Beyrouth Company Case (France v Lebanon)* [1953] ICJ Pleadings, Application instituting Proceedings, 15.

[68] *Armed Activities in the Territory of the Congo (Democratic Republic of the Congo v Burundi)* [1999] ICJ Pleadings, Application instituting Proceedings, 19.

[69] *LaGrand (Germany v USA)* (Application), 6.

[70] *LaGrand (Germany v USA)* (Memorial of Germany) vol 1, 161–162.

[71] *Fisheries Case (United Kingdom v Norway)* [1949] ICJ Pleadings, Application instituting Proceedings, 12.

[72] *Case concerning the Protection of French Nationals and Protected Persons in Egypt (France v Egypt)* [1949] ICJ Pleadings, Application instituting Proceedings, 12.

7.3 *Practical Perspectives*

These above-mentioned cases involved claims through which the Court was not requested to determine the compensation due. Neither did the applicant determine the amount of compensation through the unilateral application. Thus, the Court was requested to declare that compensation was due, without being requested to determine the amount of compensation and without any prior determination made by the applicant.

A relevant conclusion would be that in the cases that involved such claims, the remedy requested by the applicant was not necessarily compensation, even if such terminology found its place in the request of the applicant. It should be reiterated that the applicant state cannot ignore its duty to substantiate its claims for compensation, because without proper substantiation, the Court cannot grant this remedy. As a consequence, when a state requests that the Court *'adjudges and declares'* that compensation is due, without determining the amount, the remedy that the applicant is actually seeking is a declaratory judgment. In such a situation, the judicial body would not issue a judgment through which the respondent state receives a clear indication of the action that it should perform, *i.e.* the payment of a determined amount of money, but would rather declare that money is, generally, due. There is no reason to consider that such a declaration would not fall within the judicial function of the International Court.

However, it is significant to note that with respect to undetermined compensation, the case-law of the Court shows that these claims cannot lead to a judgment that would grant compensation in a determined amount. Thus, the consequences of such claims are either that the compensation is determined at a later stage (through the memorial or through the reply), or at a subsequent stage (a later judgment regarding the amount of compensation). The only other possibility is that compensation remains undetermined and, as a consequence, the applicant state receives a declaratory judgment.

7.3.3 *Compensation and Reparation*

As mentioned above, in certain cases, compensation was sought through a claim in which the Court was requested to grant reparation. However, even if the unilateral application did not expressly mention compensation, the intention of the applicant was that the Court should grant this remedy. Illustratively, in the Certain Property Case, Liechtenstein requested the Court to determine that reparation was the remedy that should be granted by the Court. However, the interpretation of its request leads to the conclusion that when referring to reparation, Liechtenstein actually requested undetermined compensation, in the following terms:

> *Liechtenstein further requests that the nature and amount of such reparation should, in the absence of agreement between the parties, be assessed and determined by the Court, if necessary, in a separate phase of the proceedings.*[73]

The link between reparation and the notions of '*damages*' firstly points to the conclusion that Lichtenstein sought compensation. Further, its request that certain '*amounts*' should be determined by the Court leads to the same conclusion. It is this last submission that undoubtedly confirms the fact that the applicant requested compensation from the International Court, even if it did not nominate the remedy as such. The Certain Property Case is not singular from this perspective, as the same approach regarding requests for compensation was followed in other cases before the International Court. Thus, in the Territorial and Maritime Dispute, the applicant requested the Court to find that Colombia should make reparation for the damage and injuries caused, in an amount determined in a subsequent phase.[74] Again, the references to the concepts of '*damages*' and its link with '*injuries*' firstly point out that the applicant requested compensation and not reparation generally. Similarly to the previously described case, the reference to '*amounts of reparation*' clearly indicates the sought remedy. The implicit intention for requesting undetermined compensation was also expressed in the Oil Platforms Case.[75]

As such, several elements should be observed when determining whether a request for reparation is for determined or undetermined compensation because, often, the applicant does not refer to this remedy as such. Thus, requests related to the payment of reparation or to the payment of compensation, without mentioning the quantum, are different from the requests related to certain amounts of reparation or certain amounts of compensation in which an express quantum is provided by the applicant. Further, these different types of requests for compensation should be considered by the Court when determining whether it should grant a certain amount of damages or whether it should render a declaratory judgment through which it would find that compensation is due.

While these determinations do not entail a complex analysis of the requests of the application, they are relevant for the proper identification of the remedy that was requested by the applicant states. In this manner the Court best

---

[73] *Certain Property (Liechtenstein v Germany)* (Application), 18.

[74] *Territorial and Maritime Dispute (Nicaragua v Colombia)* [2009] ICJ Pleadings, Reply of Nicaragua, 237–238.

[75] *Oil Platforms (Islamic Republic of Iran v USA)* (Judgment) [2003] ICJ Rep 16, 5.

7.3 *Practical Perspectives*

addresses the claim and provides relevant remedies in the disputes that are submitted before it.

7.3.3.1 Compensation for Material Damages

The first characteristic of material damages is that they are financially assess-able.[76] The Commentary to the ILC Articles further clarifies the notion of *'financially assessable'*, as such:

> The qualification 'financially assessable' is intended to exclude compensation for what is sometimes referred to as 'moral damage' to a State, i.e. the affront or injury caused by a violation of rights not associated with actual damage to property or persons: this is the subject matter of satisfaction, dealt with in Article 37.[77]

A second characteristic of material damages is that the state claiming them has the duty to substantiate them through certain specific valuation rules.[78] Therefore, the Court cannot assess ex officio the amount of compensation should the applicant not submit any arguments for a certain determined amount.

The S.S. 'Wimbledon' Case is the first case that was submitted before the Permanent Court, which involved a successful claim for compensation. In the morning of 21 March 1921, the British steamship 'Wimbledon', chartered by the French armament firm 'Les Affréteurs réunis', proceeding to Danzig with a cargo of 4,000 tons of goods (military material), was refused access to, and free passage through, the Kiel Canal by the German authorities. The argu-ment submitted by Germany was that that the cargo of the steamship 'Wimbledon' consisted of war material destined for Poland. The applicant states sought compensation, requesting the Court to adjudge and declare that reparation for loss is due, in a determined amount, estimated by the applicant in the form of a liquidated sum, with interest.[79]

Even if the Permanent Court did not specifically address the particularities of compensation as a notion, several conclusions result from the judgment in the 'Wimbledon' Case. One relevant conclusion that could be drawn by interpreting the judgment of the Permanent Court in the 'Wimbledon' Case is with respect to the valuation of compensation. The Court granted

---

[76] ILC Draft Articles with Commentaries, 91.
[77] ILC Draft Articles with Commentaries, 91, 92.
[78] Martha, The Financial Obligation in International Law, 91.
[79] S.S. 'Wimbledon' (*Great Britain et al v Germany*), 6.

124   *7 Compensation*

the said amounts, accepting the arguments that were brought by the applicant in this respect. As such, authors have confirmed that the 'Wimbledon' Case established, despite the absence of a detailed analysis of compensation,[80] certain relevant issues with respect to the assessment of compensation, such as the principle that its amount should correspond to the value that restitution in kind would bear.[81] Another issue that had arisen before the Permanent Court in the 'Wimbledon' Case was with respect to the currency of the amounts of compensation that would be granted, in the sense that if the applicant sets the currency within its claims and the responding state does not contest it, the Court should express the amounts as such.[82]

The Permanent Court decided that the German authorities were wrong in refusing access to the Kiel Canal and that the German Government was bound to repair the injury caused to the French Republic and further concluded that specific amounts were due as compensation.[83] It can therefore be concluded that the findings of the only case in which compensation was granted by the Permanent Court were confirmed by subsequent judgments of the International Court with respect to the approach towards compensation, in the sense that, firstly, it is available as a remedy of international law.

7.3.3.1.1 THE CORFU CHANNEL CASE The first case brought before the International Court represents one of the few instances in which the Court decided upon the issue of compensation for material damages and addressed its characteristics. The Corfu Channel Case arose from incidents that occurred as a result of two British destroyers striking mines in Albanian waters and suffering material damages, including serious loss of life. The Court rendered two judgments with respect to this case, the first regarding the merits of the case and a subsequent judgment related to compensation.

In its first judgment,[84] the Court concluded that it had jurisdiction to assess the amount of compensation, but also stated that it could not do so through the same judgment. This was because the Albanian Government had not yet stated which items, if any, of the various sums claimed it contested, and the United Kingdom Government had not submitted its related evidence. Great Britain requested the Court to determine through its second judgment that Albania should pay compensation.

[80] Gray, Judicial Remedies in International Law, 77.
[81] Martha, The Financial Obligation in International Law, 98.
[82] Martha, The Financial Obligation in International Law, 98.
[83] S.S. 'Wimbledon' (Great Britain et al v Germany), 33.
[84] Corfu Channel Case (Great Britain v Albania) (Merits), 26.

Great Britain requested compensation for damage to property (the two warships) and compensation for the damage caused to its nationals (the naval personnel).[85] Thus, all three heads of claim submitted by Great Britain represented material damages. The damages that were sought by Great Britain were financially assessable, as is demonstrated by the fact that the applicant had substantiated its claims. Further, this case is one of the rare disputes in the history of the International Court in which experts were employed for the verification of the valuation that was submitted by the applicant, as provided by Article 50 of the Statue of the Court. After assessing the reports of experts in this field, the Court concluded with respect to the 'Saumarez' ship, that Great Britain justified its claims related to compensation,[86] and, consequently, that they are reasonable and well founded.[87]

Considering the deaths and injuries of the naval personnel, Great Britain also requested compensation related to cost of pensions made to the victims and their dependants as well as medical treatment.[88] The Court concluded that these claims were proved to its satisfaction and granted them.[89]

Even if the Court did not explicitly address the characteristics of compensation for material damages, it can be concluded that the Court indirectly considered that, in this case, the damages that were allegedly caused must be substantiated. The determination that experts should be used in this respect and the further examination of their reports leads to the conclusion that the Court considers the amounts requested as compensation a sensitive issue, which should be carefully approached and described by the party requesting it, so that the judgment of the Court is accurate in this respect.

Certain commentators consider the judgment of the International Court to be prophetic[90] due to its findings regarding state responsibility. More so, this judgment represented, for a long period of time, the only judgment of the Court through which a liquidated amount of money was granted.[91] The Diallo Case represents the second judgment of the Court in this respect.

---

[85] *Corfu Channel Case (Great Britain v Albania)* (Compensation), 7.

[86] *Corfu Channel Case (Great Britain v Albania)* (Compensation), 9.

[87] *Corfu Channel Case (Great Britain v Albania)* (Compensation), 9.

[88] *Corfu Channel Case (Great Britain v Albania)* (Compensation), 10.

[89] *Corfu Channel Case (Great Britain v Albania)* (Compensation), 10.

[90] Mohammed Bedjaoui, 'An International Contentious Case on the Threshold of the Cold War' in Karine Bannelier, Théodore Christakis and Sarah Heathcote (eds), *The ICJ and the Evolution of International Law. The Enduring Impact of the Corfu Channel Case* (Routledge 2012) 15.

[91] Aristoteles Constantinides, 'The Corfu Channel Case in Perspective: The Factual and Political Background' in Bannelier, Christakis and Heathcote (eds), The ICJ and the Evolution of International Law, 53.

7.3.3.1.2 THE DIALLO CASE The second case in which the Court analysed material damages was the Diallo Case. This case was initiated by Guinea, which instituted proceedings against the Democratic Republic of the Congo for breaching protections granted by both the International Covenant on Civil and Political Rights and the African Charter on Human and People's Rights in its actions against Ahmadou Sadio Diallo, a Guinean national. Mr Diallo had set up two companies in the Democratic Republic of the Congo. Due to the fact that the state owed a large sum of money to his companies, he sued the state to recover the debt. As a response, the state arrested Mr Diallo in 1988. Mr. Diallo was again arrested in 1995 and 1996 with the purpose of the final expulsion from the Democratic Republic of the Congo which took place on 31 January 1996.

As a consequence, Guinea filed a claim with the Registry of the International Court, claiming that the Democratic Republic of the Congo has breached the rights of Mr Diallo guaranteed by the above-mentioned conventions. Thus, Guinea claimed USD 250,000 for moral damages, USD 6,430,148 for loss of earnings, USD 550,000 for material damages, USD 4,360,000 for loss of potential earnings and, finally, USD 500,000 for the costs of proceedings.

The Democratic Republic of the Congo argued that USD 30,000 were due for the non-pecuniary injuries caused to Mr Diallo and that no compensation for material damages was owed. Guinea submitted three heads of claim for material damages.[92] Even though the applicant included these heads of claim under compensation for material damages, it failed to substantiate its claims. As such, the Court rejected most of Guinea's amounts, considering its lack of substantiation.[93] With respect to the alleged loss of personal property, three categories were considered by the Court: furnishings of Mr Diallo's apartment, certain high-value items alleged to have been in Mr Diallo's apartment and his assets in bank accounts.

The Court first analysed the inventory that was submitted by Guinea and concluded that 'there is uncertainty about what happened to the property listed on the inventory'.[94] As a consequence, the Court found that the evidence that was submitted by Guinea had failed to prove the extent of the loss suffered by Mr Diallo. Further, the Court found that no evidence had been provided with respect to the valuation of the items that were allegedly lost by Mr Diallo. For these reasons, Guinea's claim was rejected. With respect to the allegation regarding the loss of several valuable items that were allegedly located in the

---

[92] Diallo (Republic of Guinea v Democratic Republic of the Congo) (Merits), 332.
[93] Diallo (Republic of Guinea v Democratic Republic of the Congo) (Merits), 345.
[94] Diallo (Republic of Guinea v Democratic Republic of the Congo) (Merits), 337.

apartment, the Court concluded that Guinea brought no evidence regarding the location of the said items. Thus, it held that there is no evidence regarding the items that were purchased[95] or that Mr Diallo owed these items at the time of his expulsion.[96]

Due to the fact that Guinea did not allocate any value to the items that were allegedly lost, the Court also rejected this claim. Finally, regarding the assets alleged to have been contained in bank accounts, the Court found that Guinea had failed to provide any evidence in this respect as well. Guinea offered no details regarding the total sum held in the bank, the names in which the accounts were held or the causal link between the loss of the assets and the circumstance of Mr Diallo leaving the Democratic Republic of the Congo. Regarding the head of claim related to the loss of remuneration of Mr Diallo, the Court concluded that Guinea did not properly address the evidence related to the total amount of USD 80,000 claimed, as no bank account or tax records were provided in support of this claim. Therefore, the Court did not grant any compensation for this head of claim either.

The analysis and questions that were raised by the Court in this case provide an insight into the manner in which evidence regarding compensation for material damage should be presented by the parties before the Court. Authors have argued in this respect that Guinea completely failed to substantiate the alleged loss and that the low quantum granted by the Court was, thus, justified.[97] Other cases have been resolved by the judicial body, in which compensation was part of the requested reparation, but the Court did not enter into its analysis due to the lack of substantiation. One such example is the Chorzów Factory Case, in which the Permanent Court did not analyse the quantum of compensation because 'of the insufficiency of the data presented by the parties'.[98]

7.3.3.1.3 DISPUTE REGARDING NAVIGATIONAL AND RELATED RIGHTS The dispute between Nicaragua and Costa Rica is also relevant for the analysis of compensation for material loss. The applicant in this case submitted claims for compensation in a purely declaratory manner, arguing that the Court has the power to declare that compensation is due, in situations in which the amounts are not determined by the party claiming this remedy[99].

---

[95] *Diallo (Republic of Guinea v Democratic Republic of the Congo)* (Merits), 337.
[96] *Diallo (Republic of Guinea v Democratic Republic of the Congo)* (Merits), 337.
[97] Crawford, State Responsibility, 520–521.
[98] Brownlie, 'Remedies in the International Court of Justice' 478.
[99] *Dispute regarding Navigational and Related Rights (Costa Rica v Nicaragua)* [2006] ICJ Pleadings, Memorial of Costa Rica vol 1, 141–142.

128   *7 Compensation*

To substantiate this argument, Costa Rica referred to the previous practice of the Court, mentioning the Fisheries Jurisdiction Case, in which the Court concluded that states have the possibility to seek a declaration through which the Court establishes that compensation is due.[100] However, the Court rejected the claims for compensation submitted by Costa Rica with the reasoning that the request for compensation was not substantiated by any evidence.[101] In this sense, a delimitation should be drawn between substantiation of amounts and substantiation of claims.

In cases in which states request a declaratory judgment regarding the availability of compensation as a remedy, substantiation of claims is necessary, in the sense that the applicant state should demonstrate that material loss occurred, with no further obligation to substantiate determined amounts. In cases in which states request an order for a liquidated amount, substantiation should have the scope of demonstrating a link between the damage caused and the specific quantum of compensation requested from the Court.

The availability of compensation as a remedy for any given dispute should not be interpreted in a vacuum, without linking the remedy with the facts of the case. The conclusion that the Court has reached with respect to this circumstance could be that the availability of compensation is conditioned on the substantiation of the claim, provided by the applicant. Nevertheless, it is apparent that the standard in this situation is lower than the one for substantiation of claims, in which the applicant must submit evidence regarding particular amounts.

As such, in situations in which the Court receives an application through which compensation is requested in a determined but unsubstantiated amount (such as the Diallo Case) the Court should reject such a request. However, in situations in which the Court receives an application through which the applicant requests a declaration that compensation is due (such as the Dispute regarding Navigational and Related Rights) the Court should also reject this claim for not being substantiated, but the standard applied for substantiation of claims should be lower than the standard applied for substantiation of amounts.

7.3.3.2 Compensation for Moral Damages

Compensation for moral damages is a remedy that is available before the Court. This position is generally accepted, certain commentators considering

---

[100] *Fisheries Jurisdiction Case (Germany v Iceland)* (Merits) [1974] ICJ Rep 175, 204.
[101] *Navigational and Related Rights (Costa Rica v Nicaragua)* (Judgment), 267.

in this sense that there is a general principle of international law regarding the availability of compensation for moral damages before international courts and tribunals.[102] The Commentary to the ILC Articles defines moral damages as:

> Moral damage includes such items as individual pain and suffering, loss of loved ones or personal affront associated with an intrusion on one's home or private life.[103]

The notion of 'moral damages' is also referred to as non-material damages,[104] in the sense that it does not affect property or other interests of the state or its nationals. Thus, the first characteristic of moral damages is that it is more abstract than material damages and, as a consequence, cannot be financially assessed. Another characteristic of moral damages is that there is no condition of substantiation for it to be granted by the Court. Therefore, should the applicant state not submit any clarification or evidence with respect to the quantum of moral damages, the Court has the power to determine the amount ex officio.

7.3.3.2.1 THE DIALLO CASE The Diallo Case represents the most recent case in which the Court has rendered a judgment in which it interpreted the notion of moral damages. In this case, the applicant state argued the following:

> Mr Diallo suffered moral and mental harm, including emotional pain, suffering and shock, as well as the loss of his position in society and injury to his reputation as a result of his arrests, detentions and expulsion by the DRC.[105]

It is important to stress that the applicant did not adduce any evidence in this respect. However, the Court concluded that non-material injury can be established with no requirement for specific evidence.[106] This was the sole instance in which the Court held that a state does not have to substantiate a claim for moral damages. This finding is reasonable in light of the fact that

---

[102] Matthew T Parish, Annalise K Nelson and Charles B Rosenberg, 'Awarding Moral Damages to Respondent States in Investment Arbitration' (2011) 29:1 Berkeley Journal of International Law 225, 226.

[103] ILC Draft Articles with Commentaries, 91.

[104] James Crawford, *The International Law Commission's Articles on State Responsibility: Introduction, Text and Commentaries* (Cambridge University Press 2002) 223.

[105] *Diallo (Republic of Guinea v Democratic Republic of the Congo)* (Merits), 13.

[106] *Diallo (Republic of Guinea v Democratic Republic of the Congo)* (Merits), 13.

moral damages are not financially assessable. Due to the above-mentioned arguments, the Court awarded the amount of USD 85,000 to Guinea, based on equity and reasonableness without providing any further explanation for the way it calculated this amount. Authors have considered this circumstance regrettable.[107] The Court however, performed a thorough analysis of the practice of international courts and tribunals to determine the amount that was due to Guinea.[108] Thus, even if non-material damages are difficult to assess, this type of remedy exists in international law, and it is applied as such.

It is important to mention at this point that non-material damages can take both the form of compensation and of satisfaction. In this respect it has been argued, and rightly so, that it is important to *'distinguish between a monetary payment for symbolic damages as a form of satisfaction and the payment of compensation'*.[109] The difference between moral damages as satisfaction and moral damages as compensation should be analysed through the perspective of the ILC Articles, which describe the difference between non-material damages to a state and non-material damages to individuals. The ILC Articles should be interpreted as follows:

- should non-material damage occur to states, the remedy that should be granted is satisfaction;
- should non-material damage occur to individuals, the remedy that should be granted is pecuniary compensation.[110]

It is relevant to note in this respect that the manner in which these two types of damages are assessed has not yet been addressed by the Court as such. However, what can be concluded is that, in light of the Diallo Case, equity would govern the latter.

7.3.3.3 Compensation for Direct and Indirect Injury

The notion of direct injury refers to damages that are caused to the state, directly, and not to its nationals. Therefore, in cases of direct injury, the state does not use the mechanism of diplomatic protection, but it stands before the Court representing its own rights. In this case, the injury for which the state seeks reparation was originally caused to the state.[111]

---

[107] Crawford, State Responsibility, 521.
[108] *Diallo (Republic of Guinea v Democratic Republic of the Congo)* (Merits).
[109] Quintana, Litigation at the International Court, 1147.
[110] Boleslaw Adam Boczek, *International Law: A Dictionary* (Scarecrow Press 2005) 111.
[111] Wilfried Fiedler, 'Damages' in Linda J Pike (ed), *Encyclopedia of Disputes Installment 10* (Elsevier 2015) 69.

Opinions have been expressed regarding the possibility to grant compensation for direct injuries caused to states.[112] Thus, the question as to whether a state may receive substantial reparation in situations in which its sovereignty was harmed[113] is relevant from the perspective of the scope of compensation for direct injury. In this respect, the issue is whether the Court, in cases other than those that involve diplomatic protection, should award compensation.[114] Some authors consider that compensation should be granted to states for direct injury even if no material damage has occurred. Thus, some commentators consider that a state might be entitled to compensation even in a situation in which it has not suffered any material damage.[115] Other authors criticise this approach, and consider that a violation of sovereignty with no material consequences does not entitle a state to claim compensation.[116]

The function of compensation is to compensate for the loss that was suffered by the injured state and should the Court grant any amount that would be outside the function of compensation, it would be imposing a penalty upon the responsible state.[117] The only category in which such compensation for damages other than material damages is available would be for moral damages, if they have occurred. The Court has not analysed compensation for direct injury to states throughout its jurisprudence, even if states have attempted to pursue such heads of claim. One example in which remedies for direct injury to states was addressed properly was the Corfu Channel Case in which the Court determined that satisfaction was the appropriate remedy.[118] Therefore, an appropriate remedy for direct injury to states would indeed be satisfaction, both in monetary and non-monetary forms. Authors confirm this view when arguing that:

Accordingly where a sum of money is awarded as reparation for financially non-assessable damage, one cannot speak of compensation within the meaning of Article 36 of the Articles on State Responsibility. Such remedies must be deemed to reside under Article 37 concerning 'satisfaction'.[119]

---

[112] Gray, Judicial Remedies in International Law, 85.

[113] Gray, Judicial Remedies in International Law, 86.

[114] Wittich, 'Compensation' 22–24.

[115] Gray, Judicial Remedies in International Law, 85.

[116] Gray, Judicial Remedies in International Law, 86.

[117] Bin Cheng, *General Principles of Law As Applied by International Courts and Tribunals* (Cambridge University Press 2006) 234.

[118] *Corfu Channel Case (Great Britain v Albania)* (Compensation), 36.

[119] Martha, The Financial Obligation in International Law, 431.

132   *7 Compensation*

As mentioned in the previous sections, the applicant state can request compensation in two situations: i) if it suffered a direct injury, *i.e.* where the original damages were caused to the state itself and ii) if it suffered an indirect injury, *i.e.* where the original damages were caused to its nationals. When analysing the first situation, one argument that should be considered is that *'damages are awarded not for the loss suffered by individuals but for the breach of an international obligation that rests on the defendant State, i.e. its own actual or imputed wrongful act'.*[120] As such, the notion and interpretation of diplomatic protection is relevant for the interpretation of compensation for indirect injury. The Mavrommatis Case provides an accurate interpretation of the scope of diplomatic protection. In this case, the Court concluded that *'by resorting to diplomatic action or international judicial proceedings on his behalf, a State is in reality asserting its own right'.*[121] Thus, in the cases in which compensation for indirect injury is requested, the state is restricted in claiming *'damages for wrongs it itself has suffered, and individuals are left to seek damages according to the defendant State's legal system'.*[122]

7.3.3.4 Compensation for Environmental Damages

Even if the case-law in which compensation was granted is scarce, the International Court has recently issued its judgment in the Case concerning Certain Activities carried out by Nicaragua in the Border Area between Costa Rica and Nicaragua[123] on 2 February 2018. This judgment is the first in the history of the Court in which compensation was granted for environmental damage. Various issues, stemming from the methodology for assessing compensation for environmental damage to punitive damages, were analysed by the Court through its landmark judgment.

It should be firstly noted that both parties agreed upon the circumstance that environmental damage is compensable under international law. As such Costa Rica argued that *'it is " settled" that environmental damage is compensable under international law*"[124] and Nicaragua did *'not contest Costa Rica's*

---

[120] Fiedler, 'Damages' 69.

[121] *Mavrommatis Palestine Concessions (Greece v United Kingdom)*, 12.

[122] Fiedler, 'Damages' 69.

[123] *Certain Activities Carried Out by Nicaragua in the Border Area (Costa Rica v Nicaragua) and Construction of a Road in Costa Rica along the San Juan River (Nicaragua v Costa Rica)* (Judgment) [2015] ICJ Rep, 665.

[124] *Certain Activities Carried Out by Nicaragua in the Border Area (Costa Rica v Nicaragua) and Construction of a Road in Costa Rica along the San Juan River (Nicaragua v Costa Rica)* (Judgment) [2015] ICJ Rep 665, 12.

contention that damage to the environment is compensable'.[125] Analysing the arguments of both parties with respect to environmental damage being compensation, the International Court concluded as follows in this respect:

> *The Court is therefore of the view that damage to the environment, and the consequent impairment or loss of the ability of the environment to provide goods and services, is compensable under international law. Such compensation may include indemnification for the impairment or loss of environmental goods and services in the period prior to recovery and payment for the restoration of the damaged environment.*[126]

However, even if both parties, and the Court as well, agreed and respectively concluded that compensation is applicable for environmental harm, divergent views were submitted, regarding the manner in which the Court should appreciate the interpretation of compensation in this respect. Costa Rica concluded that the *'ecosystem services approach'* method should be used by the Court when analysing compensation for environmental harm. As such, Costa Rica explained its arguments as follows:

> *the value of an environment is comprised of goods and services that may or may not be traded on the market. Goods and services that are traded on the market (such as timber) have a 'direct use value' whereas those that are not (such as flood prevention or gas regulation) have an 'indirect use value'. In Costa Rica's view, the valuation of environmental damage must take into account both the direct and indirect use values of environmental goods and services in order to provide an accurate reflection of the value of the environment. In order to ascribe a monetary value to the environmental goods and services that Nicaragua purportedly damaged, Costa Rica uses a value transfer approach for most of the goods and services affected. Under the value transfer approach, the damage caused is assigned a monetary value by reference to a value drawn from studies of ecosystems considered to have similar conditions to the ecosystem concerned.*[127]

On the other hand, Nicaragua submitted that a *'replacement value'* method should be used by the International Court when assessing compensation for

---

[125] *Certain Activities Carried Out by Nicaragua in the Border Area (Costa Rica v Nicaragua) and Construction of a Road in Costa Rica along the San Juan River (Nicaragua v Costa Rica)* (Judgment) [2015] ICJ Rep 665, 12.

[126] *Certain Activities Carried Out by Nicaragua in the Border Area (Costa Rica v Nicaragua) and Construction of a Road in Costa Rica along the San Juan River (Nicaragua v Costa Rica)* (Judgment) [2015] ICJ Rep 665, 17.

[127] *Certain Activities Carried Out by Nicaragua in the Border Area (Costa Rica v Nicaragua) and Construction of a Road in Costa Rica along the San Juan River (Nicaragua v Costa Rica)* (Judgment) [2015] ICJ Rep 665, 15.

134   7 *Compensation*

environmental damage. As such Nicaragua submitted the following argument in this respect:

> Nicaragua considers that Costa Rica is entitled to compensation 'to replace the environmental services that either have been or may be lost prior to recovery of the impacted area', which it terms the 'ecosystem service replacement cost' or 'replacement costs'. According to Nicaragua, the proper method for calculating this value is by reference to the price that would have to be paid to preserve an equivalent area until the services provided by the impacted area have recovered.[128]

The Court did not choose between the two methods that were suggested by the parties and rather decided to reach a compromise between the two arguments.[129] Even if the Court decided to take a different path, it decided to *'take into account the specific circumstances and characteristics of each case'*.[130] After rejecting both above-mentioned methods, the Court decided to accept the modified version of a third method submitted by Nicaragua, the entitled *'corrected analysis'*. The Court, however, made its own further adjustments to this manner of valuating compensation. Firstly, the Court rejected the arguments that were submitted by Costa Rica through which it requested that an appropriate calculation of the loss would have to consider a period of fifty years of recovery of the ecosystem.[131] As such, the Court concluded that the assignment of a determined period of fifty years, for various components of the ecosystem would be incorrect.[132] As such, the Court considered that fifty years cannot be considered as a relevant period for each claim submitted by Costa Rica.

Furthermore, the Court also concluded that Nicaragua's submission was inaccurate and provided arguments in the sense that compensation for

[128] *Certain Activities Carried Out by Nicaragua in the Border Area (Costa Rica v Nicaragua) and Construction of a Road in Costa Rica along the San Juan River (Nicaragua v Costa Rica)* (Judgment) [2015] ICJ Rep 665, 16.

[129] *Certain Activities Carried Out by Nicaragua in the Border Area (Costa Rica v Nicaragua) and Construction of a Road in Costa Rica along the San Juan River (Nicaragua v Costa Rica)* (Judgment) [2015] ICJ Rep 665, 17.

[130] *Certain Activities Carried Out by Nicaragua in the Border Area (Costa Rica v Nicaragua) and Construction of a Road in Costa Rica along the San Juan River (Nicaragua v Costa Rica)* (Judgment) [2015] ICJ Rep 665, 17.

[131] *Certain Activities Carried Out by Nicaragua in the Border Area (Costa Rica v Nicaragua) and Construction of a Road in Costa Rica along the San Juan River (Nicaragua v Costa Rica)* (Judgment) [2015] ICJ Rep 665, 22.

[132] *Certain Activities Carried Out by Nicaragua in the Border Area (Costa Rica v Nicaragua) and Construction of a Road in Costa Rica along the San Juan River (Nicaragua v Costa Rica)* (Judgment) [2015] ICJ Rep 665, 22.

environmental damage cannot be based on '*general incentives paid to particular individuals or groups to manage a habitat*'.[133] Given this argumentation, the Court concluded that it will undertake a different approach, by combining, to a certain degree, the two methods suggested by the parties. Thus, the Court concluded that:

> The Court considers, for the reasons specified below, that it is appropriate to approach the valuation of environmental damage from the perspective of the ecosystem as a whole, by adopting an overall assessment of the impairment or loss of environmental goods and services prior to recovery, rather than attributing values to specific categories of environmental goods and services and estimating recovery periods for each of them.[134]

7.3.4 The Implications of the Chorzów Factory Case

The Chorzów Factory Case decided by the Permanent Court has influenced the manner in which compensation is interpreted. This case is relevant with respect to the manner in which restitution in kind and compensation interact with each other, in order to reach the restoration of the status quo ante. It is also pertinent with respect to various issues that involve the clarification of compensation.

7.3.4.1 Damages to Third Parties

First of all, the Court pursued a legal rationale regarding the connection between compensation and the damage caused to the German companies. It concluded that this remedy should not include damages that were caused to third parties, and that it should be limited to the direct damage that was caused to the applicant.[135]

The Permanent Court also observed the practice of other arbitral tribunals, in establishing the principle that compensation can be claimed with respect to the damages caused to property. The Permanent Court did not refer to a

---

[133] *Certain Activities Carried Out by Nicaragua in the Border Area* (*Costa Rica v Nicaragua*) *and Construction of a Road in Costa Rica along the San Juan River* (*Nicaragua v Costa Rica*) (Judgment) [2015] ICJ Rep 665, 22.

[134] *Certain Activities Carried Out by Nicaragua in the Border Area* (*Costa Rica v Nicaragua*) *and Construction of a Road in Costa Rica along the San Juan River* (*Nicaragua v Costa Rica*) (Judgment) [2015] ICJ Rep 665, 22.

[135] *Factory at Chorzów* (*Germany v Poland*) (Merits), 31.

particular international judicial body or to a particular arbitral tribunal, as the International Court did in the Diallo Case when analysing compensation for moral damages.[136] It referred, generally, to the practice of arbitral tribunals. This approach demonstrates that since inception the Permanent Court has not acted in an isolated manner by referring exclusively to its own previous case-law but paid due consideration to the general practice regarding remedies of international law. This approach has been maintained throughout its activity and its effects can be considered positive for the predictability and coherence of the application of international law.

7.3.4.2 Lawful and Unlawful Expropriation

In the Chorzów Factory Case, the Permanent Court also analysed the manner in which compensation applies differently with respect to lawful and unlawful expropriation. This was the first case where the Permanent Court determined the manner in which compensation applies to a dispute which involves issues of unlawful seizure of property. In its judgment, the Permanent Court held that there is a difference between lawful and unlawful expropriation and that this difference produces certain effects with respect to the quantification of the amount of damages that should be granted as compensation. The Permanent Court first assessed the legal qualification of an expropriation that contravenes a treaty in force. In this respect, the Court concluded that an expropriation that is not lawful, as was in the circumstances of the case, is not an expropriation at all, but a seizure of property.[137]

Following this conclusion, the Permanent Court analysed the manner in which such a breach would be repaired through compensation. It held that it should not apply the same standard for quantifying compensation regarding seizure of property (unlawful expropriation) as it did for quantifying lawful expropriation. Thus, the Permanent Court concluded that compensation for seizure of property, or for unlawful expropriation, should not be limited to the value of the undertaking as if the responding state had legally expropriated, albeit without paying fair compensation.[138] The manner in which compensation applies differently with respect to lawful and to unlawful expropriation was further substantiated and confirmed by the doctrine.[139] It is therefore

---

[136] *Diallo (Republic of Guinea v Democratic Republic of the Congo)* (Merits).

[137] *Factory at Chorzów (Germany v Poland)* (Merits), 46.

[138] *Factory at Chorzów (Germany v Poland)* (Merits), 47.

[139] Suzy H Nikièma, 'Compensation for Expropriation', International Institute for Sustainable Development – Best Practices Series (2013), 3.

worth mentioning that for the situation in which unlawful expropriation occurs, the value of compensation would be higher in comparison with the amounts granted by the Court for acts of lawful expropriation. The Court found the following in this respect:

> *The impossibility, on which the Parties are agreed, of restoring the Chorzów factory could therefore have no other effect but that of substituting payment of the value of the undertaking for restitution; it would not be in conformity either with the principles of law or with the wish of the Parties to infer from that agreement that the question of compensation must henceforth be dealt with as though an expropriation properly so called was involved.*[140]

However, after providing that compensation for lawful expropriation differ in quantum from compensation for unlawful expropriation, the Court analysed the submissions of the parties in this respect and concluded that it cannot determine the amounts because it was not provided with sufficient data. The Court therefore concluded that the related claims are insufficiently substantiated.[141]

One reason why the Permanent Court did not go as far as suggesting the mechanism that should be applied for unlawful expropriation could be the high degree of technicality regarding the precise calculation of damages. This deduction is further supported by the fact that, in this case, the Permanent Court considered that an expert opinion would be useful for a proper quantification of damages.[142] Even if the Court did not necessarily suggest a concrete manner in which compensation would be quantified differently depending on the nature of expropriation (lawful or unlawful), the conclusion that the consequences of an unlawful expropriation should be more drastic than the ones for legal expropriation is still relevant for the interpretation and application of compensation.

7.3.4.3 Compensation and Restitution in Kind

As mentioned above, in the Chorzów Factory Case the parties agreed that restitution in kind was no longer possible[143] and therefore concluded that the proper remedy for the dispute would be compensation. Thus, the Permanent Court was limited to granting or rejecting compensation. The Permanent

---

[140] *Factory at Chorzów (Germany v Poland) (Merits)*, 48.
[141] *Factory at Chorzów (Germany v Poland) (Merits)*, 49.
[142] *Factory at Chorzów (Germany v Poland) (Merits)*, 51.
[143] *Factory at Chorzów (Germany v Poland) (Merits)*, 48.

138   7 Compensation

Court concluded that it is a principle that indemnity is a form of reparation, and further mentioned that compensation is the most usual form of reparation.[144]

The conclusion that the Permanent Court reached in this respect seems rather isolated from its own interpretation due to the fact that, in the history of the Permanent Court, compensation was requested in approximately one-third of its cases and it was granted only in the 'Wimbledon' Case;[145] in the history of the International Court, even less so.

The finding with respect to compensation being the usual form of reparation also seems to contradict the Permanent Court's subsequent findings in the Chorzów Factory Case, which are considered as being obiter dictum regarding reparation in general, and restitution in kind as being the primary remedy in international law. Thus, even if the Permanent Court considered that compensation is the most usual form of reparation, it further concluded that restitution in kind applies, or should apply, with priority.[146] Certain authors[147] consider that the Permanent Court clearly established 'the principles [which] are self-evident in suggesting the clear preference for restitution as the primary remedy for violations in international law'.[148]

However, although compensation does not appear to be the most usual form of reparation, as the Permanent Court had concluded, neither does restitution in kind. Compensation remains among the remedies that have been among the least granted by the Court throughout its case-law.

7.3.5 The Implications of the Corfu Channel Case

The Corfu Channel Case is the first case that the International Court had on its docket. Also, this case would be the only one for a long period of time in which the International Court granted compensation. The Corfu Channel Case is not exceptional in its substantial analysis of compensation because the International Court followed the judgment of the Permanent Court in the Chorzów Factory Case. However, certain relevant conclusions of the International Court have contributed to the interpretation and clarification of this remedy.

---

[144] Factory at Chorzów (Germany v Poland) (Merits), 27.
[145] Gray, Judicial Remedies in International Law, 77.
[146] Factory at Chorzów (Germany v Poland) (Merits), 47.
[147] Leckie and Huggins, Conflict and Housing, Land and Property Rights, 133.
[148] Leckie and Huggins, Conflict and Housing, Land and Property Rights, 133.

7.3.5.1 Bifurcation of Proceedings

The judgment of the Corfu Channel Case is relevant to compensation as a remedy from a procedural standpoint as well. In this case, the Court, after deciding that compensation is the appropriate remedy that should be granted to the applicant, decided to bifurcate the proceedings and hold a separate phase with respect to the determination of the quantum of compensation. The reasoning for such a determination was that the Albanian Government had not provided sufficient details with respect to its claims for compensation.[149] As a consequence, in the judgment which referred to the merits of the case, the Court concluded that it would reserve for further consideration the assessment of compensation.[150]

Bifurcation of proceedings before the International Court is the usual procedural mechanism through which the Court resolves the disputes: it first delivers a judgment regarding the merits of the case and, subject to further clarifications provided either by the parties or by designated experts, it delivers a judgment regarding the quantum of compensation. Cases such as Diallo (discussed further below) demonstrate that this approach has been followed by the Court throughout its practice.

7.3.5.2 Expert Reports

Another relevant issue with a certain degree of novelty in the Corfu Channel Case was the reliance on Article 50 of the Statute of the Court for requesting, ex officio, expert determination for a variety of issues which included the quantification of compensation. Applying the said Article, the Court submitted the following question to the experts, due to its anxiety towards the determination of technical issues that could have interfered with finding the truth.[151] The Court further relied on expert reports regarding the assessment of damages. Thus, the Court considered that the experts should evaluate and examine the submissions of the parties regarding the amount of damages in dispute.[152] The Court analysed the report that was submitted by the experts in order to decide whether or not the claims of Great Britain were well substantiated. The request for expert reports by the Court, ex officio, is rather exceptional. Throughout its case-law the International Court requested expert

---

[149] Corfu Channel Case (Great Britain v Albania) (Compensation), 5.
[150] Corfu Channel Case (Great Britain v Albania) (Merits), 36.
[151] Corfu Channel Case (Great Britain v Albania) (Order), 4–5.
[152] Corfu Channel Case (Great Britain v Albania) (Order), 4–5.

140   7 Compensation

opinions in few cases: the Corfu Channel Case and the Gulf of Maine Case[153] are such examples.

The reasons for the reluctance of the Court to appoint experts cannot be easily determined. However, it could be concluded that the Court could consider that should it appoint experts, an important portion of the dispute would be resolved by the experts and not by the Court. In this sense, the Corfu Channel Case remains *'the outstanding example of the use of experts by the ICJ. Subsequent instances have not displaced this case from its position as the leading illustration'.*[154] In the judgment on the compensation phase, the Court determined the liquidated amount that the Republic of Albania should pay to the United Kingdom.[155]

Even though the International Court decided that a fixed amount was due as compensation, it is relevant to note that this finding did not necessarily lead to a formal settlement of the dispute. Albania decided to ignore the judgment of the Court in this respect and refused to pay the said amounts until 1991, when the dispute was finally settled.[156] This approach of the responding party further demonstrates the reasons for which the Court has been rather reluctant ever since to grant compensation of a determined amount, with few exceptions, such as the Diallo Case.

7.3.6 The Implications of the Diallo Case

The judgment of the Court in the Diallo Case represents another circumstance where the Court granted compensation, in which it approached several issues for the first time: Diallo is the only case in the history of the Court in which it granted compensation for indirect moral damages. Further, with respect to the practice of the International Court regarding compensation, it is the second case in approximately sixty years in which the Court granted this remedy. Also, the Court took a novel approach with respect to its references to the practice of other international courts.

---

[153] *Delimitation of Maritime Boundary in the Gulf of Maine Area (Canada v The USA)* (Order) [1984] ICJ Rep 165.

[154] Gillian White, 'The Use of Experts by the International Court of Justice' in Robert Yewdall Jennings, Vaughn Lowe and Malgosia Fitzmaurice (eds), *Fifty Years of the International Court of Justice: Essays in Honour of Sir Robert Jennings* (Cambridge University Press 1996) 529.

[155] *Corfu Channel Case (Great Britain v Albania)* (Compensation), 10.

[156] A Mark Weisburd, *Failings of the International Court of Justice* (Oxford University Press 2016) 351.

7.3.6.1 The Burden of Proof

Generally, the burden of proof rests with the entity that submits a positive assertion, as the maxim actori incumbit probatio provides. However, it is interesting to note that the Court mentioned that it has the possibility to determine the amount of compensation by analysing the arguments of the responding state as well, accepting that the applicant might have material difficulties in assessing certain situations. Therefore, even though the applicant had the burden of proof with respect to the amounts of compensation, the Court considered that this burden was not absolute and that it had the power to make a determination on the amounts. Thus, the Court recognised that the circumstances of the expulsion of Mr Diallo justify this approach.[157] As such, the Court concluded that the general rule that a party alleging a factual framework must support its claims should be applied flexibly, as long as the responding state *'may be in a better position to establish certain facts'*.[158]

This approach was confirmed, and further clarified, by the Court in its more recent case concerning Certain Activities Carried out by Nicaragua in the Border Area. First, the Court reconfirmed the above-quoted finding,[159] reiterated its finding in the Diallo Case and concluded that the burden of proof does not always rest on the applicant state. Second, the Court further stressed that in cases regarding environmental damage *'particular issues may arise with respect to the existence of damage and causation'*[160] and that, in such cases, in which the state of science might also influence the interpretation of the factual framework of the case, *'it is for the Court to decide whether there is a sufficient causal nexus between the wrongful act and the injury suffered'*.[161]

As such, the finding of the Court in the Diallo Case related to the burden of proof has been confirmed by in its subsequent case-law. It is relevant to note, at this juncture, that the issues regarding the burden of proof are not, and should not be, interpreted restrictively by the Court. Consequently, it can be concluded that the substantiation of claims standard is subjective in nature, as it takes into consideration the capabilities of each state to fulfil it.

---

[157] Diallo (*Republic of Guinea v Democratic Republic of the Congo*) (Merits), 12.
[158] Diallo (*Republic of Guinea v Democratic Republic of the Congo*) (Merits), 12.
[159] *Certain Activities Carried Out by Nicaragua in the Border Area* (*Costa Rica v Nicaragua*) (Compensation) [2018] ICJ Rep, 15.
[160] *Certain Activities Carried Out by Nicaragua in the Border Area* (*Costa Rica v Nicaragua*) (Compensation) [2018] ICJ Rep 15.
[161] *Certain Activities Carried Out by Nicaragua in the Border Area* (*Costa Rica v Nicaragua*) (Compensation) [2018] ICJ Rep 15.

7.3.6.2 Non-material Damage and Equity

The judgment of the International Court in the Diallo Case is relevant for the interpretation and clarification of compensation due to the fact that it made a clear distinction between material and non-material damage. This judgment is also relevant, not only because it considered the availability of non-material damages, but also through the perspective of its approach towards their quantification. In this respect, the Court concluded that equitable considerations guide the quantification of damages for non-material harm, which involve flexibility and consideration of what is *'just, fair and reasonable in all the circumstances of the case'*.[162]

Due to the above-mentioned arguments, the Court awarded the amount of USD 85,000 to Guinea, based on equity and reasonableness. The reasoning for which the Court concluded that the said amount is equitable took into consideration the number of days that Mr Diallo was detained,[163] the fact that Mr Diallo was detained without being provided with the reasons for the incarceration,[164] the fact that he was not allowed to seek remedies for the incarceration,[165] that he was detained for an unjustifiably long period pending expulsion, that he was made the object of accusations that were not substantiated and that he was wrongfully expelled from the country.[166] Authors have argued that the analysis of the Court was not necessarily sufficient for the determination of the said quantum of compensation for moral damages and considered this circumstance regrettable.[167] Nevertheless, the Court performed a thorough analysis of the practice of international courts and tribunals to determine the amount that was due to Guinea,[168] and this approach is relevant and useful for such a determination. Thus, even if non-material damages are difficult to assess, *'international courts and tribunals recognize that such damages are very real'*.[169] The International Court confirmed this view through the Diallo Case, which is unique in its finding regarding moral damages granted by the Court as compensation. The finding of the International Court represents a veritable precedent in this respect.[170]

---

[162] *Diallo (Republic of Guinea v Democratic Republic of the Congo) (Merits)*, 15.

[163] *Diallo (Republic of Guinea v Democratic Republic of the Congo) (Merits)*, 11.

[164] *Diallo (Republic of Guinea v Democratic Republic of the Congo) (Merits)*, 11.

[165] *Diallo (Republic of Guinea v Democratic Republic of the Congo) (Merits)*, 11.

[166] *Ahmadou Sadio Diallo (Republic of Guinea v Democratic Republic of the Congo)*, ICJ Pleadings, Application instituting Proceedings, 7.

[167] Crawford, State Responsibility, 521.

[168] *Diallo (Republic of Guinea v Democratic Republic of the Congo) (Merits)*, 324.

[169] Martha, The Financial Obligation in International Law, 98.

[170] *Certain Activities Carried Out by Nicaragua in the Border Area (Costa Rica v Nicaragua) (Compensation)* [2018] ICJ Rep, 14.

7.4 CONCLUSION

Firstly, regarding the availability of compensation for moral damages as a remedy of international law, the Court concluded that it covers injuries that do not have a material form and that, as a consequence, non-material injury to an individual may take a variety of forms.[171] Secondly, the judgment of the Court in the Diallo Case represents a novelty with respect to the manner in which the Court assessed compensation regarding injuries caused to individuals, the Court considering equity as a valuation tool for this type of compensation. It can therefore be concluded that the finding of the Court with respect to the manner in which this remedy is interpreted represents a finding of principle[172] which should be applied in the future by the Court and by other international courts and tribunals.

It appears that the analysis of compensation does not imply difficulties when interpreted in abstracto, as a concept. Its definition, function, categories and means of assessment are without many controversies. However, the specificities of each case and the fact that the International Court does not yet have a substantial body of case-law in this respect prove that certain characteristics of compensation need further address.[173] The recent case-law of the International Court and the manner in which states frame their requests for this remedy, both with respect to compensation for material and non-material damages, lead to the conclusion that further clarifications regarding it shall be made available by the Court in its future case-law.

It can be concluded with respect to compensation that, although the case-law of the International Court is rather limited regarding this remedy, it is the one towards which the Court has manifested its greatest care. Perhaps due to the technicalities and typologies of compensation, the International Court has provided relevant findings that clarified certain notions, such as the manner in which compensation is addressed by experts, the burden of proof or compensation for moral damages and the use of equity in its evaluation.

Even if compensation does not involve the same limitations as restitution in kind, such as material possibility and a proportionate burden, one important hurdle must be surpassed by states claiming this remedy: that of substantiation

---

[171] *Certain Activities Carried Out by Nicaragua in the Border Area* (*Costa Rica v Nicaragua*) (Compensation) [2018] ICJ Rep, 13.

[172] Guiguo Wang, *International Investment Law: A Chinese Perspective*, (Routledge 2015) 495.

[173] John Barker, 'The Different Forms of Reparation: Compensation' in James Crawford, Alain Pellet and Simon Olleson (eds), *The Law of International Responsibility* (Oxford University Press 2010) 603.

of claims. As such, perhaps the reasons for which requests for undetermined compensation, in which the quantum of damages is not requested, are more apposite before the International Court of Justice, especially because the damages caused in interstate relations often entail a high degree of complexity. The Court seems more comfortable in determining that compensation is due, without assessing a determined quantum.

8

Satisfaction

8.1 INTRODUCTION

The availability of satisfaction before the Court is undisputed. What is presently established is that satisfaction is the appropriate remedy for injuries that are directly caused to states and cannot be quantified because they are not material.[1] As such, state parties to disputes submitted before the Court request this remedy and the Court grants satisfaction, if certain conditions are met. Authors confirm this view, and conclude that the general practice of the Court shows that it grants satisfaction through the awarding of declaratory judgments,[2] and that satisfaction is usually granted for moral damages caused to states.[3] However, even if satisfaction is available before the Court, the manner in which it is interpreted is rather controversial.

Among the remedies that are available before the Court, satisfaction is among the broadest in scope, since, currently, a precise mechanism through which satisfaction is achieved cannot necessarily be drawn up. Compensation, restitution in kind and specific performance prove to be more straightforward in this respect, as these remedies have specific means of application.

Authors have argued that the measures of reparation provided by satisfaction are designed to calibrate the norms regarding state responsibility for violations that cannot be addressed by the classic forms of restitution and compensation.[4] Thus, satisfaction is a more abstract remedy which can be morphed and adapted in accordance with the specificities of each case, provided that

---

[1] Gray, Judicial Remedies in International Law, 41.
[2] McIntyre, 'Declaratory Judgments' 146.
[3] Martha, The Financial Obligation in International Law, 429.
[4] Gentian Zyberi, 'The International Court of Justice and Applied Forms of Reparation for International Human Rights and Humanitarian Law Violations' (2011) 7:1 Utrecht Law Review 204, 211.

compensation or restitution cannot be applied. In this sense, satisfaction could be considered, at times, an exceptional remedy that becomes applicable only if restitution and compensation are unavailable. This clear delimitation of the applicability of satisfaction does not necessarily represent the reality before the Court, as states seem more comfortable with satisfaction rather than with restitution or compensation.

Furthermore, the declaration of wrongfulness as satisfaction is the remedy that the Court has granted most throughout its history, either on a stand-alone basis or in conjunction with other remedies. Whilst satisfaction is a remedy that is distinct from restitution and compensation in scope, it has certain similarities with the latter, especially because satisfaction may be pecuniary in nature.[5] Therefore, one feature that sets satisfaction apart from other remedies, except from compensation, is that it can be both non-pecuniary and pecuniary in nature. The specificities of satisfaction as a remedy before the International Court shall be analysed below.

Satisfaction as a remedy before the International Court and the Permanent Court has not been often requested by the parties, nor granted by the Court. More so, it appears that in the few disputes in which the Court has granted this remedy, it has interpreted and applied it in a different manner than that of the ILC Articles.[6] The approach that the Court has taken towards satisfaction as a remedy has led authors like Amerasinghe to conclude that the legal status of satisfaction is yet uncertain.[7]

This conclusion has merit, as the inconsistencies regarding the interpretation and clarification of satisfaction as a remedy have been amplified by the fact that the International Court attributes a meaning to satisfaction that was not necessarily envisioned by the ILC Articles. The meaning attributed to satisfaction by the ILC Articles entails that the state which committed the breach of an international obligation should provide satisfaction, if the Court considers this remedy appropriate. Nevertheless, the Court seems to consider that satisfaction can be granted without any action on behalf of the responsible state.

Even if satisfaction is a well-established remedy of international law, the case-law of the Court shows that states rarely request satisfaction as a remedy. Furthermore, the Permanent Court and the International Court have rarely granted this remedy for breaches of international law. These circumstances have sometimes led to drastic opinions, such as the one expressed by Judge

---

[5] García Amador, Sohn and Baxter, Recent Codification of State Responsibility Law, 102.

[6] ILC Draft Articles with Commentaries, 105.

[7] Amerasinghe, Jurisdiction of Specific International Tribunals, 417.

8.2 Theoretical Perspectives 147

Azavedo in the Corfu Channel Case, who concluded that satisfaction should no longer be considered a form of reparation due to its volatile nature.[8] Nevertheless, even if the availability of satisfaction as a remedy of international law is accepted, not only does the Court seem rather indecisive with respect to the interpretation of satisfaction as a remedy but state practice further complicates the manner in which satisfaction is interpreted.[9] The following sections shall assess the established types of satisfaction.

8.2 THEORETICAL PERSPECTIVES

8.2.1 *The Definition and Function of Satisfaction*

The characteristics of satisfaction are not as tangible as those of compensation and restitution, it being considered as a broader aspect of reparation.[10] The reason why satisfaction is more abstract than other remedies is that its interpretation implies that the responsible state should express its regret for breaching international law. Another relevant aspect for the difficulty of interpreting the scope of satisfaction is that this remedy did not receive a coherent understanding throughout the last centuries.[11] As such, expressing regret could cover a wide range of possibilities that have the final function of appeasing the injured state. Due to its nature and given the above-mentioned considerations, satisfaction has been defined as being *'any measure which the responsible state is bound to take under customary international law or under an agreement of the parties to a dispute, apart from restitution and compensation'.*[12] This definition is rather vague and not necessarily accurate, especially because it assimilates satisfaction with remedies that reside outside the scope of restitution and compensation. The reasoning for this assimilation might have been the fact that satisfaction, as a recognition of the illegal act, is included, to a certain degree, in other remedies, cessation being such an example. Nevertheless, if this should be the case the same conclusion could be reached regarding restitution and compensation, if the state that committed an international wrong would implement these remedies. Satisfaction should not be defined by reference to other remedies of international law, as it is independent and it has a precise function.

---

[8] *Corfu Channel Case (Great Britain v Albania)* (Merits) (Dissenting Opinion of Judge Azevedo).

[9] Gray, Judicial Remedies in International Law, 42.

[10] Crawford, Brownlie's Principles, 574.

[11] McIntyre, 'Declaratory Judgments' 146.

[12] Crawford, Brownlie's Principles, 574.

148   *8 Satisfaction*

As such, satisfaction could be defined as a recognition, either formal or informal, of the illegal acts that led to breaches of international obligations.

It is generally accepted that satisfaction is a rather exceptional[13] remedy. Article 37(2) of the ILC Articles confirms this view, as it provides that satisfaction is appropriate insofar as reparation cannot be achieved through restitution or compensation. Thus, *'only if those two forms have not provided full reparation may satisfaction be required'*.[14]

The wording of Article 37(1) is identical to the wording of Article 36 and Article 35 of the ILC Articles in the sense that the responsible state has the obligation to provide satisfaction, compensation or restitution. It must therefore be noted that satisfaction, first and foremost, is a form of reparation, and that, in this respect, it is no different from compensation and restitution. It must also be noted that, in accordance with the ILC Articles, satisfaction may repair injury in ways that restitution and compensation cannot. In other words, if the injury is non-material and is caused directly to the state, since this type of injury cannot be repaired either by restitution (as there is no restorable object) or by compensation (as moral damages caused directly to the state cannot be financially assessed), satisfaction should suffice.

A first characteristic of the function of satisfaction could therefore be the reparation of injuries that restitution and compensation are unable to redress. However, satisfaction should not be limited to this exceptional role before the Court. Authors, referring to the judgment of the Court in the Corfu Channel Case,[15] have argued that satisfaction should not always be interpreted as an alternative to compensation, especially in situations in which compensation is not requested.[16]

The distinction between pecuniary and non-pecuniary satisfaction is therefore relevant for determining its function. The Commentary to the ILC Articles provides that satisfaction is *'a remedy for those injuries not financially assessable which amount to an affront to the State'*.[17] However, referring to pecuniary satisfaction, some authors have concluded that satisfaction can be interpreted as de facto compensation for moral damages to the state.[18] It would

---

[13] Crawford, Brownlie's Principles, 574.

[14] McIntyre, 'Declaratory Judgments' 146.

[15] *Corfu Channel Case (Great Britain v Albania)* (Compensation), 244.

[16] Pierre d'Argent, 'Reparation and Compliance' in Karine Bannelier, Theodore Christakis and Sarah Heathcote (eds), *The ICJ and the Evolution of International Law: The Enduring Impact of the Corfu Channel Case* (Routledge 2012), 336.

[17] ILC Draft Articles with Commentaries, 106.

[18] Crawford, State Responsibility, 527.

be rather difficult to assimilate satisfaction with compensation, since, even if satisfaction takes a pecuniary form, it is a remedy that cannot be financially assessed. The amount due as pecuniary satisfaction can however be determined by the Court based on equitable considerations, given the moral character of the injury.

Therefore, even if pecuniary satisfaction has similarities with compensation, a more appropriate view is the one that considers satisfaction as an independent remedy, and that referring to satisfaction as a typology of compensation might cause difficulties of interpretation.[19] As such, the function of satisfaction is to *'appease the injured state'*[20] through public apologies.

8.2.2 *Types of Satisfaction*

An exhaustive list of mechanisms through which satisfaction would repair the non-material injury caused to a state is yet to be drawn. Due to its function, satisfaction is a remedy that should not be limited to a given set of modalities in which it would be achieved and injured states should have the freedom to determine what action is best suited to satisfy them. In this sense, while compensation is granted through monetary relief and restitution through the restoration of good, individuals or legislation, satisfaction is represented by a wide range of forms through which non-material damage is repaired.[21] This is further confirmed by the ILC Articles, as there is no provision of an exhaustive list through which satisfaction could be achieved; the enumeration provided by Article 37 is illustrative when providing that this remedy is attained through *'an acknowledgement of the breach, an expression of regret, a formal apology or another appropriate modality'*.[22] In this sense, authors have concluded that the common measures in which satisfaction could be achieved are *'apologies, punishment of the guilty, assurances as to the future and pecuniary satisfaction'*.[23] However, it can be concluded that the most appropriate classification of satisfaction is into two main categories: i) non-pecuniary satisfaction and ii) pecuniary satisfaction.[24]

---

[19] Quintana, Litigation at the International Court, 1147.
[20] Eibe Riedel, 'Satisfaction' in Pike (ed), *Encyclopedia of Disputes Installment* 10, 383.
[21] Crawford, Brownlie's Principles, 574.
[22] ILC Draft Articles with Commentaries, 106.
[23] Amerasinghe, Jurisdiction of Specific International Tribunals, 418.
[24] García Amador, Sohn and Baxter, Recent Codification of State Responsibility Law, 103.

8.3 PRACTICAL PERSPECTIVES

8.3.1 *The Availability of Satisfaction*

The dispute in the Corfu Channel Case which was submitted before the Court, entailed that a number of British warships were damaged due to existing mines in the waters of Albania. The United Kingdom sought compensation for its losses, while Albania sought satisfaction.[25]

An underlying reason for which Albania requested this type of remedy could be considered the fact that no injury was caused to it as a result of the breach of sovereignty rights. As such, requests for other more coercive remedies, such as restitution in kind or compensation, would have been redundant. Deciding upon the above-mentioned request of Albania, the Court concluded that its declaratory judgment, which confirmed that a breach of international law occurred on behalf of the United Kingdom, represents proper satisfaction for Albania.[26] The manner in which the Court has determined that its declaration would constitute an appropriate form of satisfaction has been contested. Commentators have argued in this sense that the Court cannot substitute itself for the applicant and determine a different mechanism of applying a remedy.[27] Nevertheless, the findings of the Court in this case have been referred to by the International Court throughout its practice as obiter dicta. Thus, in the Case Concerning the Application of the Convention on the Prevention and Punishment of the Crime of Genocide, the Court has confirmed the view that was expressed in the Corfu Channel Case, and concluded that a declaration of wrongfulness represents appropriate satisfaction.[28]

It is therefore important to note that the Corfu Channel Case represents the first case that established that satisfaction can be granted by the Court by means of a declaratory judgment. Few opinions have been expressed against the availability of satisfaction as apologies, one being that of Judge Azavedo in his dissenting opinion of the Corfu Channel Case, which concluded that the Court should '*break away from the familiar medieval procedure*'.[29] Judge

---

[25] *Corfu Channel Case (Great Britain v Albania)* [1948] ICJ Pleadings, Counter-memorial submitted by the Government of the People's Republic of Albania, 146.

[26] *Corfu Channel Case (Great Britain v Albania)* (Merits), 36.

[27] Kolb, The International Court of Justice, 920.

[28] *Application of the Convention on the Prevention and Punishment of the Crime of Genocide (Bosnia and Herzegovina v Serbia and Montenegro)* (Judgment), 195.

[29] *Corfu Channel Case (Great Britain v Albania)* (Merits) (Dissenting Opinion of Judge Azevedo), 36.

8.3 *Practical Perspectives* 151

Azavedo further clarified his point and concluded that a breach of international law could not remain without a remedy, considering that:

> There remains only one moral sanction that can be applied without disregarding the absence of a claim for the assessment of damages.
>
> The matter cannot be left to the future; for the sanction must re ipsa be found in the Judgment. This will be purely declaratory, and will state that the United Kingdom's conduct was contrary to international law and in every way abnormal.[30]

However, the fact that this remedy is becoming obsolete is not necessarily an argument that would render the judgments of the Court that grant this remedy contrary to international law. As has been previously stated, the more established remedies of compensation and restitution have become rather exceptional before the International Court. This circumstance should not mean, however, that they should no longer be regarded as remedies, but it merely describes a certain evolutionary trend. The same applies for satisfaction. Thus, the following, more flexible view has merit:

> A remedy on these lines and with this purpose, rather than 'satisfaction' properly so called, would provide a means of protecting the interests which in fact call for the protection of international law in cases involving responsibility of this kind.[31]

Another case that confirms the availability of satisfaction before the Court, applied through declaratory judgments, is the case concerning the Application of the Convention on the Prevention and Punishment of the Crime of Genocide. Through the statement of facts, the applicant state sought to establish that the People and State of Bosnia and Herzegovina had suffered from the crime of genocide, as defined by the 1948 Genocide Convention.[32]

As a consequence, the applicant state argued that it was entitled to compensation for the damages caused,[33] and did not refer to satisfaction as a potential remedy. Nevertheless, the Court concluded that satisfaction represented the appropriate remedy. The Court concluded that even if the obligation to prevent the crime of genocide was clearly breached, a link of causality

---

[30] *Corfu Channel Case* (*Great Britain v Albania*) (Merits) (Dissenting Opinion of Judge Azevedo), 36.

[31] García Amador, Sohn and Baxter, Recent Codification of State Responsibility Law, 128.

[32] *Application of the Convention on the Prevention and Punishment of the Crime of Genocide* (*Bosnia and Herzegovina v Serbia and Montenegro*) (Application Instituting Proceedings), para 135.

[33] *Application of the Convention on the Prevention and Punishment of the Crime of Genocide* (*Bosnia and Herzegovina v Serbia and Montenegro*) (Judgment), 64.

between the breach and the damage should be proven by the applicant state.[34] Consequently, the Court concluded that even if reparation was due, without any link of causality compensation could not be granted, but that satisfaction, in lieu of the former, was the appropriate remedy.[35] However, the Court decided to refer to the finding related to compensation provided in one of its previous cases, where it granted satisfaction through a declaratory judgment, in the Corfu Channel Case, as justifying the applicability of satisfaction in this dispute.[36]

This case demonstrates the fact that satisfaction could be considered as being a secondary remedy which applies in the cases where the primary remedies, such as compensation or restitution, prove to be impossible to grant. In other words, the availability of satisfaction before the Court is presently established. However, the scope of its application, related to pecuniary and non-pecuniary satisfaction, is not.

8.3.2 Non-pecuniary Satisfaction

Non-pecuniary satisfaction represents the norm before the Court. According to Article 37 of the ILC Articles, satisfaction can take the following forms of acknowledging the breach and any other forms deemed appropriate by the Court. It could, therefore, be considered that the ILC Articles confirm the opinions that envisage non-pecuniary satisfaction as the typical form, and pecuniary satisfaction as the exception,[37] the latter being included in the second category, *i.e.* forms deemed appropriate by the Court. Even if not provided through Article 37, the Commentary to the ILC Articles provides that non-pecuniary satisfaction could be granted for certain serious violations of international law, such as territorial integrity, attacks on ships or aircraft or on members of diplomatic missions.[38] Although the list of examples through which satisfaction could be granted is non-exhaustive, two main mechanisms[39] through which satisfaction has often been granted by the Court exist:

i) a declaration of wrongdoing, delivered by the Court;

or

ii) an apology, delivered by the responding state.

---

[34] *Application of the Convention on the Prevention and Punishment of the Crime of Genocide (Bosnia and Herzegovina v Serbia and Montenegro)* (Judgment), 195.

[35] *Application of the Convention on the Prevention and Punishment of the Crime of Genocide (Bosnia and Herzegovina v Serbia and Montenegro)* (Judgment), 195.

[36] *Application of the Convention on the Prevention and Punishment of the Crime of Genocide (Bosnia and Herzegovina v Serbia and Montenegro)* (Judgment), 195.

[37] Martha, The Financial Obligation in International Law, 431.

[38] ILC Draft Articles with Commentaries, 106.

[39] Martha, The Financial Obligation in International Law, 439.

8.3.2.1 Declaration of Wrongdoing

Non-pecuniary satisfaction is often granted through a declaration of the Court through which the wrongdoing of the responding state is acknowledged.[40] The Commentary of the ILC Articles confirms that the declaration of wrongfulness is the most common form of satisfaction.[41] The Corfu Channel Case[42] and the Application of the Genocide Convention Case,[43] through which the Court determined that such a declaration was sufficient reparation, are relevant from this perspective.

The Corfu Channel Case represents the locus clasicus for satisfaction as a remedy of international law and for its granting through a declaratory judgment.[44] The finding of the Court in the Corfu Channel Case is often referred to when interpreting non-pecuniary satisfaction granted through declaratory relief. In this, the Court concluded that Great Britain was responsible for violating the sovereignty of Albania through an operation in its national waters, although no material damage was caused by this action. The Court determined that its declaration is in itself a manner in which satisfaction was applied as a remedy of international law.[45] What is relevant in this case is that the respondent explicitly requested the Court to conclude that satisfaction should be granted by the Court.[46]

It is important to note that the Court did not act ex officio when determining the appropriate remedy, this being the reason for which certain authors disagree with the finding of the Court in this case, arguing that the Court did not grant satisfaction because this remedy should be delivered by the responding state and not by the Court through a declaration of wrongdoing.[47] Nevertheless, the practice of the Court confirms that it has issued several judgments in which it considered that its declaration of wrongfulness represents satisfaction. The Application of the Genocide Convention Case is such an instance.

In the Application of the Genocide Convention Case, the Court considered that a declaration of wrongfulness was the suitable remedy even where

---

[40] Crawford, State Responsibility, 530.
[41] ILC Draft Articles with Commentaries, 107.
[42] Corfu Channel Case (Great Britain v Albania) (Compensation), 244.
[43] Application of the Convention on the Prevention and Punishment of the Crime of Genocide (Bosnia and Herzegovina v Serbia and Montenegro) (Judgment).
[44] D'Argent, 'Reparation and Compliance' 336.
[45] Corfu Channel Case (Great Britain v Albania) (Merits), 35.
[46] Corfu Channel Case (Great Britain v Albania) (Merits), 12.
[47] McIntyre, 'Declaratory Judgments' 147.

the responding state requested compensation. The Court therefore followed the structure of the ILC Articles, first determining that compensation was unsuitable, and afterwards concluding that satisfaction is the appropriate remedy.[48] However, quoting the finding of the Corfu Channel Case regarding satisfaction, the Court concluded that the applicant has the right to reparation for non-material damages by means of satisfaction, which would further be granted through a declaration of wrongfulness.[49] The two above-mentioned cases are examples for non-pecuniary satisfaction that was provided by the Court to the applicant state without imposing any duty of apology directed towards the responding state. The mere declaration of wrongfulness of the Court was considered sufficient, as this manner of granting satisfaction fulfils the function of this remedy, *i.e.* to appease the injured state.

8.3.2.2 Apologies

Non-pecuniary satisfaction could also be granted through an apology of the responding state by which it admits that it has breached an international obligation, delivered to the applicant state. It is therefore important for the purposes of non-pecuniary satisfaction that the wrongful act is acknowledged, either by the Court in the case of declaratory relief, or by the responding state in the case of apologies. One case through which the characteristics of non-pecuniary satisfaction were expressed by the applicant state was the Borchgrave Case,[50] in which Belgium requested the Permanent Court to determine that the responding state should order Spain to express its excuses and regrets for breaching international law.[51] The Court did not review the merits of the case in order to determine whether this remedy was appropriate,[52] but the request of Belgium is considered by certain authors as representative of the interpretation of non-pecuniary satisfaction,[53] as it focuses on the idea of acknowledgement of wrongdoing.

Cases also exist where apologies have been expressed by the respondent state. In the LaGrand Case,[54] in which the relevance of an apology as

---

[48] *Application of the Convention on the Prevention and Punishment of the Crime of Genocide (Bosnia and Herzegovina v Serbia and Montenegro)* (Judgment), 195.

[49] *Application of the Convention on the Prevention and Punishment of the Crime of Genocide (Bosnia and Herzegovina v Serbia and Montenegro)* (Judgment), 195.

[50] *The Borchgrave Case (Belgium v Spain)* PCIJ Rep Series A/B No. 73.

[51] *The Borchgrave Case (Belgium v Spain)* PCIJ Rep Series A/B No. 73, 165.

[52] The case was discontinued due to the fact that the parties reached an agreement.

[53] Kaczorowska, Public International Law, 484.

[54] *LaGrand (Germany v USA)* (Judgment).

reparation for a wrongful act was extensively disputed by the parties to this dispute, Germany did not request apologies, but assurances and guarantees of non-repetition.[55] Nevertheless, the USA considered that the apologies that were presented to the Government of Germany were sufficient reparation for the wrongful act[56] and that further remedies would be inappropriate.

The Court, however, concluded in this respect that the determination of apologies as a form of satisfaction is analysed on a case-by-case basis.[57] Therefore, even if the Court granted a different remedy, it strengthened the idea that satisfaction in the form of an apology is a remedy that can be granted in certain cases.

8.4 CONCLUSION

Some authors have criticised satisfaction as a remedy, arguing that *'state practice on the award of satisfaction shows the lack of objective standards in this area'*.[58] However, even if this argument is taken to be valid, a lack of objective standards does not imply that satisfaction should not be granted or that it is not a proper remedy. Indeed, the lack of objective standards or clear methodology of application has not proven to be a bar for the grant of restitution in kind or compensation, before the Court.

To conclude, *'even if Graefrath considers these forms of satisfaction "anachronistic", and Judge Azevedo described them in Corfu Channel as "mediaeval"*[59] and the modes in which satisfaction has been granted by the Court have been broad and various, this remedy is often granted, be it in the form of apologies or in the form of declaratory relief. Further, the judgment of the Court in the Corfu Channel continues to be a leading authority for other courts and tribunals[60] for the remedy of satisfaction. These above-mentioned cases demonstrate the manner in which satisfaction is currently interpreted. Thus, one form in which satisfaction is granted is as provided by the 'I'm Alone' Case, in which the responding state was ordered to present apologies to

---

[55] *LaGrand (Germany v USA)* (Judgment), 472.

[56] *LaGrand (Germany v USA)* (Judgment), 473.

[57] *LaGrand (Germany v USA)* (Judgment), 489.

[58] Gray, Judicial Remedies in International Law, 42.

[59] Bernard Graefrath, 'Responsibility and Damages Caused: Relationship between Responsibility and Damages' in The Hague Academy of International Law (ed), *Collected Courses of the Hague Academy of International Law vol 185* (Brill/Nijhoff 1984) 19, 85; and *Corfu Channel Case (Great Britain v Albania) (Separate Opinion of Judge Azevedo)*, 114, as cited in McIntyre, 'Declaratory Judgments' 147.

[60] D'Argent, 'Reparation and Compliance' 335.

the applicant state. The other form, which has been repeatedly confirmed by the Court, is through a declaration of wrongfulness. The ILC Articles provide a different approach towards satisfaction, namely that this remedy should be ordered by the Court and that it should be provided by the state that has committed a breach of international law. The opinion expressed by the Court in the sense that a declaration of wrongfulness also means satisfaction would indeed render the latter obsolete. It is important to reiterate the fact that the purpose of satisfaction as a remedy is that the responsible state acknowledges that it has breached international law, and not only that the Court concludes that such a breach has occurred.

9

The Case Law of International Courts and Tribunals

9.1 INTRODUCTION

The interpretation and application of remedies by the International Court is complex, particularly in the context of the proliferation of international courts and tribunals and the fragmentation of international law. As such, the clarification of the remedies of international law has been developed by the International Court through references, especially in its recent case-law, by reference to the jurisprudence of other international courts and tribunals. More so, states also refer to such case-law in order to justify their claims for remedies of international law.

Consequently, even if the focus of this book is the study of the remedies of international law as applied by the International Court, it would not be complete without a brief analysis of the most relevant cases of other international courts and tribunals that contributed to the interpretation and clarification of the remedies of international law.

9.2 ASSESSING MORAL DAMAGES

One issue that was clarified by the International Court by referring to the case-law of other international courts and tribunals was the mechanisms through which moral damages are assessed. As mentioned, the judgment in the Diallo Case represents a novelty in this sense, as it is one of the very few instances in which the Court referred explicitly to the findings of other international courts and tribunals.

It must be noted that the Court relied on its previous practice related to compensation. Thus, the cases that influenced the decision of the Court in the Diallo Case were the Chorzów Factory Case and the Corfu Channel

Case.[1] These references are natural because these two cases are among the few that interpreted and clarified certain characteristics of compensation. This approach is rather intuitive because these judgments represent what the Court considered, throughout its jurisprudence, to be good law.[2] Thus, as its previous case-law indicates, the Court first decided that the parties should reach an agreement with respect to the amount of compensation due. Provided that the said agreement would have failed, the Court decided that it shall analyse and determine the amounts of compensation that should be paid by the Democratic Republic of the Congo.[3]

When determining the manner in which the moral damages granted to Mr Diallo should be assessed, the Court referred to the case-law of other international courts, such as the European Court of Human Rights or the Inter-American Court of Human Rights, in the following terms:

> *Equitable considerations have guided their quantification of compensation for non-material harm. For instance, in Al-Jedda v. United Kingdom, the Grand Chamber of the European Court of Human Rights stated that, for determining damage, '[i]ts guiding principle is equity, which above all involves flexibility and an objective consideration of what is just, fair and reasonable' [...]*
>
> *Similarly, the Inter-American Court of Human Rights has said that the payment of a sum of money as compensation for non-pecuniary damages may be determined by that court 'in reasonable exercise of its judicial authority and on the basis of equity'.[4]*

This approach is rather singular in the case-law of the Court as it has rarely relied on a particular international jurisdiction, especially a court that deals with the law of human rights.

More so, the Court referred, explicitly, to a judgment of an arbitral tribunal in the Lusitania cases.[5] As such, it concluded that the Court does not have the power to determine the amount of moral damages without justification. In this case, with respect to quantification of compensation for moral damages, the Court confirmed that arbitral practice considers that *'quantification of compensation for non-material injury necessarily rests on equitable considerations'.[6]*

---

[1] *Diallo (Republic of Guinea v Democratic Republic of the Congo)* (Merits), 11.
[2] Lauterpacht, The Development of International Law, 14.
[3] *Diallo (Republic of Guinea v Democratic Republic of the Congo)* (Merits), 598.
[4] *Diallo (Republic of Guinea v Democratic Republic of the Congo)* (Merits) 324, 11.
[5] *Opinion in the Lusitania Cases (United States/Germany)* (1923) RIAA vol 7, 32–44.
[6] *Opinion in the Lusitania Cases (United States/Germany)* (1923) RIAA vol 7, 32–44.

9.3 PECUNIARY SATISFACTION

The Court has never granted pecuniary satisfaction for direct injuries to states throughout its case-law. However, the Commentary to the ILC Articles addresses this type of satisfaction and describes it as being 'the award of symbolic damages for non-pecuniary injury'.[7] The differences between pecuniary satisfaction and compensation are relevant from the perspective of their scope.[8] Even if money is granted in both circumstances by the Court, authors have argued that their purposes are different, in the sense that pecuniary satisfaction is granted for moral damages[9] or for non-material injury caused to states.[10] Even if the Court has not yet resolved a case in which pecuniary satisfaction was granted, the I'm Alone Case[11] and the Rainbow Warrior Case are examples of cases in which this remedy has been granted in interstate disputes. The I'm Alone Case represents one of the few cases in which pecuniary satisfaction has been granted in an interstate dispute. In this case, the Joint Commission concluded that no compensation should be provided for the loss of a ship and of its cargo, but that pecuniary satisfaction, in the form of an apology and of a liquidated amount of USD 25,000 , should be paid by the responding state.[12]

This case represents one of the very few circumstances in which an international tribunal granted both pecuniary and non-pecuniary satisfaction. The finding of the Joint Commission has been criticised, as several authors consider that in this case pecuniary satisfaction was, in fact, punitive.[13] However, there is no indication of such a conclusion in the merits of the case; the only reference that would lead to the conclusion that the Tribunal granted punitive damages being the word 'amend' from the dispositif of its judgment. Therefore, the view that considers the 'I'm Alone' Case as a rather unusual one in which an international Tribunal has granted pecuniary satisfaction to a state[14] is preferable.

---

[7] ILC Draft Articles with Commentaries, 106.

[8] Clarisse Barthe-Gay, 'Réflexions sur la satisfaction en droit international' 113.

[9] Crawford, State Responsibility, 528.

[10] Quintana, Litigation at the International Court, 1147.

[11] S.S. 'I'm Alone' (Canada/United States) (1933/1935) 3 RIAA vol 3, 1609–1618.

[12] S. S. 'I'm Alone' (Canada/United States) (Arbitral Award), 1618.

[13] Alexander Orakhelashvili, 'Peremptory Norms for International Wrongful Acts' (2003) 3:1 Baltic Yearbook of International Law 19, 46; Shelton, Remedies in International Human Rights Law, 160.

[14] Gray, Judicial Remedies in International Law, 43.

9.3.1 The S.S. 'I'm Alone' Case

Although a Joint Commission established under the auspices of the United Nations resolved this dispute, it can be used as a reference for the clarification of satisfaction, as a remedy of international law, especially because, as previously mentioned, the Court presently observes the practice of other judicial bodies when it delivers its judgments.

On 22 March 1929, a Canadian ship, the 'I'm Alone', was sunk by the US vessel 'Dexter', at a distance that exceeded 200 miles from the coast. The 'I'm Alone' was illegally transporting alcohol to the USA. A ship of the USA intentionally sank the 'I'm Alone'. As a consequence, both the 'I'm Alone' and its cargo were lost, and one person lost their life. The 'I'm Alone' Case represents one of the few cases in which pecuniary satisfaction has been granted in an interstate dispute. In this sense, the Joint Commission concluded that compensation is not applicable in this case regarding the loss of the ship or the cargo but that the act of sinking was an unlawful act and, as a consequence, that:

> The United States of America ought formally to acknowledge its illegality, and to apologize to His Majesty's Canadian Government;
> and, further, that as a material amend in respect of the wrong the United States of America should pay the sum of $25,000 to His Majesty's Canadian Government; and they recommend accordingly.[15]

This finding provides relevant insight regarding the difference between compensation and pecuniary satisfaction, especially because the Commission considered that compensation is not applicable but still granted a determined amount of money. Nevertheless, the differences between pecuniary satisfaction and compensation for moral damages are still difficult to establish, especially because the jurisprudence of international courts and tribunals is rather limited in this sense. As such, the challenge is to delimit what exceeds material compensation as pecuniary satisfaction.[16] In this sense, future cases might arise in which the Court grants determined amounts of compensation that do not fully represent the calculable financial loss of a state.

9.3.2 The Rainbow Warrior Case

The Rainbow Warrior Case is perhaps one of the most referred to awards in the jurisprudence of the Court, as it contains important findings that clarified

---

[15] S.S. 'I'm Alone' (Canada/United States) (Arbitral Award).
[16] Amerasinghe, Jurisdiction of Specific International Tribunals, 418.

the interpretation of the remedies of international law, such as compensation, satisfaction or cessation. This case was decided by an arbitral tribunal, that was seized by New Zealand, which submitted arguments in the sense that France breached its agreements resulted from a decision issued by the Secretary General of the UN.

Regarding compensation, the tribunal in the Rainbow Warrior Case analysed a request submitted by New Zealand, through which it requested the Tribunal to find that it is entitled to compensation *'for the violation of sovereignty and the affront and insult that that involved'*.[17] The Tribunal considered that it can deliver an order for monetary compensation, if international obligations were breached, even though no material damage was caused.[18] As such, even if the Tribunal qualified the monetary relief in this case as compensation, it can be considered that a more appropriate approach would have been to qualify it as pecuniary satisfaction, as the injury was directly caused to the state and the damage suffered was not financially assessable. However, it must be noted that at the time the decision was rendered, the practice of international tribunals in respect of pecuniary satisfaction was not as developed as it is now. Further, the work of the ILC, which clarified the conceptual confusion between compensation and pecuniary satisfaction,[19] had not yet impacted the law of state responsibility.

Regarding satisfaction, even if pecuniary satisfaction has never been granted by the Court or by the Permanent Court if International Justice and only rarely by other international tribunals, it is a remedy which is available to states for direct non-material damage and, in future cases, the Court might consider such a remedy appropriate. The decision in the Rainbow Warrior Case is relevant, as this judgment represents an important example in which satisfaction as a remedy was analysed by an international tribunal in an interstate dispute. The Tribunal concluded the following with respect to the applicability of satisfaction:

> *There is a long established practice of States and International Courts and Tribunals of using satisfaction as a remedy or form of reparation (in the wide sense) for the breach of an international obligation. This practice relates particularly to the case of moral or legal damage done directly to the State especially as opposed to the case of damage to persons involving international responsibilities.*[20]

---

[17] *Rainbow Warrior (New Zealand v France)* (Arbitral Award) [1990] RIAA vol 20, 271.
[18] *Rainbow Warrior (New Zealand v France)* (Arbitral Award) [1990] RIAA vol 20, 272.
[19] Martha, The Financial Obligation in International Law, 431.
[20] *Rainbow Warrior (New Zealand v France)* [1990], 272.

The award of the tribunal in The Rainbow Warrior Case[21] is an example[22] that confirms the practice of the Court, because it also concluded that a declaration of wrongfulness would lead to satisfaction. However, the Tribunal provided a brief interpretation regarding the manner in which moral damage can be repaired through apologies. The Arbitral Tribunal concluded that a declaration of wrongfulness would suffice,[23] the scope of satisfaction being thus reached, even if the responding state did not formally express its apologies or regrets. However, this case is relevant as it further demonstrates that states often consider satisfaction through apology as being an appropriate remedy.

Regarding cessation, the Tribunal in the Rainbow Warrior arbitration determined that it has an inherent power to find that cessation can be sought before it, and further established that two conditions should be met for cessation to be granted, *'namely that the wrongful act has a continuing character and that the violated rule is still in force at the time in which the order is issued'.*[24]

9.3.3 *The Lusitania Cases*

The origin of the dispute in the Lusitania Cases was the sinking of the British ship 'Lusitania' by a German submarine, during the period of American Neutrality.

First, the Commission in the Lusitania Cases confirmed that the terminology of compensation is not necessarily coherent throughout international practice. As such, it provided that compensation is often referred to as *'reparation, indemnity, recompense'*,[25] but that in assessing the amounts due no punitive character should be taken into consideration, as this remedy is not concerned with *'the punishment of a wrongdoer but only with the naked question of fixing the amount which will compensate for the wrong done'.*[26] In this sense, the Opinion of the Lusitania Cases further clarified the notion of moral damages and the manner in compensation should be assessed in this sense.

Even if brief in its analysis, the award of the Arbitral Tribunal in the Lusitania Cases deserves attention regarding the clarification of the notion

---

[21] *Rainbow Warrior (New Zealand v France)* [1990], 275.
[22] ILC Draft Articles with Commentaries, 106.
[23] ILC Draft Articles with Commentaries, 215.
[24] *Rainbow Warrior (New Zealand v France)* [1990], 270.
[25] *Opinion in the Lusitania Cases (United States/Germany)*, 35.
[26] *Opinion in the Lusitania Cases (United States/Germany)*, 35.

of moral damages and the compensation granted in this respect.[27] It is relevant, therefore, to point out that the Arbitral Tribunal concluded that compensation represents a form of reparation which is linked with the suffered injury so that the injured state is made whole.[28] Moral damages were interpreted as being designed to redress *'mental suffering, injury to applicant's feelings, humiliation, shame, degradation, loss of social position, or injury to his credit or reputation'*.[29]

More so, the Opinion in the Lusitania Cases clarified that compensation for moral damages does not depend on the substantiation of such claims, especially because no mathematical formula could be used in this sense. As such, it was considered, and rightly so, that to apply the substantiation standard to moral damages would necessarily imply a denial of *'the fundamental principle that there exists a remedy for the direct invasion of every right'*.[30]

9.4 CONCLUSION

The fragmentation of international law and the proliferation of international courts and tribunals should not be ignored for addressing the manner in which certain concepts apply before these institutions. As such, the practice of the International Court, especially during its recent activity, observes the findings of other courts and tribunals which clarified certain concepts, remedies of international law included.

This approach is a positive novelty for the practice of the Court. The Court should further rely in its following judgments on observing the practice of other international courts and, vice versa, other international courts should also observe the practice of the International Court. This would bring coherence in the interpretation and application of certain concepts throughout the various judicial bodies that resolve international disputes.[31]

---

[27] The Lusitania Case is often referred to by the Commentary to the ILC Articles.

[28] *Opinion in the Lusitania Cases (United States/Germany)*, 39.

[29] *Opinion in the Lusitania Cases (United States/Germany)*, 40.

[30] *Opinion in the Lusitania Cases (United States/Germany)*, 36.

[31] L Boisson de Chazournes, 'Plurality in the Fabric of International Courts and Tribunals: The Threads of a Managerial Approach' (2017) 28:1 European Journal of International Law 13, 14.

Conclusions

The International Court has contributed to the interpretation of remedies through its jurisprudence. Several aspects of the remedies available before the Court have been clarified through its practice and, consequently, states now have more reasonable expectations when they submit a dispute before the Court. The consistency that the Court has demonstrated in its interpretation of the remedies available before it has enhanced predictability in the manner in which the Court applies and clarifies the remedies that are requested by the parties appearing before it. Illustratively, if at the beginning of the Permanent Court's activity its jurisdiction to grant remedies was disputed by the respond-ing states,[1] this is no longer an issue before the Court. Further, while in the past it was unclear whether remedies such as compensation for moral damages could be granted by the Court, the International Court has now clarified that such remedies are available.[2] As demonstrated throughout this book, various issues regarding remedies have been resolved by the Court through its related findings of principle.

Nevertheless, even though the Court has clarified an important number of issues related to remedies, there still remain aspects that require further elucidation. While a general framework of remedies exists in international law, which is fortified by international legal instruments such as the ILC Articles,[3] there still remains scope for a more detailed analysis of this particular area. The conclusion that the remedies of international law available before the Court are presently underdeveloped is confirmed by scholars such as

---

[1] *Free Zones of Upper Savoy and District of Gex (France v Switzerland)* (Judgment); *Factory at Chorzów (Germany v Poland)* (Jurisdiction), 24.
[2] *Diallo (Republic of Guinea v Democratic Republic of the Congo)* (Merits), 324.
[3] ILC Draft Articles with Commentaries.

Gray[4] and Brownlie.[5] The reason for this occurrence is that while the judgments of the Court often contain lengthy clarifications on the substance of the dispute, its findings related to the interpretation and clarification of the available remedies remain secondary and lead to certain uncertainties regarding their availability, applicability and interpretation. The contributions of authors such as James Crawford with respect to the interpretation of remedies of international law are, thus, relevant and are among the few that contain important clarifications. This said, the interpretation of certain remedies of international law remains to be further developed.

The book endeavoured to determine whether the Court applies, as such, the remedies of international law or whether the judicial body adopts a different approach. It attempted to map the differences in approach that stem from the Court's practical purpose of resolving disputes and the theoretical perspective preferred by the International Law Commission. The intention in this respect was to isolate the Court from the more general field of international dispute settlement and to test the manner in which the general model of remedies of international law codified by the International Law Commission is applied before the principal judicial body of the United Nations.

It can be concluded that the Court has a unique approach regarding the application of remedies, which deviates from the path prescribed by the ILC Articles. In general terms, the practice of the Court reflects the general framework provided by the ILC Articles, as the remedies included therein are accepted as such by the Court, in the sense that the existence of a determined list of remedies is confirmed by the practice before the Court. However, in specific terms, the rules of the ILC Articles do not fit neatly into each other, at least with respect to certain remedies.[6] The conceptual interpretation of some remedies, and the procedural implications related to others, are understood by the Court in accordance with the specificities of the disputes submitted before it. Further, while the reasons for the preference given to certain remedies appear readily from a reading of the Court's jurisprudence in some instances, in others they are less evident.

With respect to the general approach of the Court towards the resolution of disputes submitted before it, it appears that the Court behaves in a manner different from a regular court or tribunal, at least with respect to the remedies that it has granted throughout its jurisprudence. Though the Court resolves

---

[4]   Gray, Judicial Remedies in International Law, 1.
[5]   Brownlie, 'Remedies in the International Court of Justice' 557.
[6]   Gray, 'The Choice between Restitution and Compensation' 413–423.

disputes and issues judgments (akin to an arbitral tribunal), its activity has to take into consideration a multitude of factors, including, but not limited to, legal and political constraints. The fact that the disputes submitted before the Court subsume a multiplicity of legal and political considerations influences the manner in which the Court resolves the disputes that are submitted before it, as well as the mechanisms applied for restoring the situation as it existed before the occurrence of the breach of an international obligation. That is not to say that the Court is overly preoccupied with the political implications of the disputes submitted before it. Its primary endeavour is to fulfil its function, that is to *'decide, in accordance with international law, such disputes as are submitted before it'*, as prescribed by Article 38 of the Statute of the International Court.

The manner in which the remedies of international law are interpreted and applied is, however, strictly connected with the function of the Court, i.e., that of being the judicial organ of the United Nations. It has been argued, in this sense, that *'the ICJ actively services and participates in achieving and accomplishing the principles of the UN. It plays an important role in achieving the central purpose of the UN, namely, the maintenance of international peace and security through its constructive contribution to the peaceful settlement of disputes.'*[7] Therefore, the fact that the Court considers the manner in which its judgments contribute to the maintenance of international peace influences the application of remedies with respect to the disputes submitted before it. The connection between the Court and the United Nations is the reason why the Court has been more circumspect in granting coercive remedies, and correctly so. The fact that states often seem to accept the findings of the Court with respect to the remedies through which the Court resolves the legal issues submitted before it is also relevant. As such, a further differentiator is that the Court resolves disputes between states and that *'the sovereign character, common to all states, dictates or constrains the mechanisms for resolving claims by one state against another and for collective enforcement of the law'*.[8]

The function of the Court is therefore complex and manifests its effect throughout the resolution of the dispute, perhaps most of all at the stage of remedies. One reason for which the Court has been rather reluctant to grant certain remedies[9] provided by the ILC Articles is that the judgments that grant such remedies require subsequent action and monitoring, inter alia, in the

---

[7] MSM Amr, *The Role of the International Court of Justice as the Principal Judicial Organ of the United Nations* (Kluwer Law International 2003) 277.

[8] RK Gardiner, *International Law* (Pearson Education Limited 2003) 450.

[9] Crawford, 'Flexibility in the Award of Reparation' 693.

form of negotiations regulating the said action[10] between states. Therefore, even though the Court cannot guarantee compliance of states with its judgments,[11] it does factor this into its decision-making process. The member states of the United Nations accept that the judgments of the Court are binding, in accordance with Article 59 of the Statute of the Court and, further, that they have an obligation *'to comply with the decisions of the International Court'*, in accordance with Article 94 (1) of the Charter of the United Nations. However, even if subtle, the contribution of the Court with respect to compliance with its judgments should not be disregarded. The Court fulfils this function by observing the manner in which states behave in the adjudicatory phase and in the post-adjudicatory phase as well.

The Court has described and clarified its function in several of its judgments, including in the Northern Cameroons Case, where it concluded that *'[t]he function of the Court is to state the law, but it may pronounce judgment only in connection with concrete cases where there exists at the time of the adjudication an actual controversy involving a conflict of legal interests between the parties'.*[12] This finding is further confirmed by Rosenne, who concludes that *'it cannot be too often emphasized that the Court is a court of justice and not of ethics or morals or of political expediency. Its function is to declare the law, jus dicere'.*[13] The above-mentioned conclusions with respect to the function of the Court and the scope of its declarations of wrongfulness should not be interpreted restrictively. A conclusion that the Court ignores the political implications of the disputes submitted before it would be too detached from its practice. The fact that the Court observes the manner in which its judgments on remedies impact the future negotiations is confirmed by its case-law. The practice of the Court confirms that it does so given that a wide range of judgments issued by the Court invite the parties to negotiate in the post-adjudication phase.

Perhaps an even better understanding of the scope of the function of the International Court has been elucidated in the Case of the Free Zones of Upper Savoy and District of Gex, in which the Permanent Court concluded that:

> the judicial settlement of international disputes, with a view to which the Court has been established, is simply an alternative to the direct and friendly settlement of such disputes between the Parties; as consequently it is for the

[10] Rosenne, The Law and Practice of the International Court, vol 1, 195.
[11] Rosenne, The Law and Practice of the International Court, vol 1, 198.
[12] *Northern Cameroons (Cameroon v United Kingdom)* (Preliminary Objections), 33.
[13] Rosenne, The Law and Practice of the International Court, vol 1, 169.

Court to facilitate, so far as is compatible with its Statute, such direct and friendly settlement.[14]

A more recent view in this respect is that of Judge Tomka stating that '*it should be emphasized that the Court can play an important role in assisting parties in peacefully settling their disputes prior to rendering a judgment on the merits, even if the proceedings before the Court are eventually discontinued prior to the commencement of public hearings*'.[15] Thus, the Court is a complex dispute settlement institution, which is also a facilitator of amicable political settlement of international disputes between states. This function of the Court is manifested in the different phases that a dispute submitted before it entails. In the discharge of its functions, the Court looks towards the past (by deciding whether a wrongful act occurred), towards the present (by contributing to the amicable settlement of the disputes during its proceedings) and also towards the future (by paying due consideration to the manner in which its judgments are implemented). It can, thus, be validly concluded that the exercise of the function of the International Court should not necessarily be conditioned upon a judgment being issued, but upon the final resolution of the dispute.

However, when the parties to a dispute do not reach settlement prior to the delivery of the judgment, as often happens, the Court makes its best efforts to ensure that its judgment, once issued, is respected and implemented by the responding state. The Court does so by issuing judgments that contain appropriate remedies which observe the particularities of each case. This approach is relevant from the fact that, often, '*States, in contemplating the resolution of a dispute, will invariably consider all the relevant circumstances and may resort to the Court as a part of a broader strategy.*'[16] As such, the resolution of a dispute is essential for the Court, and the mechanism through which the dispute is resolved or the procedural moment in which the dispute is resolved is secondary, or a means to an end.

The meaning of '*deciding in accordance with international law*' is, therefore, wide and does not impose upon the Court any particular mechanism, or action, through which it would decide the cases that are brought before it, except for applying the sources of international law provided by Article 38 of its Statute read with Article 36, which includes reparation within the jurisdiction

---

[14] *Case of the Free Zones of Upper Savoy and District of Gex* (Order) [1929] PCIJ Series A No. 22, 13.

[15] Peter Tomka, 'The Role of the International Court of Justice in World Affairs: Successes and Challenges', with Special Reference to OAS Member States and the Pact of Bogotá (Lecture Series of the Americas, 10 April 2014) 14.

[16] Tomka, 'The Role of the International Court of Justice in World Affairs' 14.

of the Court. Presently, the Court understands Article 38 of its Statute to mean that it best decides the disputes submitted before it through declaratory judgments, which represent the norm before the Court. The declaratory judgment is well suited to fulfil the role of the Court as it also denotes its preventive function in the vaudeville of international law.[17] It has been argued in this respect that '*as a measure of preventive justice, the declaratory judgment probably has its greatest efficacy. It is designed to enable parties to ascertain and establish their legal relations so as to conduct themselves accordingly and thus to avoid the necessity of future litigation*'.[18] It is also relevant to note that the states party to the disputes submitted before the Court are satisfied with the declaratory judgments it renders, and often accept its findings related to remedies with no need for future negotiations related to compliance or implementation.

The manner in which the Court approaches the application of the remedies of international law constantly and consistently contributes towards the clarification of this particular area of interest. The statement of Sir Hersch Lauterpacht, that '*Judicial settlement may, given the will of the parties, prove the starting-point for a required change of the law. But before such change is attempted it may be necessary to determine what the law is*',[19] is relevant, because it best describes the activity of the Court, at least with respect to the remedies of international law. The Court declares the law and, in doing so, further influences the direction of its change and enhances its development.

[17] Charles de Visscher, *Aspects récents du droit procédural de la Cour internationale de Justice* (A Pedone 1966) 187.

[18] Borchard, 'Declaratory Judgment' 105, 110.

[19] Lauterpacht, The Function of Law, 338.

APPENDICES

APPENDIX 1

Requests Submitted before the Permanent Court of International Justice through Special Agreements

No.	Case	Relief Sought	Type of Relief
1.	**Treaty of Neuilly, 1924**	*'submit to the Permanent Court of International Justice, [...], the dispute which has arisen between them in connection with the jurisdiction of the arbitrator appointed [...]'*	Declaratory
2.	**Lotus, 1926**	*'(1) Has Turkey, [...], acted in conflict with the principles of international law – and if so, what principles – [...]'.'(2) Should the reply be in the affirmative, what pecuniary reparation is due [...]?'*	Declaratory Compensation
3.	**Serbian Loans, 1928**	*'(a) Whether, [...], the latter is entitled to effect in paper francs the service of [...], as it has hitherto done; (b) or whether, on the contrary, the Government of the Kingdom of the Serbs, Croats and Slovenes, as held by the French bondholders, is under an obligation to pay in gold or in foreign currencies and at the places indicated hereinafter, the amount [...]: [...] Lastly, how the value of the gold franc is to be determined [...].'*	Declaratory Specific Performance
4.	**Brazilian Loans, 1927**	*'With regard to the Brazilian Federal Government's 5 % loan of 1909 (Port of Pernambuco), 4 % loan of 1910, and 4 % loan of 1911, is payment of coupons [...] to be effected by delivery to the French holders, in respect of each franc, of the value corresponding, in the currency of the place of payment at the rate of exchange on the day, to one-twentieth of a gold piece weighing 6.45161 grammes of 900/1000 fineness, or is such payment or repayment to be effected as hitherto in paper francs, that is to say, in the French currency which is compulsory legal tender?'*	Declaratory
5.	**Free Zones of Upper Savoy and the District of Gex, 1928**	*'it shall rest with the Permanent Court of International Justice to decide whether, as between Switzerland and France, Article 435, paragraph 2, of the Treaty of Versailles, with its annexes, has abrogated or has for its object the abrogation of the provisions [...][...]'*	Declaratory

6.	Territorial Jurisdiction of the International Commission of the River Oder, 1928	'Does the jurisdiction of the International Commission of the Oder extend, [. . .], to [. . .], and, if so, what is the principle laid down which must be adopted for the purpose of determining the upstream limits of the Commission's jurisdiction?'	Declaratory
7.	Delimitation of the Territorial Waters between Castellorizo and the Coasts of Anatolia, 1929	NA	NA
8.	Lighthouses, 1931	'to give its decision upon the question whether the contract [. . .] was duly entered into and is accordingly operative as regards the Greek Government [. . .]'.	Declaratory Specific performance
9.	Oscar Chinn, 1934	'1. [. . .] were the above-mentioned measures complained of by the Government of the United Kingdom in conflict with the international obligations of the Belgian Government towards the Government of the United Kingdom? 2. [. . .] what is the reparation to be paid by the Belgian Government to the Government of the United Kingdom?'	Declaratory Compensation
10.	Lighthouses in Crete and Samos, 1936	'Whether the contract concluded on April 1st/14th, 1913, between the French firm Collas & Michel, [. . .] was duly entered into and is accordingly operative [. . .]'	Declaratory Specific Performance
11.	Borchgrave, 1937	'[. . .] whether, having regard to the circumstances of fact and of law concerning the case, the responsibility of the Spanish Government is involved.'	Declaratory

APPENDIX 2

Judgments of the Permanent Court of International Justice in the Cases Submitted through Special Agreements

No.	Case	Judgment	Type of Relief Granted
1.	**Treaty of Neuilly, 1924**	*'That [...] should be interpreted as authorizing claims in respect of acts committed even outside Bulgarian territory as constituted before October 11th, 1915, and in respect of damage incurred by claimants [...];* *That reparation due on this ground is within the scope of the reparation contemplated in [...]'*	Declaratory
2.	**Lotus, 1927**	*'(1) that, [...] Turkey, by instituting criminal proceedings in pursuance of Turkish law against Lieutenant Demons, [...] has not acted in conflict with the principles of international law, contrary to Article 15 of the Convention of Lausanne of July 24th, 1923, respecting conditions of residence and business and jurisdiction;* *(2) that, consequently, there is no occasion to give judgment on the question of the pecuniary reparation [...].'*	Declaratory
3.	**Serbian Loans, 1929**	*'(1) That, [...] the holders of bonds of this loan are entitled, whatever their nationality may be, to obtain, at their free choice, payment of the nominal amount of their coupons due for payment but not paid and of those subsequently falling due [...];* *(3) That the value of the gold franc shall be fixed between the "Parties, for the above-mentioned payments, as equivalent to that of a weight of gold corresponding to the twentieth part of a piece of gold weighing 6 grammes 45161, 900/1000 fine."'*	Declaratory Specific Performance
4.	**Brazilian Loans, 1929**	*'That [...] payment of coupons [...] must be effected by delivery to the French holders in respect of each franc [...]'*	Declaratory

(continued)

No.	Case	Judgment	Type of Relief Granted
5.	'Free Zones of Upper Savoy and the District of Gex', 1932	*'That, as between France and Switzerland, Article 435, paragraph 2, of the Treaty of Versailles, with its Annexes, neither has abrogated nor is intended to lead to the abrogation of the provisions [. . .] regarding the customs and economic régime of the free zones of Upper Savoy and the Pays de Gex. [. . .]'*	Declaratory
6.	Territorial Jurisdiction of the International Commission of the River Oder, 1929	*'(1) [. . .] the jurisdiction of the International Commission of the Oder extends to the sections of the Warthe (Warta) and Netze (Notec) which are situated in Polish territory.* *(2) The principle laid down, which must be adopted for the purpose of determining the upstream limits of the Commission's jurisdiction, is the principle laid down in Article 331 of the Treaty of Versailles.'*	Declaratory
7.	Delimitation of the Territorial Waters between Castellorizo and the Coasts of Anatolia, 1933	*'Declares that the proceedings begun in regard to the case concerning the delimitation of the territorial waters between the island of Castellorizo and the coasts of Anatolia are thus terminated [. . .].'*	NA
8.	Lighthouses, 1934	*'decides that the contract of [. . .] was duly entered into and is accordingly operative [. . .].'*	Declaratory Specific Performance
9.	Oscar Chinn, 1934	*'decides that the measures taken and applied [. . .] are not, having regard to all the circumstances of the case, in conflict with the international obligations [. . .]'*	Declaratory
10.	Lighthouses in Crete and Samos, 1937	*'decides that the contract concluded on [. . .] was duly entered into and is accordingly operative as regards [. . .]'*	Declaratory Specific Performance
11.	Borchgrave, 1928	*'[. . .] places on record the discontinuance by the Belgian and Spanish Governments of the proceedings instituted by the Special Agreement filed on March 5th, 1937; [. . .].'*	NA

APPENDIX 3

Requests Submitted before the Permanent Court of International Justice through Unilateral Applications

No.	Case	Request for Relief	Type
1.	S.S. 'Wimbledon', 1923	*'That the German authorities wrongfully refused on March 21st, 1921, free access [...]';* *That the German Government shall make reparation for the loss incurred [...]'*	Declaratory Compensation
2.	Interpretation of Judgment No. 3, 1924	*'(a) the possible existence, according to the terms of the judgment, of Bulgarian property in Greece which might be used to realize sums awarded by the arbitrator; [...].'*	Declaratory
3.	Mavrommatis Jerusalem Concessions, 1924	Not available. However, the request for relief is paraphrased in the Judgment of the Court as follows: *'the Government of Palestine and consequently also the Government of His Britannic Majesty have, since 1921, wrongfully refused to recognize to their full extent the rights acquired by M. Mavrommatis under the contracts and agreements [...] shall make reparation for the consequent loss incurred by the said Greek subject [...].'*	Declaratory Compensation
4.	Certain German Interests in Polish Upper Silesia (Merits), 1925	*'1. (a) that Article 2 of the Polish Law of July 14th, 1920, constitutes a measure of liquidation [...].'*	Declaratory
5.	Denunciation of the Treaty of 2 November 1865 between China and Belgium, 1926	*'To give judgment, [...] to the effect that the Government of the Chinese Republic is not entitled unilaterally to denounce the Treaty of November 2nd, 1865;'*	Declaratory

6.	Interpretation of Judgments Nos. 7 and 8, 1927	'(1) that in Judgment No. 7 the Court reserved to the Polish Government the right to annul [...] the Agreement of December 24th, 1919 [...]'	Declaratory
7.	Rights of Minorities in Upper Silesia, 1928	'that Articles 74, 106 and 131 of the German–Polish Convention relating to Upper Silesia of May 15th, 1922, establish [...];'	Declaratory
8.	Factory at Chorzów (Merits), 1927	'(1) that by reason of its attitude [...] the Polish Government is under an obligation to make good the consequent damage sustained [...];'	Compensation
9.	Interpretation of the Statute of the Memel Territory, 1932	'To decide [...] (1) whether the Governor of the Memel Territory has the right to dismiss the President of the Directorate; (2) in the case of an affirmative decision, whether this right only exists under certain conditions or in certain circumstances, and what those conditions or circumstances are; [...].'	Declaratory
10.	Legal Status of the South-Eastern Territory of Greenland, 1932	NA	NA
11.	Prince von Pless Administration, 1932	'(1) that the attitude of the Polish Government and authorities [...] is in conflict with Articles 67 and 68 of the Geneva Convention; [...].'	Declaratory
12.	Legal Status of Eastern Greenland, 1931	'the promulgation of the above-mentioned declaration of occupation and any steps taken in this respect by the Norwegian Government constitute a violation of the existing legal situation and are accordingly unlawful and invalid'.	Declaratory

(continued)

No.	Case	Request for Relief	Type
13.	**Appeals from Certain Judgments of the Hungaro/Czechoslovak Mixed Arbitral Tribunal, 1932**	*'appealing from the judgments of December 21st, 1931, of the Hungaro-Czechoslovak Mixed Arbitral Tribunal concerning questions of jurisdiction in the case of Alexander Semsey and others v. the State of Czechoslovakia (No. 321) and in the case of Wilhelm Fodor v. the State of Czechoslovakia (No. 752)'* *'appealing from the judgment of April 13th, 1932, of the Hungaro-Czechoslovak Mixed Arbitral Tribunal upon merits in the case of the Ungarzsche Hanfund Flachsindustrie v. (1) the State of Czechoslovakia, and (2) the Flax Spinners' Association (No. 127)'*	Declaratory
14.	**Polish Agrarian Reform and German Minority, 1933**	*'The German Government requests the Permanent Court of International Justice to declare that violations of the Treaty of June 28th, 1919, have been committed to the detriment of Polish nationals of German race and to order reparation to be made.'*	Declaratory Reparation
15.	**Appeal from a Judgment of the Hungaro/Czechoslovak Mixed Arbitral Tribunal, 1933**	*' That, in its judgment No. 221 delivered on February 3rd, 1933, the Hungaro-Czechoslovak Mixed Arbitral Tribunal wrongly decided that [...];* *Alternatively: To invite the Mixed Arbitral Tribunal to conform to the principles laid down by*	Declaratory Specific performance

		the Court for the interpretation of Articles [...], and to deliver a fresh judgment in case No. 221, dismissing the Applicant's claim; [...].'	
16.	Pajzs, Czáky, Esterházy, 1935	*'2. [...] that the Mixed Arbitral Tribunal has jurisdiction to adjudicate upon the claims [...]. B. Alternatively or cumulatively, as the Court may see fit: [...] 2. To order the Kingdom of Yugoslavia, in particular: (a) in its attitude and proceedings, strictly to conform to [...]; (b) to make good the damage and refund the costs and expenses occasioned to Hungarian nationals [...];'*	Declaratory Specific performance Compensation
17.	Losinger, 1935	*'I. To declare that the Government of the Kingdom of Yugoslavia cannot [...] release itself from the observance of an arbitration clause in a contract [...].'*	Declaratory
18.	Diversion of Water from the Meuse, 1937	*'[...] (a) the construction by Belgium of works [...] is contrary to the Treaty of May 12th, 1863; [...] II. To order Belgium (a) to discontinue all the works [...] '*	Declaratory Cessation Restitution in kind
19.	Phosphates in Morocco, 1936	*' (a) that the monopolization of the Moroccan phosphates, [...] is inconsistent with the international obligations of [...], and that it must for that reason be annulled [...]; [...] (d) that additional pecuniary compensation is due [...]'*	Declaratory Compensation

(continued)

No.	Case	Request for Relief	Type
20.	**Panevezys-Saldutiskis Railway, 1937**	'1. *That the Lithuanian Government has wrongfully refused to recognize the rights of* [...], *and to compensate that company for the illegal seizure and operation of this line.* [...].'	Declaratory Compensation
21.	**Electricity Company of Sofia and Bulgaria, 1938**	'(A) *to declare that the State of Bulgaria has failed in its international obligations* [...] (B) *and to order the requisite reparation in respect of the above-mentioned acts to be made.*'	Declaratory Reparation
22.	**Société Commerciale de Belgique, 1938**	'(1) *to declare that the Greek Government* [...] *has violated its international obligations;* (2) *to assess the amount of the compensation due* [...]'.	Declaratory Specific Performance Compensation

APPENDIX 4

Judgments of the Permanent Court of International Justice in the Cases Submitted through Unilateral Applications

No.	Case	Judgment	Type of Relief Granted
1.	S.S. 'Wimbledon', 1923	'1. That the German authorities [...], were wrong in refusing access to the Kiel Canal to the S.S. "Wimbledon"; [...] 5. that the German Government shall therefore pay to the Government of the French Republic, at Paris, in French francs, the sum of [...]'	Declaratory Compensation
2.	Interpretation of Judgment No. 3 1925	'That the request of the Greek Government for an authoritative interpretation of the judgment [...] cannot be granted.'	Rejected request
3.	Mavrommatis Jerusalem Concessions, 1925	'1. That the concessions granted to [...] are valid; [...] That therefore the Greek Government's claim for an indemnity must be dismissed; [...]'	Declaratory Rejected compensation claim
4.	Certain German Interests in Polish Upper Silesia (Merits), 1926	'(1) That the application both of [...], constitutes, [...] a measure contrary to Article 6 and the following articles of that Convention;[...].'	Declaratory
5.	Denunciation of the Treaty of 2 November 1865 between China and Belgium, 1929	'Declares that the proceedings begun in regard to the said suit are thus terminated;'	NA
6.	Interpretation of Judgments Nos. 7 and 8, 1927	That, in Judgment No. 7, the Court did not reserve to the Polish Government the right of asking by process of law, even after the rendering of that Judgment and with application to that particular case, for a declaration that [...].'	Declaratory
7.	Rights of Minorities in Upper Silesia (Minority Schools), 1928	'[...] (2) that Articles [...] bestow upon every national the right freely to [...]'	Declaratory

8.	Factory at Chorzów (Merits), 1928	'(1) gives judgment to the effect that, [. . .] the Polish Government is under an obligation to pay [. . .] a compensation corresponding to. [. . .]'	Compensation
9.	Interpretation of the Statute of the Memel Territory, 1932	'(1) that the Governor of the Memel Territory is entitled, for the protection of the interests of the State, to dismiss the President of the Directorate in case of serious acts which violate [. . .];'	Declaratory
10.	Legal Status of the South-Eastern Territory of Greenland, 1933	'Declares that the proceedings in regard to [. . .], are terminated; [. . .].'	NA
11.	Prince von Pless Administration, 1933	'[. . .] declares that the proceedings begun by [. . .] are terminated; [. . .].'	NA
12.	Legal Status of Eastern Greenland, 1933	(1) decides that the declaration of occupation [. . .], constitute a violation of the existing legal situation and are accordingly unlawful and invalid; [. . .].'	Declaratory
13.	Appeals from Certain Judgments of the Hungaro/Czechoslovak Mixed Arbitral Tribunal, 1933	'Taking note of [. . .] declares that the proceedings begun by the Applications of the Czechoslovak Government are terminated; [. . .].'	NA
14.	Polish Agrarian Reform and German Minority, 1933	'[. . .] declares that the proceedings begun by the Application of the German Government are terminated; [. . .].'	NA
15.	Appeal from a Judgment of the Hungaro/Czechoslovak Mixed Arbitral Tribunal, 1933	'[. . .] (2) decides that [. . .] the Hungaro-Czechoslovak Mixed Arbitral Tribunal has rightly decided (a) that it is competent to [. . .]; and (b) that the Czechoslovak Government is bound to restore [. . .].'	Declaratory

(continued)

(continued)

No.	Case	Judgment	Type of Relief Granted
16.	Pajzs, Czáky, Esterházy, 1936	'[...] (3) decides that the attitude of [...] has been consistent with the provisions of [...];'	Declaratory Rejected other claims
17.	Losinger, 1936	'places on record [...] that the Swiss and Yugoslav Governments are discontinuing the proceedings. [...]'	NA
18.	Diversion of Water from the Meuse, 1937	'Rejects the various submissions of the Memorial [...]. Rejects the submissions of the aforesaid counter-claim.'	Rejected all claims
19.	Phosphates in Morocco, 1938	'the Application filed on March 30th, 1936, [...] cannot be entertained.'	Rejected as inadmissible
20.	Panevezys-Saldutiskis Railway, 1939	'Declares that the objection [...] is well founded, and declares that the claim presented by [...] cannot be entertained.'	Rejected as inadmissible
21.	Electricity Company of Sofia and Bulgaria (Belgium v. Bulgaria)	NA	NA
22.	Société Commerciale de Belgique, 1939	'1. Admits submission A of the Belgian Government and submission No. 3 of the Greek Government and, noting the agreement between the Parties, states that the arbitral awards [...] are definitive and obligatory; [...].'	Declaratory Specific Performance

APPENDIX 5

Requests Submitted before the International Court of Justice through Special Agreements

No.	Case	Special Agreement Provision	Type of Relief
1.	**Corfu Channel, 1948**	'(1) Is Albania responsible under international law for [. . .] and is there any duty to pay compensation? (2) Has the United Kingdom under international law violated the sovereignty of the Albanian People's Republic [. . .] and is there any duty to give satisfaction?'	Declaratory Compensation Satisfaction
2.	**Asylum, 1949**	'was Colombia competent, as the country granting asylum, to qualify the offence for the purposes of said Asylum. [. . .].'	Declaratory
3.	**Minquiers and Ecrehos, 1951**	'The Court is requested to determine whether the sovereignty over the islets and rocks (in so far as they are capable of appropriation) of the Minquiers and Ecrehos groups, respectively belongs to [. . .].'	Declaratory
4.	**Sovereignty over Certain Frontier Land, 1957**	'The Court is requested to determine whether the sovereignty over the parcels shown in the survey [. . .], belongs to [. . .].'	Declaratory
5.	**North Sea Continental Shelf, 1967** *Proceedings joined with North Sea Continental Shelf (Federal Republic of Germany v. Netherlands) on 26 April 1968	'What principles and rules of international law are applicable to the delimitation [. . .]?'	Declaratory
6.	**North Sea Continental Shelf, 1967** Proceedings joined with North Sea Continental Shelf (Federal Republic of Germany v. Denmark) on 26 April 1968	'What principles and rules of international law are applicable to the delimitation [. . .]?'	Declaratory

7.	Continental Shelf, 1978	'Quels sont les principes et règles du droit international qui peuvent être appliqués pour la délimitation de la? [...]'	Declaratory
8.	Delimitation of the Maritime Boundary in the Gulf of Maine Area, 1981	'What is the course of the single maritime boundary that divides [...].'	Declaratory
9.	Continental Shelf, 1981	'What principles and rules of international law are applicable to the delimitation of [...]'	Declaratory
10.	Frontier Dispute, 1983	'Quel est le tracé de la frontière entre la République de Haute-Volta et la République du Mali dans la zone contestée telle qu'elle est définie ci-après?'	Declaratory
11.	Land, Island and Maritime Frontier Dispute, 1986	'1. To delimit the boundary line in the zones or sections [...]. 2. To determine the legal situation of the islands and maritime spaces.'	Declaratory
12.	Territorial Dispute, 1990	'[...] to decide upon the limits of their respective territories in accordance with the rules of international law [...]'	Declaratory
13.	Gabčíkovo –Nagymaros Project, 1993	'(1) [...] (a) whether the Republic of Hungary was entitled to suspend and subsequently abandon, in 1989, the works [...]. (2) The Court is also requested to determine the legal consequences, including the rights and obligations for the Parties, arising from its Judgment [...]'	Declaratory Specific Performance Reparation

(continued)

No.	Case	Special Agreement Provision	Type of Relief
14.	Kasikili/Sedudu Island, 1996	'The Court is asked to determine [...] the boundary between Namibia and Botswana around Kasikili/ Sedudu Island and the legal status of the island.'	Declaratory
15.	Sovereignty over Pulau Ligitan and Pulau Sipadan, 1998	'The Court is requested to determine [...], whether sovereignty over Pulau Ligitan and Pulau Sipadan belongs to [...].'	Declaratory
16.	Frontier Dispute, 2002	' a) déterminer le tracé de la frontière entre la [...]'	Declaratory
17.	Sovereignty over Pedra Branca/Pulau Batu Puteh, Middle Rocks and South Ledge, 2003	'The Court is requested to determine whether sovereignty over [...] belongs to [...]'	Declaratory
18.	Frontier Dispute, 2010	'The Court is requested to: 1. determine the course of the boundary between the two countries;[].'	Declaratory
19.	Guatemala's Territorial, Insular and Maritime Claim, 2015	'The Parties request the Court to determine any and all legal claims of Guatemala against Belize to land and insular territories and to any maritime areas pertaining to these territories, to declare the rights therein of both Parties, and to determine the boundaries between their respective territories and areas.'	Declaratory

APPENDIX 6

Judgments of the International Court of Justice in the Cases Submitted through Special Agreements

No.	Case	Judgment	Type
1.	**Corfu Channel, 1949**	'*Gives judgment that the People's Republic of Albania is responsible under international law for the explosions [...], and for the damage and loss of human life [...]* *Reserves for further consideration the assessment of the amount of compensation [...]* *Gives judgment that by reason of the acts of the British Navy [...] the United Kingdom violated the sovereignty of the People's Republic of Albania, and that this declaration by the Court constitutes in itself appropriate satisfaction.*' Judgment on compensation: '*[...] Fixes the amount of compensation due from the People's Republic of Albania to the United Kingdom at £ 843,947.*'	Declaratory Satisfaction Compensation
2.	**Asylum, 1950**	'*[...]Finds that the grant of asylum by the Colombian Government to Victor Raúl Haya de la Torre was not made in conformity with Article 2, paragraph 2 ('First'), of that Convention.*'	Declaratory
3.	**Minquiers and Ecrehos, 1953**	'*[...] finds that the sovereignty over the islets and rocks of the Ecrehos and Minquiers groups, [...], belongs to the United Kingdom.*'	Declaratory

4.	Sovereignty over Certain Frontier Land, 1959	'[...] finds that sovereignty over the plots shown in [...] belongs to the Kingdom of Belgium.'	Declaratory
5.	North Sea Continental Shelf, 1969 Proceedings joined with North Sea Continental Shelf (Federal Republic of Germany v. Netherlands) on 26 April 1968	'(C) the principles and rules of international law applicable to the delimitation are as follows: [...].'	Declaratory
6.	North Sea Continental Shelf (Federal Republic of Germany v. Netherlands) 1969 Proceedings joined with North Sea Continental Shelf (Federal Republic of Germany v. Denmark) on 26 April 1968	'[...] (C) the principles and rules of international law applicable to the delimitation [...] are as follows: [...].'	Declaratory
7.	Continental Shelf, 1982	'A. The principles and rules of international law applicable for the delimitation, [...] are as follows: [...].'	Declaratory
8.	Delimitation of the Maritime Boundary in the Gulf of Maine Area, 1984	'That the course of the single maritime boundary [...] shall be defined by geodetic lines connecting the points with the following co-ordinates: [...].'	Declaratory
9.	Continental Shelf, 1985	'[...] A. The principles and rules of international law applicable for the delimitation, [...] are as follows: [...].'	Declaratory
10.	Frontier Dispute, 1986	'[...] A. That the frontier line between Burkina [...] is as follows: [...].'	Declaratory
11.	Land, Island and Maritime Frontier Dispute, 1992	'Decides that the boundary line between [...] is as follows: [...].'	Declaratory

(continued)

(continued)

No.	Case	Judgment	Type
12.	**Territorial Dispute, 1994**	'(1) Finds that the boundary between [...] is defined by the Treaty of [...]; (2) Finds that the course of that boundary is as follows: [...].'	Declaratory
13.	**Gabčíkovo–Nagymaros Project, 1997**	'A. [...] Finds that Hungary was not entitled to suspend and subsequently abandon, in 1989, the works on the Nagymaros Project [...] B. [...] Finds that Hungary and Slovakia must negotiate in good faith [...] and must take all necessary measures to ensure the achievement of the objectives of the Treaty of 16 September 1977, in accordance with such modalities as they may agree upon; [...] D. [...] Finds that [...] Hungary shall compensate Slovakia for the damage sustained by Czechoslovakia and by Slovakia [...] and Slovakia shall compensate Hungary for the damage it has sustained [...].'	Declaratory Specific performance Compensation
14.	**Kasikili/Sedudu Island, 1999**	'(1) [...] Finds that the boundary between [...] follows the line of [...];'	Declaratory
15.	**Sovereignty over Pulau Ligitan and Pulau Sipadan, 2002**	'Finds that sovereignty over Pulau Ligitan and Pulau Sipadan belongs to Malaysia.'	Declaratory

16.	Frontier Dispute, 2005	'(1) Finds that the boundary between [. . .] takes the following course: [. . .].'	Declaratory
17.	Sovereignty over Pedra Branca/Pulau Batu Puteh, Middle Rocks and South Ledge, 2008	'Finds that sovereignty over Pedra Branca/ Pulau Batu Puteh belongs to the Republic of Singapore; [. . .].'	Declaratory
18.	Frontier Dispute, 2013	'[. . .] Decides that, [. . .], the course of the frontier between Burkina Faso and the Republic of Niger takes the form of a straight line; [. . .].'	Declaratory
19.	Guatemala's Territorial, Insular and Maritime Claim, 2013	Note: judgment is pending.	NA

APPENDIX 7

Requests Submitted before the International Court of Justice through Unilateral Applications

No.	Case Name (Parties)	Request in Unilateral Application	Type
1.	**Fisheries, 1949**	'[...] (a) to declare the principles of international law to be applied in defining the base-lines [...]; (b) to award damages to the Government of the United Kingdom [...].'	Declaratory Compensation
2.	**Protection of French Nationals and Protected Persons in Egypt, 1949**	'that the measures taken by the Egyptian Government [...] are contrary to the principles of international law and to the Convention of Montreux of May 8th, 1937 [...] that compensation for the damage suffered by the French Government in the person of the victims of the said measures is due by the Government of Egypt.'	Declaratory Compensation
3.	**Rights of Nationals of the United States of America in Morocco, 1950**	'that the privileges of the nationals of the United States of America in Morocco are only those which result from the text of [...], and that, [...], there is nothing to justify the granting to the nationals of the United States of preferential treatment which would be contrary to the provisions of the treaties; [...].'	Declaratory

(continued)

No.	Case Name (Parties)	Request in Unilateral Application	Type
4.	**Request for Interpretation of the Judgment of 20 November 1950 in the Asylum Case, 1950**	'*Must the Judgment of November 20th, 1950, be interpreted in the sense that the qualification made by the Colombian Ambassador of the offence attributed to M. Haya de la Torre, was correct, and that, consequently, it is necessary to recognize that the above-mentioned qualification, in so far as it has been confirmed by the Court, has legal effect? [. . .].*'	Declaratory
5.	**Haya de la Torre, 1950**	'*[. . .] to determine the manner in which effect shall be given to the Judgment of November 20th, 1950; [. . .].*'	Declaratory
6.	**Ambatielos, 1951**	'*[. . .] 1. That the arbitral procedure [. . .] must receive application in the present case; 2. That the Commission of Arbitration provided for in the said Protocol shall be constituted within a reasonable period, to be fixed by the Court. [. . .].*'	Specific performance
7.	**Anglo-Iranian Oil Co., 1951**	'*(a) To declare that the Imperial Government of Iran are under a duty to submit the dispute between themselves and the Anglo-Iranian Oil Company, Limited, to arbitration [. . .], and to accept and carry out any award issued as a result of such arbitration.*'	Declaratory Satisfaction Compensation

		(b) Alternatively, *[. . .] (iv) To adjudge that the Imperial* *Government of Iran should give full* *satisfaction and indemnity for all acts* *committed in relation to [. . .] and to* *determine the manner of such satisfaction* *and indemnity.'*	
8.	**Nottebohm, 1951**	*'I. That the Government of Guatemala* *restore to Mr. Friedrich Nottebohm his* *[. . .].* *II. That in case such restitution should* *prove impossible for reasons of physical* *destruction or for other reasons, the* *Government of Guatemala pay Mr.* *Friedrich Nottebohm compensation [. . .].* *III. That the Government of Guatemala* *pay Mr. Friedrich Nottebohm* *compensation for [. . .]* *V. That the Government of Guatemala* *should agree to reinstate upon Mr.* *Friedrich Nottebohm his registration as a* *citizen of Liechtenstein. [. . .].'*	Restitution in kind/ alternative: compensation Compensation
9.	**Monetary Gold Removed from Rome in 1943, 1953**	*'(1) that the Governments of the French* *Republic, Great Britain and Northern* *Ireland and the United States of America* *should deliver to Italy any share of the* *monetary gold that might be due to Albania* *under [. . .].'*	Compensation

(continued)

No.	Case Name (Parties)	Request in Unilateral Application	Type
10.	**Electricité de Beyrouth Company**, 1953	*'That the alterations of the situation of the Société Électricité de Beyrouth made unilaterally by the Lebanese Government are contrary to the undertaking given [...] That the Lebanese Government is under an obligation to enter into negotiations [...]*	Declaratory Specific Performance (negotiations)
11.	**Treatment in Hungary of Aircraft and Crew of United States of America**, 1954	*'that the Court decide that the accused Governments are jointly and severally liable to the United States for the damage caused; that the Court award damages in favour of the United States Government [...]'*	Declaratory Compensation
12.	**Treatment in Hungary of Aircraft and Crew of United States of America**, 1954	*'that the Court decide that the accused Governments are jointly and severally liable to the United States for the damage caused; that the Court award damages in favour of the United States Government [...].'*	Declaratory Compensation Reparation
13.	**Aerial Incident of 10 March 1953**, 1955	*'that the Court find that the Czechoslovak Government is liable to the United States Government for the damage caused; that the Court award damages in favour of the United States Government [...].'*	Declaratory Compensation Reparation
14.	**Antarctica**, 1955	*'(1) that the United Kingdom, as against the Republic of Argentina, possesses, and at all material dates has possessed, valid and*	Declaratory Cessation Specific performance

	Declaratory	Cessation	Specific performance	Compensation	Reparation
15. Antarctica, 1955	subsisting legal titles to the sovereignty over all the territories comprised [...] (3) that the Republic of Argentina is bound to respect the United Kingdom's sovereignty over the territories comprised of [...], to cease her pretensions to exercise sovereignty in or relative to those territories and, [...], to withdraw from them all or any Argentine personnel and equipment.' (1) that the United Kingdom, as against the Republic of Chile, possesses, and at all material dates has possessed, valid and subsisting legal titles to the sovereignty of [...] (3) that the Republic of Chile is bound to respect the United Kingdom's sovereignty over [...], to cease her pretensions to exercise sovereignty in, or relative to those territories and, [...], to withdraw from them all or any Chilean personnel or equipment.'				
16. Aerial Incident of 7 October 1952, 1955				'that the Soviet Government is liable to the United States Government for the damages caused; that the Court award damages in favour of the United States Government against the Soviet Government in the sum of [...].'	

(continued)

No.	Case Name (Parties)	Request in Unilateral Application	Type
17.	**Certain Norwegian Loans, 1955**	*'That the international loans issued by [. . .] stipulate in gold the amount of the borrower's obligation for the service of coupons and redemption of bonds; [. . .].'*	Declaratory
18.	**Right of Passage over Indian Territory, 1955**	*'(a) To recognize and declare that Portugal is the holder or beneficiary of a right of passage between its territory of [. . .], and that this right comprises the faculty of [. . .]. (c) To adjudge that India should put an immediate end to this de facto situation by allowing Portugal to exercise the above-mentioned right of passage [. . .].'*	Declaratory Cessation
19.	**Application of the Convention of 1902 Governing the Guardianship of Infants, 1957**	*'That the measure taken and maintained [. . .], the 'skyddsuppfostran' instituted and maintained by the decrees of [. . .], is not in conformity with the obligations binding [. . .]; That Sweden is under an obligation to end this measure.'*	Declaratory Cessation
20.	**Interhandel, 1957**	*'1. that the Government of the United States of America is under an obligation to restore the assets [. . .]; 2. in the alternative, that the dispute is one which is fit for submission for judicial*	Restitution in kind Declaratory

		settlement, arbitration or conciliation under the conditions which it will be for the Court to determine.'	
21.	Aerial Incident of 27 July 1955, 1957	'(a) that the People's Republic of Bulgaria is responsible under international law [. . .]; (b) To determine the amount of compensation due; [. . .].'	Declaratory Compensation
22.	Aerial Incident of 27 July 1955, 1957	'that the Court find that the Bulgarian Government is liable to the United States Government for the damage caused; that the Court award damages in favour of the United States Government against the Bulgarian Government in the sum of [. . .].'	Declaratory Compensation Reparation
23.	Aerial Incident of 27 July 1955, 1957	'(a) to declare that the People's Republic of Bulgaria is responsible to the Government of the United Kingdom under international law for the losses sustained [. . .]; (b) to award damages [. . .] in the amount of [. . .]	Declaratory Compensation Reparation
24.	Arbitral Award Made by the King of Spain on 23 December 1906, 1958	'1. that failure by the Government of Nicaragua to give effect to the arbitral award [. . .] constitutes a breach of an international obligation [. . .]; 2. that the Government of the Republic of Nicaragua is under an obligation to give effect to the award made [. . .] and in particular to comply with any measures for this purpose which it will be for the Court to determine.'	Declaratory Specific performance

(continued)

(continued)

No.	Case Name (Parties)	Request in Unilateral Application	Type
25.	Aerial Incident of 4 September 1954, 1958	'It will request that the Court find that the Soviet Government is liable to the United States Government for the damages caused; that the Court award damages in favour of the United States Government against the Soviet Government in the sum of [. . .]'	Declaratory Compensation Reparation
26.	Barcelona Traction, Light and Power Company, Limited, 1958	'I. que les mesures, actes, décisions et omissions des organes de l'État espagnol en vertu desquels la Barcelona Traction a été déclare en faillite et ses biens liquidés dans les circonstances relevées dans la présente requête, sont contraires au droit des gens et que l'État espagnol est responsable du préjudice qui en est résulté; II. que l'État espagnol est en conséquence tenu de rétablir intégralement la [. . .] et qu'il est tenu de plus d'assurer l'indemnisation de cette société pour tous autres préjudices [. . .]. III. Subsidiairement, dire qu'au cas où la e restitutio in integrum demande ci-dessus s'avérerait en tout ou partie impossible, a raison notamment d'obstacles constitutionnels l'État espagnol serait tenu de verser à l'État belge une indemnité équivalant à la valeur des biens, droits et intérêts dont. [. . .]'.	Declaratory Restitution in kind Compensation

204

27.	Compagnie du Port, des Quais et des Entrepôts de Beyrouth and Société Radio-Orient, 1959	'that the alterations of the situation of [...] are, in the circumstances in which they were made, contrary to the undertaking given in [...] – that the Lebanese Government is under an obligation to make good the damage suffered [...]'	Declaratory Compensation
28.	Aerial Incident of 7 November 1954, 1957	'that the Court find that the Soviet Government is liable to the United States Government for the damages caused; that the Court award damages in favour of the United States Government against the Soviet Government in the amount of [...]'	Declaratory Compensation Reparation
29.	Temple of Preah Vihear, 1959	(1) that the Kingdom of Thailand is under an obligation to withdraw the detachments of armed forces [...]; (2) that the territorial sovereignty over the Temple of Preah Vihear belongs to the Kingdom of Cambodia.'	Specific performance Declaratory
30.	South West Africa, 1960 Proceedings joined with South West Africa (Liberia v. South Africa)	'[...] B. The Union of South Africa remains subject to the international obligations set forth in [...]; that the General Assembly of the United Nations is legally qualified to exercise the supervisory functions [...]; and that the Union is under an obligation	Declaratory Specific Performance Cessation

(continued)

No.	Case Name (Parties)	Request in Unilateral Application	Type
		to submit to the supervision and control of the General Assembly with regard to the exercise of the Mandate. [...] *F. The Union, in administering the Territory, has practised apartheid, [...]; that such practice is in violation of [...]; and that the Union has the duty forthwith to cease the practice of apartheid in the Territory. [...].'*	
31.	**South West Africa (Liberia v. South Africa) 1960** Proceedings joined with South West Africa (Ethiopia v. South Africa)	**Idem No. 30**	Declaratory Cessation
32.	**Northern Cameroons, 1961**	*'Dire et juger, [...] que le Royaume-Uni, dans l'application de l'Accord de Tutelle du 13 décembre 1946, n'a pas respecté certaines obligations [...].'*	Declaratory
33.	**Barcelona Traction, Light and Power Company, Limited (New Application: 1962), 1962**	*'1° dire et juger que les mesures, actes, décisions et omissions des organes de l'État espagnol décrits dans la présente requête sont contraires au droit des gens et que l'État espagnol est tenu, à l'égard de la Belgique, de réparer le préjudice qui en est résulté pour les ressortissants belges,*	Declaratory Compensation

personnes physiques et morales, actionnaires de la Barcelona Traction; [...] 3° dire et juger, au cas où l'effacement des conséquences des actes incriminés se révélerait impossible, que l'État espagnol sera tenu deverser l'État belge, à titre d'indemnité [...].'

34.	Appeal Relating to the Jurisdiction of the ICAO Council, 1971	'to adjudge and declare [...] that the aforesaid decision of the Council is illegal, null and void, or erroneous, on the following grounds or any others: [...].'	Declaratory
35.	Fisheries Jurisdiction, 1972	'(a) That there is no foundation in international law for the claim by Iceland to be entitled to extend its fisheries jurisdiction [...]; and that its claim is therefore invalid; and [...].'	Declaratory
36.	Fisheries Jurisdiction, 1972	'(a) that the unilateral extension by Iceland of its zone of exclusive fisheries jurisdiction to 50 nautical miles from the present baseline, [...] would have no basis in international law and could therefore not be opposed[...];'	Declaratory
37.	Nuclear Tests (Australia v. France), 1973	'that, [...] the carrying out of further atmospheric nuclear weapon tests in the South Pacific Ocean is not consistent with applicable rules of international law.	Declaratory Cessation

(continued)

No.	Case Name (Parties)	Request in Unilateral Application	Type
		And to order that the French Republic shall not carry out any further such tests.'	
38.	**Nuclear Tests (New Zealand v. France), 1973**	*'That the conduct [...] constitutes a violation of New Zealand's rights under international law, and that these rights will be violated by any further such tests.'*	Declaratory
39.	**Trial of Pakistani Prisoners of War, 1973**	*'(1) That Pakistan has an exclusive right to exercise jurisdiction over the one hundred and ninety-five Pakistani nationals [...] and that no other Government or authority is competent to exercise such jurisdiction. [...].'*	Declaratory
40.	**Aegean Sea Continental Shelf, 1976**	*(i) that the Greek islands [...] are entitled to the portion of the continental shelf which appertains to them according to the applicable principles and rules of international law; [...] (vi) that Turkey shall not continue any further activities as described above in subparagraph (iv) within the areas of the continental shelf which the Court shall adjudge appertain to Greece.'*	Declaratory Cessation
41.	**United States Diplomatic and Consular Staff in Tehran, 1979**	*'(a) That the Government of Iran [...], violated its international legal obligations*	Declaratory Specific performance Compensation

			Declaratory	Cessation	Compensation
		to the United States as provided by [. . .] (b) That [. . .], the Government of Iran is under a particular obligation immediately to secure the release of all United States nationals currently being detained within the premises of the United States Embassy in Tehran and to assure that all such persons and all other United States nationals in Tehran are allowed to leave Iran safely; (c) That the Government of Iran shall pay [. . .] reparation [. . .].'			
42.	Military and Paramilitary Activities in and against Nicaragua, 1984	'(a) That the United States, [. . .], has violated and is violating its express charter and treaty obligations to Nicaragua and, in particular, its charter and treaty obligations under: [. . .] (g) That, [. . .] the United States is under a particular duty to cease and desist immediately: [. . .] (h) That the United States has an obligation to pay [. . .] reparations for damages [. . .].'	Declaratory	Cessation	Compensation
43.	Application for Revision and Interpretation of the Judgment of 24 February 1982 in the Case concerning	'That there is a new fact of such a character as to lay the Judgment open to revision within the meaning of Article 61 of the	Declaratory		

(continued)

209

No.	Case Name (Parties)	Request in Unilateral Application	Type
	the Continental Shelf (Tunisia/Libyan Arab Jamahiriya) (Tunisia v. Libyan Arab Jamahiriya) 1984	*Statute of the Court; [...]* *That there is cause to construe the Judgment of 24 February 1982 and to correct an error;* *That the starting-point for the line of delimitation is the point where the outer limit of the territorial sea of the Parties is [...].'*	
44.	Border and Transborder Armed Actions, 1986	*'(a) that the acts and omissions of Costa Rica in the material period constitute breaches of the various obligations of customary international law and the treaties specified in [...];* *(b) that Costa Rica is under a duty immediately to cease and to refrain [...];* *(c) that Costa Rica is under an obligation to make reparation [...]'*	Declaratory Cessation Reparation
45.	Border and Transborder Armed Actions, 1986	*'(a) that the acts and omissions of Honduras in the material period constitute breaches of the various obligations of customary international law and the treaties specified in [...];* *(b) that Honduras is under a duty immediately to cease and to refrain [...];*	Declaratory Cessation Reparation

		(c) that Honduras is under an obligation to make reparation [...].'	
46.	**Elettronica Sicula S.p.A., 1987**	*'(a) that the Government of Italy has violated the Treaty of [...]; and (b) that the Government of Italy is responsible to pay compensation to the United States in an amount to be determined by the Court [...]'*	Declaratory Compensation
47.	**Maritime Delimitation in the Area between Greenland and Jan Mayen, 1988**	*'(a) to decide, in accordance with international law, where a single line of delimitation shall be drawn between Denmark's and Norway's fishing zones and continental shelf areas in the waters between Greenland and Jan Mayen; [...].'*	Declaratory
48.	**Aerial Incident of 3 July 1988, 1989**	*'(a) that the ICAO Council decision is erroneous in that [...]. (c) that the Government of the United States is responsible to pay compensation [...]'*	Declaratory Compensation
49.	**Certain Phosphate Lands in Nauru, 1989**	*'that Australia has incurred an international legal responsibility and is bound to make restitution or other appropriate reparation to Nauru for the damage and prejudice suffered. Nauru further requests that the nature and amount of such restitution or reparation should, in the absence of agreement between the Parties, be assessed and determined by the Court, if necessary, in a separate phase of the proceedings.'*	Declaratory Restitution Reparation

(continued)

No.	Case Name (Parties)	Request in Unilateral Application	Type
50.	**Arbitral Award of 31 July 1989, 1989**	*'that that so-called decision is inexistent in view of the fact that one of the two arbitrators making up the appearance of a majority in favour of the text of the 'award', has, by a declaration appended to it, expressed a view in contradiction with the one apparently adopted by the vote; [. . .].'*	Declaratory
51.	**East Timor, 1991**	*'(1) that, first, the rights of the people of East Timor [. . .] are opposable to Australia, which is under an obligation not to disregard them, but to respect them. [. . .] (4) that [. . .], Australia has incurred international responsibility and has caused damage, for which it owes reparation to the people of East Timor and to Portugal, [. . .]. (5) that Australia is bound, [. . .], to cease from all breaches of the rights and international norms referred to [. . .], until such time as the people of East Timor shall have exercised its right to self-determination, under the conditions laid down by the United Nations: [. . .].'*	Declaratory Reparation Cessation
52.	**Maritime Delimitation between Guinea-Bissau and Senegal, 1991**	*'What should be, [. . .], the line (to be drawn on a map) delimiting all the maritime territories [. . .].'*	Declaratory

53.	Passage through the Great Belt, 1991	*'(a) that there is a right of free passage through the Great Belt which applies to all ships entering and leaving Finnish ports and shipyards; [...]* *(d) that Denmark and Finland should start negotiations, in good faith, [...]'*	Declaratory Specific performance
54.	Maritime Delimitation and Territorial Questions between Qatar and Bahrain, 1991	*'I. To adjudge and declare in accordance with international law* *(A) that the State of Qatar has sovereignty over the Hawar islands; [...].'*	Declaratory
55.	Questions of Interpretation and Application of the 1971 Montreal Convention arising from the Aerial Incident at Lockerbie, 1992	*'(a) that Libya has fully complied with all of its obligations under the Montreal Convention; [...]* *(c) that the United Kingdom is under a legal obligation immediately to cease and desist [...].'*	Declaratory Cessation
56.	Questions of Interpretation and Application of the 1971 Montreal Convention arising from the Aerial Incident at Lockerbie, 1992	*'(a) that Libya has fully complied with all of its obligations under the Montreal Convention; [...]* *(c) that the United States is under a legal obligation immediately to cease and desist [...].'*	Declaratory Cessation
57.	Oil Platforms, 1992	*'[...] (b) that in attacking and destroying the oil platforms [...], the United States breached its obligations; [...]* *(d) that the United States is under an obligation to make reparations; [...].'*	Declaratory Compensation

(continued)

No.	Case Name (Parties)	Request in Unilateral Application	Type
		Counterclaims: '1. That [. . .] the Islamic Republic of Iran breached its obligations to the United States [. . .] 2. That the Islamic Republic of Iran is accordingly under an obligation to make full reparation to the United States [. . .].'	
58.	Application of the Convention on the Prevention and Punishment of the Crime of Genocide, 1993	'(a) that Yugoslavia (Serbia and Montenegro) has breached, and is continuing to breach, its legal obligations toward the People and State of Bosnia and Herzegovina under Articles [. . .]; (q) that Yugoslavia (Serbia and Montenegro) and its agents and surrogates are under an obligation to cease and desist [. . .]: (r) that Yugoslavia (Serbia and Montenegro) has an obligation to pay Bosnia and Herzegovina, in its own right and as parens patriae for its citizens, reparations for damages [. . .].'	Declaratory Cessation Compensation
59.	Land and Maritime Boundary between Cameroon and Nigeria, 1994	'(a) that sovereignty over the Peninsula of Bakassi is Cameroonian, by virtue of international law, and that that Peninsula	Declaratory Cessation Compensation

		is an integral part of the territory of Cameroon; [...] (e) that in view of these breaches of legal obligation, mentioned above, the Federal Republic of Nigeria has the express duty of putting an end to [...]; (e') that, [...], reparation in an amount to be determined by the Court is due [...].'	
60.	Fisheries Jurisdiction, 1995	'A. that the Court declare that the legislation of Canada, [...], is not opposable to the Kingdom of Spain; B. that Canada is bound to refrain from any repetition of the acts complained of, and to offer to the Kingdom of Spain the reparation that is due, in the form of an indemnity; [...].'	Declaratory Guarantee of non-repetition Compensation
61.	Request for an Examination of the Situation in Accordance with Paragraph 63 of the Court's Judgment of 20 December 1974 in the Nuclear Tests, 1995	'(1) that the conduct of the proposed nuclear tests will constitute a violation of the rights under international law of New Zealand, as well as of other States; [...].'	Declaratory
62.	Vienna Convention on Consular Relations, 1998	'(1) that the United States, [...] violated its international legal obligations to Paraguay [...] (2) that Paraguay is therefore entitled to restitutio in integrum; [...]'	Declaratory Restitution in kind Specific performance Guarantee of non-repetition

(continued)

No.	Case Name (Parties)	Request in Unilateral Application	Type
		(4) that the United States is under an international legal obligation to carry out in conformity with the foregoing international legal obligations any future detention of or criminal proceedings against Angel Francisco Breard or any other Paraguayan national in its territory, [. . .] *(2) the United States should restore the status quo ante, that is, re-establish the situation that existed before the detention of, proceedings against, and conviction and sentencing of Paraguay's national in violation of the United States' international legal obligations took place; and* *(3) the United States should provide Paraguay a guarantee of the non-repetition of the illegal acts.'*	
63.	**Request for Interpretation of the Judgment of 11 June 1998 in the Case concerning the Land and Maritime Boundary between Cameroon and Nigeria, 1998**	*'that the Court's Judgment of 11 June 1998 is to be interpreted as meaning that: so far as concerns the international responsibility which Nigeria is said to bear for certain alleged incidents: (a) the dispute before the Court does not include any alleged incidents other than (at*	Declaratory

		most) *those specified in Cameroon's Application of 29 March 1994 and Additional Application of 6 June 1994; [. . .].'*	
64.	**Ahmadou Sadio Diallo, 1998**	*'To order the authorities of the Democratic Republic of the Congo to make an official public apology to the State of the Republic of Guinea; [. . .]* *To order that the Congolese State pay to the State of Guinea on behalf of its national, Mr. Diallo Ahmadou Sadio, the sums [. . .];* *To order that the said State return to the Applicant all the non-monetary assets set out in the list of miscellaneous claims; [].'*	Satisfaction Compensation Restitution in kind
65.	**LaGrand, 1999**	*'(1) that the United States, [. . .] violated its international legal obligations to Germany [. . .],* *(2) that Germany is therefore entitled to reparation, [. . .]* *(4) that the United States is under an international obligation to carry out in conformity with the foregoing international legal obligations any future detention of or criminal proceedings against any other German national in its territory, [. . .];* *(2) the United States should provide*	Declaratory Reparation Specific performance Satisfaction Compensation Restitution in kind Guarantee of non-repetition

(continued)

No.	Case Name (Parties)	Request in Unilateral Application	Type
		reparation, in the form of compensation and satisfaction, *(3) the United States should restore the status quo ante in the case of Walter LaGrand, [. . .]; and* *(4) the United States should provide Germany a guarantee of the non-repetition of the illegal acts.'*	
66.	**Legality of Use of Force (Serbia and Montenegro v. Belgium), 1999**	*'[. . .] The Kingdom of Belgium has acted against the Federal Republic of Yugoslavia in breach of its obligation not to use force against another State; [. . .]* *The Kingdom of Belgium is obliged to stop immediately the violation [. . .];* *The Kingdom of Belgium is obliged to provide compensation for the damage done [. . .]'*	Declaratory Cessation Compensation
67.	**Legality of Use of Force (Serbia and Montenegro v. Canada), 1999**	*'[. . .] Canada has acted against the Federal Republic of Yugoslavia in breach of its obligation not to use force against another State; [. . .]* *Canada is obliged to stop immediately the violation [. . .];* *Canada is obliged to provide compensation for the damage done [. . .].'*	Declaratory Cessation Compensation

			Declaratory	Cessation	Compensation
68.	Legality of Use of Force (Serbia and Montenegro v. France), 1999	'[…] the Republic of France has acted against the Federal Republic of Yugoslavia in breach of its obligation not to use force against another State; […] The Republic of France is obliged to stop immediately the violation […]; The Republic of France is obliged to provide compensation for the damage done […]'	Declaratory	Cessation	Compensation
69.	Legality of Use of Force (Serbia and Montenegro v. Germany), 1999	'[…] the Federal Republic of Germany has acted against the Federal Republic of Yugoslavia in breach of its obligation not to use force against another State; […] The Federal Republic of Germany is obliged to stop immediately the violation […]; The Federal Republic of Germany is obliged to provide compensation for the damage […]'	Declaratory	Cessation	Compensation
70.	Legality of Use of Force (Serbia and Montenegro v. Italy), 1999	'[…] the Republic of Italy has acted against the Federal Republic of Yugoslavia in breach of its obligation not to use force against another State; The Republic of Italy is obliged to stop immediately the violation […]; The Republic of Italy is obliged to provide compensation for the damage done […]'	Declaratory	Cessation	Compensation

(continued)

No.	Case Name (Parties)	Request in Unilateral Application	Type
71.	**Legality of Use of Force (Serbia and Montenegro v. Netherlands), 1999**	'[...] *the Kingdom of the Netherlands has acted against the Federal Republic of Yugoslavia in breach of its obligation not to use force against another State; [...]* *The Kingdom of the Netherlands is obliged to stop immediately the violation [...];* *The Kingdom of the Netherlands is obliged to provide compensation for the damage done [...]*'	Declaratory Cessation Compensation
72.	**Legality of Use of Force (Serbia and Montenegro v. Portugal), 1999**	'[...] *Portugal has acted against the Federal Republic of Yugoslavia in breach of its obligation not to use force against another State; [...]* *Portugal is obliged to stop immediately the violation [...];* *- Portugal is obliged to provide compensation for the damage done [...].*'	Declaratory Cessation Compensation
73.	**Legality of Use of Force (Yugoslavia v. Spain), 1999**	'[...] *the Kingdom of Spain has acted against the Federal Republic of Yugoslavia in breach of its obligation not to use force against another State; [...]* *- The Kingdom of Spain is obliged to stop immediately the violation [...];* *- The Kingdom of Spain is obliged to provide compensation for the damage done [...]*'	Declaratory Cessation Compensation

74.	Legality of Use of Force (Serbia and Montenegro v. United Kingdom), 1999	'[. . .] The United Kingdom of Great Britain and Northern Ireland has acted against the Federal Republic of Yugoslavia in breach of its obligation not to use force against another State; [. . .] - The United Kingdom of Great Britain and Northern Ireland is obliged to stop immediately the violation [. . .]; - The United Kingdom of Great Britain and Northern Ireland is obliged to provide compensation for the damage done [. . .].'	Declaratory Cessation Compensation
75.	Legality of Use of Force (Yugoslavia v. United States of America), 1999	'[. . .] The United States of America has acted against the Federal Republic of Yugoslavia in breach of its obligation not to use force against another State; [. . .] - The United States of America is obliged to stop immediately the violation [. . .]; - The United States of America is obliged to provide compensation for the damage done [. . .]'	Declaratory Cessation Compensation
76.	Armed Activities on the Territory of the Congo (Democratic Republic of the Congo v. Burundi), 1999	'(a) Burundi is guilty of an act of aggression within the meaning of [. . .]; (1) all Burundian armed forces participating in acts of aggression shall forthwith vacate the territory [. . .]; (3) the Democratic Republic of the Congo is entitled to compensation [. . .], in addition to its claim for the restitution of all property removed.'	Declaratory Specific performance Compensation Restitution in kind

(continued)

No.	Case Name (Parties)	Request in Unilateral Application	Type
77.	**Armed Activities on the Territory of the Congo (Democratic Republic of the Congo v. Uganda), 1999**	'*(a) Uganda is guilty of an act of aggression within the meaning of [...];* *(1) all Ugandan armed forces participating in acts of aggression shall forthwith vacate the territory [...];* *(3) the Democratic Republic of the Congo is entitled to compensation [...], in addition to its claim for the restitution of all property removed.*'	Declaratory Specific performance Compensation Restitution in kind
78.	**Armed Activities on the Territory of the Congo (Democratic Republic of the Congo v. Rwanda), 1999**	'*(a) Rwanda is guilty of an act of aggression within the meaning of [...];* *(3) the Democratic Republic of the Congo is entitled to compensation [...], in addition to its claim for the restitution of all property removed.*'	Declaratory Specific performance Compensation Restitution in kind
79.	**Application of the Convention on the Prevention and Punishment of the Crime of Genocide, 1999**	'*(1) that the Federal Republic of Yugoslavia has breached its legal obligations toward the people and Republic of Croatia under Articles [...];* *(b) that the Federal Republic of Yugoslavia has an obligation to pay to the Republic of Croatia, in its own right and as parens patriae for its citizens, reparations for damages to [...].*'	Declaratory Compensation

80.	**Aerial Incident of 10 August 1999, 1999**	*'(a) that the acts of India (as stated above) constitute breaches of the various obligations under […];* *(b) that India is under an obligation to make reparations to the Islamic Republic of Pakistan for the loss of the aircraft and as compensation […]'*	Declaratory Compensation
81.	**Territorial and Maritime Dispute between Nicaragua and Honduras in the Caribbean Sea, 1999**	*'Accordingly, the Court is asked to determine the course of the single maritime boundary between […].* *Whilst the principal purpose of this Application is to obtain a declaration concerning the determination of the maritime boundary or boundaries, the Government of Nicaragua reserves the right to claim compensation […].* *Nicaragua also reserves the right to claim compensation for any natural resources that may have been extracted or may be extracted in the future to the south of the line of delimitation that will be fixed by the Judgment of the Court.'*	Declaratory Reserved the right to claim compensation
82.	**Arrest Warrant of 11 April 2000, 2000**	*'The Court is requested to declare that the Kingdom of Belgium shall annul the international arrest warrant […].'*	Restitution in kind

(continued)

No.	Case Name (Parties)	Request in Unilateral Application	Type
83.	**Application for Revision of the Judgment of 11 July 1996 in the Case concerning Application of the Convention on the Prevention and Punishment of the Crime of Genocide (Bosnia and Herzegovina v. Yugoslavia), Preliminary Objections (Yugoslavia v. Bosnia and Herzegovina), 2001**	'*there is a new fact of such a character as to lay the case open to revision under Article 61 of the Statute of the Court. Furthermore, Applicant is respectfully asking the Court to suspend proceedings regarding the merits of the case until a decision on this Application is rendered.*'	Declaratory
84.	**Certain Property, 2001**	'*that Germany has incurred international legal responsibility and is bound to make appropriate reparation to Liechtenstein for the damage and prejudice suffered. [. . .].*'	Declaratory Reparation
85.	**Territorial and Maritime Dispute, 2001**	'*First, that the Republic of Nicaragua has sovereignty over the islands of [. . .]; [. . .] the Government of Nicaragua reserves the right to claim compensation [. . .]*'	Declaratory Reserved the right to claim compensation
86.	**Armed Activities on the Territory of the Congo (New Application: 2002) (Democratic Republic of the Congo v. Rwanda), 2002**	'1) *toute force armée rwandaise à la base de l'agression doit quitter sans délai le territoire de la République Démocratique du Congo; afm de permettre à la population congolaise de jouir pleinement de ses droits à la paix, à la sécurité, à ses ressources et au développement; [. . .]*'	Cessation Specific performance Compensation

		3) *la République Démocratique du Congo a droit à obtenir du Rwanda le dédommagement de tous actes de pillages, destructions, massacres, déportations de biens et des personnes et autres méfaits qui sont imputables au Rwanda et pour lesquels la République Démocratique du Congo se réserve le droit de fixer ultérieurement une évaluation précise des préjudices, outre la restitution des biens emportés.'*	
87.	**Application for Revision of the Judgment of 11 September 1992 in the Case concerning the Land, Island and Maritime Frontier Dispute, 2002**	*'[...] (c) [...], to proceed to the revision of the Judgment of 11 September 1992, so that a new Judgment will determine the boundary line [...]:'*	Declaratory
88.	**Avena and Other Mexican Nationals, 2003**	*'(1) that the United States, [...], violated its international legal obligations to Mexico, [...];* *(2) that Mexico is therefore entitled to restitutio in integrum; [...]* *(4) that the United States is under an international legal obligation to carry out in conformity with the foregoing international legal obligations any future detention of or criminal proceedings against the 54 Mexican nationals on death row or any other Mexican national in its territory, [...];*	Declaratory Reparation Specific performance Guarantee of non-repetition

(continued)

No.	Case Name (Parties)	Request in Unilateral Application	Type
		(4) the United States, in light of the pattern and practice of violations set forth in this Application, must provide Mexico a full guarantee of the non-repetition of the illegal acts.'	
89.	**Certain Criminal Proceedings in France,** 2003	*'that the French Republic shall cause to be annulled the measures of investigation and prosecution taken [...]: [...].'*	Restitution in kind
90.	**Maritime Delimitation in the Black Sea,** 2004	*'to draw in accordance with the international law, [...], a single maritime boundary between [...]'*	Declaratory
91.	**Dispute regarding Navigational and Related Rights,** 2005	*'that Nicaragua is in breach of its international obligations [...].* *In particular the Court is requested to adjudge and declare that, by its conduct, Nicaragua has violated: [...]* *Further, the Court is requested to determine the reparation which must be made [...]'*	Declaratory Reparation
92.	**Status vis-à-vis the Host State of a Diplomatic Envoy to the United Nations,** 2006	*'(a) clarify the rights and duties [...], with regard to Permanent Missions and their diplomatic personnel; [...]* *(j) that the Respondents and their agents and surrogates are under an obligation to cease and desist immediately [...];*	Declaratory Cessation Compensation

		(k) that the Respondents have an obligation to pay the Applicants, the Commonwealth of Dominica, in their own right and as parens patriae for their citizens, reparations for damages [...]'	
93.	**Pulp Mills on the River Uruguay, 2006**	*'1. that Uruguay has breached the obligations incumbent upon it under [...]: 3. that Uruguay shall cease its wrongful conduct and comply scrupulously in future with the obligations incumbent upon it; and 4. that Uruguay shall make full reparation for the injury caused by its breach of [...]'*	Declaratory Cessation Reparation
94.	**Certain Questions of Mutual Assistance in Criminal Matters, 2006**	*'(a) that the French Republic is under an international legal obligation to foster all co-operation aimed at promoting the speedy disposition of the 'Case against X for the murder of Bernard Borrel', in compliance with the principle of sovereign equality between States, as laid down in [...]; (c) that the French Republic is under an international legal obligation to execute the international letter rogatory [...]; (h) that the French Republic is under an obligation immediately to cease and desist [...]: [...]*	Declaratory Specific performance Cessation Reparation Guarantee of non-repetition

(continued)

No.	Case Name (Parties)	Request in Unilateral Application	Type
		(i) that the French Republic owes reparation [. . .]; *(j) that the French Republic shall give the Republic of Djibouti a guarantee that such wrongful acts will not reoccur. [. . .]'*	
95.	Maritime Dispute, 2008	*'to determine the course of the boundary between the maritime zones of the two States in accordance with international law [. . .].'*	Declaratory
96.	Aerial Herbicide Spraying, 2008	*'(A) Colombia has violated its obligations under international law by [. . .];* *(B) Colombia shall indemnify Ecuador for any loss or damage caused: [. . .]* *(C) Colombia shall [. . .]* *(ii) forthwith, take all steps necessary to prevent, on any part of its territory, the use of any toxic herbicides in such a way that they could be deposited onto the territory of Ecuador; [. . .].'*	Declaratory Compensation Specific performance
97.	Request for Interpretation of the Judgment of 31 March 2004 in the Case concerning Avena and Other Mexican Nationals (Mexico v. United States of America) (Mexico v. United States of America), 2008	*'that the obligation incumbent upon the United States [. . .] constitutes an obligation of result as it is clearly stated in the Judgment [. . .];* *and that, pursuant to the foregoing obligation of result,*	Declaratory Reparation Specific performance

1. the United States must take any and all steps necessary to provide the reparation of review and reconsideration mandated by the Avena Judgment; and
2. the United States must take any and all steps necessary to ensure that no Mexican national entitled to review and reconsideration under the Avena Judgment is executed [. . .]'

| 98. | Application of the International Convention on the Elimination of All Forms of Racial Discrimination (Georgia v. Russian Federation), 2008 | 'that the Russian Federation, [. . .], has violated its obligations under CERD by: [. . .] The Republic of Georgia, on its own behalf and as parens patriae for its citizens, respectfully requests the Court to order the Russian Federation to take all steps necessary to comply with its obligations under CERD, including: (a) immediately ceasing all military activities [. . .], and immediate withdrawing of all Russian military personnel from the same; (b) taking all necessary and appropriate measures to ensure the prompt and effective return of IDPs to South Ossetia and Abkhazia in conditions of safety and security; [. . .] (e) paying full compensation [. . .]; [. . .].' | Declaratory Cessation Specific performance Compensation |

(continued)

No.	Case Name (Parties)	Request in Unilateral Application	Type
99.	**Application of the Interim Accord of 13 September 1995, 2008**	'*(i) [...] that the Respondent, through its State organs and agents, has violated its obligations under Article 11, paragraph 1, of the Interim Accord; (ii) to order that the Respondent immediately take all necessary steps to comply with its obligations under Article 11, paragraph 1, of the Interim Accord, and to cease and desist from objecting [...]'*	Declaratory Specific performance Cessation
100.	**Jurisdictional Immunities of the State, 2008**	'*(1) by allowing civil claims based on violations of international humanitarian law by the German Reich during World War II from September 1943 to May 1945, to be brought against the Federal Republic of Germany, committed violations of obligations under international law in that it has failed to respect the jurisdictional immunity which the Federal Republic of Germany enjoys under international law; [...] Accordingly, the Federal Republic of Germany prays the Court to adjudge and declare that: [...]*'	Declaratory Specific performance

(5) the Italian Republic must, by means of its own choosing, take any and all steps to ensure that all the decisions of its courts and other judicial authorities infringing Germany's sovereign immunity become unenforceable; [...].'

| 101. | Questions relating to the Obligation to Prosecute or Extradite, 2009 | ' [...] *the Republic of Senegal is obliged to bring criminal proceedings against Mr. H. Habré [...];*' | Specific performance |
| 102. | Certain Questions concerning Diplomatic Relations, 2009 | *'that Brazil does not have the right to allow the premises of its Mission in Tegucigalpa to be used to promote manifestly illegal activities by Honduran citizens who have been staying within it for some time now and that it shall cease to do so. Just as Brazil rightly demands that the Honduran authorities guarantee the security and inviolability of the Mission premises, Honduras demands that Brazil's diplomatic staff stationed in Tegucigalpa devote themselves exclusively to the proper functions of the Mission and not to actions constituting interference in the internal affairs of another State. [...] the Government of Honduras reserves the right to claim reparation for any damage resulting from the actions of Brazil, of its Mission, and of the Honduran persons sheltered by it in the Mission.'* | Declaratory |

(continued)

No.	Case Name (Parties)	Request in Unilateral Application	Type
103.	**Jurisdiction and Enforcement of Judgments in Civil and Commercial Matters, 2009**	*'Switzerland [. . .] is breaching the Lugano Convention, in particular [. . .] Switzerland shall take all appropriate steps to enable the judgment by the Belgian courts on the contractual and non-contractual liability of [. . .] to be recognized in Switzerland in accordance with the Lugano Convention [. . .];'*	Declaratory Specific performance
104.	**Whaling in the Antarctic, 2010**	*'that Japan is in breach of its international obligations [. . .] [] that Japan: (a) cease implementation of [. . .]; (b) revoke any authorizations, permits or licences allowing the activities which are the subject of this application to be undertaken; and (c) provide assurances and guarantees that it will not take any further action under [. . .]'*	Declaratory Cessation Specific performance Guarantee of non-repetition
105.	**Certain Activities carried out by Nicaragua in the Border Area, 2010**	*'that Nicaragua is in breach of its international obligations as referred to [. . .]. The Court is also requested to determine the reparation which must be made by Nicaragua, in particular in relation to any measures of the kind referred to in paragraph 41 above.'*	Declaratory Reparation

#	Case	Request	Remedy
106.	**Request for Interpretation of the Judgment of 15 June 1962 in the Case concerning the Temple of Preah Vihear,** 2011	*'The obligation incumbent upon Thailand to 'withdraw any military or police forces, or other guards or keepers, stationed by her at the Temple, or in its vicinity on Cambodian territory,' (second paragraph of the operative clause) is a particular consequence of [. . .].'*	Declaratory
107.	**Construction of a Road in Costa Rica along the San Juan River (Nicaragua v. Costa Rica),** 2011 Proceedings joined with Certain Activities carried out by Nicaragua in the Border Area (Costa Rica v. Nicaragua) on 17 April 2013	*'that Costa Rica has breached:* *(a) Its obligation not to violate Nicaragua's territorial integrity [. . .];* *Furthermore, Nicaragua requests the Court to adjudge and declare that Costa Rica must:* *(a) Restore the situation to the status quo ante;* *(b) Pay for all damages caused including the costs added to the dredging of the San Juan River; [. . .]* *(a) Cease all the constructions underway that affect or may affect the rights of Nicaragua;* *(b) Produce and present to Nicaragua an adequate environmental impact assessment with all the details of the works.'*	Declaratory Compensation Cessation Compensation Specific performance
108.	**Obligation to Negotiate Access to the Pacific Ocean,** 2011	*'(a) Chile has the obligation to negotiate with Bolivia in order to reach an agreement granting Bolivia a fully sovereign access to the Pacific Ocean;*	Declaratory Specific performance

(continued)

No.	Case Name (Parties)	Request in Unilateral Application	Type
		(b) Chile has breached the said obligation; *(c) Chile must perform the said obligation in good faith, promptly, formally, within a reasonable time and effectively, to grant Bolivia a fully sovereign access to the Pacific Ocean.'*	
109.	Question of the Delimitation of the Continental Shelf between Nicaragua and Colombia beyond 200 nautical miles from the Nicaraguan Coast, 2013	*'The precise course of the maritime boundary between Nicaragua and Colombia in the areas of the continental shelf which appertain to each of them beyond the boundaries determined by the Court in its Judgment of 19 November 2012. The principles and rules of international law that determine the rights and duties of the two States in relation to the area of overlapping continental shelf claims [...]'*	Declaratory
110.	Alleged Violations of Sovereign Rights and Maritime Spaces in the Caribbean Sea, 2013	*'that Colombia is in breach of:* *– its obligation not to use or threaten to use force [...];* *– and that, consequently, Colombia is bound to comply with the Judgment of 19 November 2012, wipe out the legal and material consequences of its internationally wrongful acts, and make full reparation for the harm caused by those acts.'*	Declaratory Specific performance Reparation

| 111. | Questions relating to the Seizure and Detention of Certain Documents and Data, 2013 | 'That the seizure by Australia of the documents and data violated (i) the sovereignty of Timor-Leste and (ii) its property and other rights under international law and any relevant domestic law; [...] That Australia must immediately return to the nominated representative of Timor-Leste any and all of the aforesaid documents and data, and destroy beyond recovery every copy of such documents and data that is in Australia's possession or control, and ensure the destruction of every such copy that Australia has directly or indirectly passed to a third person or third State; That Australia should afford satisfaction to Timor-Leste in respect of the above-mentioned violations of its rights under international law and any relevant domestic law, in the form of a formal apology as well as the costs incurred by Timor-Leste in preparing and presenting the present Application.' | Declaratory Restitution in kind Specific performance Satisfaction |
| 112. | Maritime Delimitation in the Caribbean Sea and the Pacific Ocean, 2013 | 'to determine the complete course of a single maritime boundary between all the maritime areas appertaining, respectively, to [...].' | Declaratory |

(continued)

No.	Case Name (Parties)	Request in Unilateral Application	Type
113.	**Obligations concerning Negotiations relating to Cessation of the Nuclear Arms Race and to Nuclear Disarmament (Marshall Islands v. India), 2014**	*'a) that India has violated and continues to violate its international obligations [...];* *to order India to take all steps necessary to comply with its obligations under customary international law [...]'*	Declaratory Specific performance
114.	**Obligations concerning Negotiations relating to Cessation of the Nuclear Arms Race and to Nuclear Disarmament (Marshall Islands v. Pakistan), 2014**	*'a) that Pakistan has violated and continues to violate its international obligations [...]* *to order Pakistan to take all steps necessary to comply with its obligations under customary international law [...]'*	Declaratory Specific performance
115.	**Obligations concerning Negotiations relating to Cessation of the Nuclear Arms Race and to Nuclear Disarmament (Marshall Islands v. United Kingdom), 2014**	*'a) that the United Kingdom has violated and continues to violate its international obligations [...];* *to order the United Kingdom to take all steps necessary to comply with its obligations under [...]'*	Declaratory Specific performance
116.	**Maritime Delimitation in the Indian Ocean, 2014**	*'to determine, on the basis of international law, the complete course of the single maritime boundary [...].'*	Declaratory
117.	**Dispute over the Status and Use of the Waters of the Silala, 2016**	*'(a) The Silala River system, together with the subterranean portions of its system, is an international watercourse, the use of which is governed by customary international law; [...]*	Declaratory Specific performance

(d) Bolivia has an obligation to take all appropriate measures to prevent and control pollution and other forms of harm to Chile [. . .]; [. . .].'

| 118. | **Immunities and Criminal Proceedings, 2016** | 'a) *En ce qui concerne le non-respect de la souveraineté de la République de Guinée équatoriale par la République française:* i) *de dire et juger que la République française a manqué à son obligation de [. . .];* b) *En ce qui concerne le Second Vice-Président de la République de Guinée équatoriale chargé de la Défense et de la Sécurité de l'État: [. . .]* ii) *d'ordonner à la République française de prendre toutes les mesures nécessaires pour mettre fin à toutes les procédures en cours contre le Second Vice-Président de la République de Guinée équatoriale chargé de la Défense et de la Sécurité de l'État; [. . .]* c) *En ce qui concerne l'immeuble sis au 42 Avenue Foch, à Paris: [. . .]* d) *En conséquence de l'ensemble des violations par la République française de ses obligations internationales dues à la* | Declaratory Specific performance Compensation |

(continued)

No.	Case Name (Parties)	Request in Unilateral Application	Type
		République de Guinée équatoriale: [. . .] *ii) d'ordonner à la République française de payer à la République de Guinée équatoriale une pleine réparation [. . .].*	
119.	**Certain Iranian Assets, 2016**	'*[. . .] b. [. . .] the USA has breached its obligations to Iran [. . .];* *c. That the USA shall ensure that no steps shall be taken based on the executive, legislative and judicial acts (as referred to above) at issue in this case which are, to the extent determined by the Court, inconsistent with the obligations of the USA to Iran under the Treaty of Amity; [. . .]* *f. That the USA is under an obligation to make full reparations to Iran for the violation of its international legal obligations [. . .];*'	Declaratory Specific performance Compensation
120.	**Land Boundary in the Northern Part of Isla Portillos, 2017** Proceedings joined with Maritime Delimitation in the Caribbean Sea and the Pacific Ocean (Costa Rica v. Nicaragua) on 2 February 2017	'*a. To determine the precise location of the land boundary [. . .]* *Costa Rica reserves its right to seek any further remedies with respect to any damage that Nicaragua has or may cause to its territory.*'	Declaratory Specific performance Reserved right to claim compensation for damages

121.	Application of the International Convention for the Suppression of the Financing of Terrorism and of the International Convention on the Elimination of All Forms of Racial Discrimination, 2017	'[...] that the Russian Federation, [...] has violated its obligations under the Terrorism Financing Convention by: [...] Ukraine respectfully requests the Court to order the Russian Federation to comply with its obligations [...]: a. Immediately and unconditionally cease and desist [...]; b. Immediately make all efforts to ensure that all weaponry provided to such armed groups is withdrawn from Ukraine; [] g. Make full reparation [...]; 138. Ukraine respectfully requests the Court to order the Russian Federation to comply with its obligations under the CERD, including: [...] b. Immediately restore the rights of [...]'	Declaratory Specific performance Cessation Reparation Restitution in kind
122.	Application for revision of the Judgment of 23 May 2008 in the Case concerning Sovereignty over Pedra Branca/Pulau Batu Puteh, Middle Rocks and South Ledge, 2017	'That there exists a new fact of such a nature as to be a decisive factor within the meaning of Article 61 of the Statute of the Court; [...].'	Declaratory
123.	Jadhav, 2017	'(1) A relief by way of immediate suspension of the sentence of death awarded to the accused.	Specific performance Restitutio in integrum Declaratory

(continued)

No.	Case Name (Parties)	Request in Unilateral Application	Type
		(2) A relief by way of restitution in interregnum by declaring that the sentence of the military court arrived at, [...] is violative of international law and the provisions of the Vienna Convention, and [...] *(4) If Pakistan is unable to annul the decision, then this Court to declare the decision illegal being violative of international law and treaty rights and restrain Pakistan from acting in violation of the Vienna Convention and international law by giving effect to the sentence or the conviction in any manner, and directing it to release the convicted Indian National forthwith.'*	
124.	Request for Interpretation of the Judgment of 23 May 2008 in the Case concerning Sovereignty over Pedra Branca/Pulau Batu Puteh, Middle Rocks and South Ledge, 2017	*'(a) 'The waters surrounding Pedra Branca/ Pulau Batu Puteh remain within the territorial waters of Malaysia' ; and (b) 'South Ledge is located in the territorial waters of Malaysia, and consequently sovereignty over South Ledge belongs to Malaysia'.*	Declaratory

125.	Arbitral Award of 3 October 1899, 2018	'(a) The 1899 Award is valid and binding upon Guyana and Venezuela, and the boundary established by that Award and the 1905 Agreement is valid and binding upon Guyana and Venezuela; [...] (c) Venezuela shall immediately withdraw from and cease [...]; (d) Venezuela shall refrain from threatening or using force against [...], and shall not interfere with any Guyanese or Guyanese- authorized activities in those areas; [...].'	Declaratory Cessation Specific performance
126.	Application of the International Convention on the Elimination of All Forms of Racial Discrimination, 2018	'[...] that the UAE, [...] has violated its obligations under [...]. to order the UAE to take all steps necessary to comply with its obligations under CERD and, inter alia: a. Immediately cease and revoke the discriminatory measures [...], ; [...] e. Restore rights of Qataris to [...], and put in place measures to ensure those rights are respected; f. Provide assurances and guarantees of non-repetition of the UAE's illegal conduct; and g. Make full reparation, including compensation, for the harm [...]'	Declaratory Cessation Specific performance Restitution in kind Guarantees of non-repetition Reparation/ compensation

(continued)

No.	Case Name (Parties)	Request in Unilateral Application	Type
127.	Appeal Relating to the Jurisdiction of the ICAO Council under Article 84 of the Convention on International Civil Aviation, 2018	'(1) *That the decision of the ICAO Council dated 29 June 2018 reflects a manifest failure to act judicially on the part of the ICAO Council, and a manifest lack of due process in the procedure adopted by the ICAO Council;* [...]'	Declaratory
128.	Appeal Relating to the Jurisdiction of the ICAO Council under Article II, Section 2, of the 1944 International Air Services Transit Agreement, 2018	'(1) *That the decision of the ICAO Council dated 29 June 2018 reflects a manifest failure to act judicially on the part of the ICAO Council, and a manifest lack of due process in the procedure adopted by the ICAO Council;* [...]'	Declaratory
129.	Alleged Violations of the 1955 Treaty of Amity, Economic Relations, and Consular Rights, 2018	'(a) *The USA, has breached its obligations to Iran under* [...]; *(b) The USA shall, by means of its own choosing, terminate the 8 May sanctions without delay;* [...] *(d) The USA shall ensure that no steps shall be taken to circumvent the decision* [...] *and will give a guarantee of non-repetition of its violations of the Treaty of Amity; (e) The USA shall fully compensate Iran for the violation of its international legal obligations* [...]'	Declaratory Specific performance Guarantee of non-repetition Compensation

130.	Relocation of the United States Embassy to Jerusalem, 2018	'51. *that the relocation, to the Holy City of Jerusalem, of the United States Embassy in Israel is in breach of the Vienna Convention on Diplomatic Relations.* 52. *The State of Palestine further requests the Court to order the United States of America to withdraw the diplomatic mission from the Holy City of Jerusalem and to conform to the international obligations flowing from the Vienna Convention on Diplomatic Relations.* 53. *In addition, the State of Palestine asks the Court to order the United States of America to take all necessary steps to comply with its obligations, to refrain from taking any future measures that would violate its obligations and to provide assurances and guarantees of non-repetition of its unlawful conduct.*'	Declaratory Specific performance Guarantees of non-repetition
131.	Application of the Convention on the Prevention and Punishment of the Crime of Genocide, 2019	'[...] *Myanmar: has breached and continues to breach its obligations under* [...]; *– must cease forthwith any such ongoing internationally wrongful act and fully respect its obligations under* [...];	Declaratory Cessation Specific performance Reparation Guarantees of non-repetition

(*continued*)

No.	Case Name (Parties)	Request in Unilateral Application	Type
		– must ensure that persons committing genocide are punished by a competent tribunal [...]; *– must perform the obligations of reparation [...]* *– must offer assurances and guarantees of non-repetition of violations of the Genocide Convention, in particular the obligations provided under [...]*	

APPENDIX 8

Judgments of the International Court of Justice in the Cases Submitted through Unilateral Applications

No.	Case Name and Parties	Judgment of the Court	Type
1.	Fisheries, 1951	*'Finds [...] that the method [...] is not contrary to international law; [...]'*	Declaratory
2.	Protection of French Nationals and Protected Persons in Egypt, 1951	Discontinued	NA
3.	Rights of Nationals of the United States of America in Morocco, 1952	*'[...] Finds that the United States of America is entitled, [...] to exercise in the French Zone of Morocco consular jurisdiction in all disputes [...];'*	Declaratory
4.	Request for Interpretation of the Judgment of 20 November 1950 in the Asylum Case, 1950	*'Declares the request for interpretation [...] to be inadmissible.'*	NA
5.	Haya de la Torre, 1951	*'[...] finds that Colombia is under no obligation to surrender Victor Raúl Haya de la Torre to the Peruvian authorities; [...] finds that the asylum [...], ought to have ceased after the delivery of the Judgment of November 20th, 1950, and should terminate.*	Declaratory Specific performance
6.	Ambatielos, 1953	*' [...] finds that the United Kingdom is under an obligation to submit to arbitration, [...] the difference as to the validity, under the Treaty of 1886, of the Ambatielos claim.'*	Specific performance
7.	Anglo-Iranian Oil Co., 1952	The Court found that it lacked jurisdiction.	NA

8.	Nottebohm, 1955	*'Holds that the claim submitted by the Government of the Principality of Liechtenstein is inadmissible.'*	NA
9.	Monetary Gold Removed from Rome in 1943, 1954	*'[...] finds that the jurisdiction conferred upon it [...] does not, in the absence of the consent of Albania, authorize it to adjudicate upon the first Submission in the Application of the Italian Government; [...].'*	NA
10.	Electricité de Beyrouth Company, 1954	Discontinued at France's request.	NA
11.	Treatment in Hungary of Aircraft and Crew of United States of America, 1954	*'the Court finds that it has not before it any acceptance by the Government of the Hungarian People's Republic of the jurisdiction of the Court [...]'*	NA
12.	Treatment in Hungary of Aircraft and Crew of United States of America, 1954	*'the Court finds that it has not before it any acceptance by the Government of the Union of Soviet Socialist Republics of the jurisdiction of the Court [...]'*	NA
13.	Aerial Incident of 10 March 1953, 1956	*'the Court finds that it has not before it any acceptance by the Government of the Czechoslovak Republic of the jurisdiction of the Court [...]'*	NA
14.	Antarctica (United Kingdom v. Argentina), 1956	*'the Court finds that it has not before it any acceptance by the Government of Argentina of the jurisdiction of the Court [...]'*	NA

(continued)

No.	Case Name and Parties	Judgment of the Court	Type
15.	**Antarctica (United Kingdom v. Chile) 1956**	*'the Court finds that it has not before it any acceptance by the Government of Chile of the jurisdiction of the Court [...]'*	NA
16.	**Aerial Incident of 7 October 1952, 1956**	*'the Court finds that it has not before it any acceptance by the Government of the Union of Soviet Socialist Republics of the jurisdiction of the Court [...]'*	NA
17.	**Certain Norwegian Loans, 1957**	*'by twelve votes to three, finds that it is without jurisdiction to adjudicate [...]'*	NA
18.	**Right of Passage over Indian Territory, 1960**	*'[...] finds that Portugal had in 1954 a right of passage over intervening Indian territory between the enclaves of [...];'*	Declaratory
19.	**Application of the Convention of 1902 Governing the Guardianship of Infants, 1958**	*'[...] rejects the claim of the Government of the Netherlands.'*	Rejected the claim
20.	**Interhandel, 1959**	*'[...] upholds the Third Preliminary Objection and holds that the Application of the Government of the Swiss Confederation is inadmissible.'*	NA
21.	**Aerial Incident of 27 July 1955 (Israel v. Bulgaria), 1959**	*'finds that it is without jurisdiction to adjudicate upon the dispute [...]'*	NA
22.	**Aerial Incident of 27 July 1955 (United States of America v. Bulgaria), 1960**	Discontinued due to request from United States.	NA
23.	**Aerial Incident of 27 July 1955 (United Kingdom v. Bulgaria), 1959**	Discontinued due to request from United Kingdom.	NA

24.	Arbitral Award Made by the King of Spain on 23 December 1906, 1960	'finds that the Award made by the King of Spain on 23 December 1906 is valid and binding and that Nicaragua is under an obligation to give effect to it.'	Declaratory Specific performance
25.	Aerial Incident of 4 September 1954, 1958	'the Court finds that it has not before it any acceptance by the Government of the Union of Soviet Socialist Republics of the jurisdiction of the Court to deal with the dispute [...].'	NA
26.	Barcelona Traction, Light and Power Company, Limited, 1961	Discontinued at the request of the Belgian Government.	NA
27.	Compagnie du Port, des Quais et des Entrepôts de Beyrouth and Société Radio-Orient, 1960	Discontinued due to settlement between the parties.	NA
28.	Aerial Incident of 7 November 1954, 1959	'the Court finds that it has not before it any acceptance by the Government of the Union of Soviet Socialist Republics of the jurisdiction of the Court to deal with the dispute [...]'	NA
29.	Temple of Preah Vihear, 1962	'[...] finds that the Temple of Preah Vihear is situated in territory under the sovereignty of Cambodia; [...] that Thailand is under an obligation to withdraw any military or police forces, or other guards or keepers, stationed by her at the Temple, or in its vicinity on Cambodian territory; [...]	Declaratory Specific performance Restitution in kind

(continued)

No.	Case Name and Parties	Judgment of the Court	Type
		that Thailand is under an obligation to restore to Cambodia any objects of the kind specified in [...]'	
30.	**South West Africa** Proceedings joined with South West Africa (Liberia v. South Africa), 1966	*'by the President's casting vote – the votes being equally divided, decides to reject the claims of the Empire of Ethiopia and the Republic of Liberia.'*	Claims rejected
31.	**South West Africa (Liberia v. South Africa)** Proceedings joined with South West Africa (Ethiopia v. South Africa), 1966	*'by the President's casting vote – the votes being equally divided, decides to reject the claims of the Empire of Ethiopia and the Republic of Liberia.'*	Claims rejected
32.	**Northern Cameroons, 1963**	*'[...] The Court finds that the proper limits of its judicial function do not permit it to entertain the claims submitted to it [...]'* ‘	NA
33.	**Barcelona Traction, Light and Power Company, Limited, 1970**	*'Since no jus standi before the Court has been established, it is not for the Court in its Judgment to pronounce upon any other aspect of the case, on which it should take a decision only if the Belgian Government had a right of protection in respect of its nationals, shareholders in Barcelona Traction. [...]*	Claim rejected

		The Court rejects the Belgian Government's claim by fifteen votes to one, twelve votes of the majority being based on the reasons set out in the present Judgment.'	
34.	Appeal Relating to the Jurisdiction of the ICAO Council, 1972	*'[...] (2) holds the Council of the International Civil Aviation Organization to be competent to entertain the Application and Complaint laid before it by the Government of Pakistan on 3 March 1971; and in consequence, rejects the appeal made to the Court by the Government of India against the decision of the Council assuming jurisdiction in those respects.'*	Declaratory
35.	Fisheries Jurisdiction (United Kingdom of Great Britain and Northern Ireland v. Iceland), 1974	*'(1) finds that the Regulations concerning the Fishery Limits off Iceland (Reglugerio urn jîskveiailandhelgi jslands) promulgated by the Government of Iceland on 14 July 1972 and constituting a unilateral extension of the exclusive fishing rights of Iceland to 50 nautical miles from the baselines specified therein are not opposable to the Government of the United Kingdom; [...] (3) holds that the Government of Iceland and the Government of the United Kingdom are under mutual obligations to undertake negotiations in good faith for the*	Declaratory Specific performance

(continued)

No.	Case Name and Parties	Judgment of the Court	Type
		equitable solution of their differences concerning their respective fishery rights [. . .]; *(4) holds that in these negotiations the Parties are to take into account, inter alia:* [. . .].'	
36.	**Fisheries Jurisdiction (Federal Republic of Germany v. Iceland), 1974**	'*(1) finds that the Regulations concerning* [. . .] *are not opposable to the Government of the Federal Republic of Germany;* [. . .] *(3) holds that the Government of Iceland and the Government of the Federal Republic of Germany are under mutual obligations to undertake negotiations in good faith for the equitable solution of their differences concerning their respective fishery rights* [. . .];'	Declaratory Specific performance
37.	**Nuclear Tests (Australia v. France), 1974**	'*finds that the claim of Australia no longer has any object and that the Court is therefore not called upon to give a decision thereon.*'	NA
38.	**Nuclear Tests (New Zealand v. France), 1974**	'*finds that the claim of New Zealand no longer has any object and that the Court is therefore not called upon to give a decision thereon.*'	NA

39.	Trial of Pakistani Prisoners of War, 1973	Discontinued at the request of Pakistan due to settlement and ongoing negotiations.	NA
40.	Aegean Sea Continental Shelf, 1978	*'finds that it is without jurisdiction to entertain the Application filed by the Government of the Hellenic Republic on 10 August 1976.'*	NA
41.	United States Diplomatic and Consular Staff in Tehran, 1980	*'1. [...] Decides that the Islamic Republic of Iran, [...], has violated in several respects, and is still violating, obligations owed by it to the United States of America [...];* *3. [...] Decides that the Government of the Islamic Republic of Iran must immediately take all steps to redress the situation [...]: (a) must immediately terminate the unlawful detention [...];* *5. [...] Decides that the Government of the Islamic Republic of Iran is under an obligation to make reparation [...];'*	Declaratory Specific performance Reparation
42.	Military and Paramilitary Activities in and against Nicaragua, 1986	*'[...] (3) [...] Decides that the United States of America, [...], has acted, against the Republic of Nicaragua, in breach of its obligation under customary international law not to intervene in the affairs of another State; [...]* *(12) [...] Decides that the United States of America is under a duty immediately to cease and to refrain from all such acts [...];*	Declaratory Cessation Reparation

(continued)

No.	Case Name and Parties	Judgment of the Court	Type
		(13) [. . .] Decides that the United States of America is under an obligation to make reparation [. . .];	
43.	**Application for Revision and Interpretation of the Judgment of 24 February 1982 in the Case concerning the Continental Shelf, 1985**	*'[. . .] (2) Declares, by way of interpretation of the Judgment of 24 February 1982, that the meaning and scope of that part of the Judgment which relates to the first sector of the delimitation are to be understood according to paragraphs 32 to 39 of the present Judgment; [. . .].'*	Declaratory
44.	**Border and Transborder Armed Actions, 1987**	Discontinued by Nicaragua due to agreement signed between the parties.	NA
45.	**Border and Transborder Armed Actions, 1992**	Discontinued by Nicaragua due to out-of-court agreement between the parties.	NA
46.	**Elettronica Sicula S.p.A., 1989**	*'[. . .] (2) [. . .] Finds that the Italian Republic has not committed any of the breaches, alleged in the said Application [. . .]* *(3) [. . .] Rejects, accordingly, the claim for reparation [. . .].'*	Declaratory Rejects reparation, due to rejection of main claim
47.	**Maritime Delimitation in the Area between Greenland and Jan Mayen, 1993**	*'Decides that, within the limits defined [. . .],* *the delimitation line that divides the continental shelf and fishery zones of the*	Declaratory

		Kingdom of Denmark and the Kingdom of Norway is to be drawn as set out in paragraphs [. . .]'	
48.	Aerial Incident of 3 July 1988, 1996	Discontinued by agreement of the parties due to settlement.	NA
49.	Certain Phosphate Lands in Nauru, 1993	Discontinued by agreement of the parties due to settlement.	NA
50.	Arbitral Award of 31 July 1989, 1993	*'[. . .] (3) [. . .] Rejects the submission of the Republic of Guinea-Bissau [. . .]; and, on the submission to that effect of the Republic of Senegal, finds that the Arbitral Award of 31 July 1989 is valid and binding [. . .].'*	Declaratory
51.	East Timor, 1995	*'Finds that it cannot in the present case exercise the jurisdiction [. . .].'*	NA
52.	Maritime Delimitation between Guinea-Bissau and Senegal, 1995	Discontinued at the request of Guinea-Bissau due to out-of-court agreement.	NA
53.	Passage through the Great Belt, 1992	Discontinued at the request of Finland due to settlement.	NA
54.	Maritime Delimitation and Territorial Questions between Qatar and Bahrain, 2001	*'(1) [. . .] Finds that the State of Qatar has sovereignty over Zubarah; [. . .].'*	Declaratory
55.	Questions of Interpretation and Application of the 1971 Montreal Convention arising from the Aerial Incident at Lockerbie, 2003	Discontinued by the agreement of the parties.	NA

(continued)

(continued)

No.	Case Name and Parties	Judgment of the Court	Type
56.	**Questions of Interpretation and Application of the 1971 Montreal Convention arising from the Aerial Incident at Lockerbie (Libyan Arab Jamahiriya v. United States of America)** 2003	Discontinued by the agreement of the parties.	NA
57.	**Oil Platforms**, 2003	*'(1) [...] Finds that the actions of the United States of America against Iranian oil platforms on 19 October 1987 and 18 April 1988 cannot be justified as measures necessary to protect the essential security interests of the United States of America [...].* *finds further that the Court cannot however uphold the submission of the Islamic Republic of Iran that those actions constitute a breach of the obligations of the United States of America under [...] and that, accordingly, the claim of the Islamic Republic of Iran for reparation also cannot be upheld; [...].'*	Declaratory Rejects reparation
58.	**Application of the Convention on the Prevention and Punishment of the Crime of Genocide**, 2007	*'[...] (2) [...] Finds that Serbia has not committed genocide [...]; (5) [...] Finds that Serbia has violated the obligation to prevent genocide [...];'*	Declaratory Specific performance Satisfaction: the judgment itself Rejected compensation and Guarantees of non-repetition

(8) [...] Decides that Serbia shall immediately take effective steps to ensure full compliance with its obligation [...];
(9) [...] Finds that, as regards the breaches by Serbia of the obligations referred to in subparagraphs (5) and (7) above, the Court's findings in those paragraphs constitute appropriate satisfaction, and that the case is not one in which an order for payment of compensation, or, in respect of the violation referred to in subparagraph (5), a direction to provide assurances and guarantees of non-repetition would be appropriate.'

| 59. | **Land and Maritime Boundary between Cameroon and Nigeria, 2002** | *'I. (A) [...] Decides that the boundary between the Republic of Cameroon and the Federal Republic of Nigeria in the Lake Chad area is delimited by [...]; [...] V. (A) [...] Decides that the Federal Republic of Nigeria is under an obligation expeditiously and without condition to withdraw its administration and its military and police forces from the territories, which fall within the sovereignty of the Republic of Cameroon [...];'* | Declaratory Specific performance |

(continued)

No.	Case Name and Parties	Judgment of the Court	Type
60.	Fisheries Jurisdiction, 1998	'Finds that it has no jurisdiction to adjudicate upon the dispute brought before it'	NA
61.	Request for an Examination of the Situation in Accordance with Paragraph 63 of the Court's Judgment of 20 December 1974 in the Nuclear Tests, 1995	'(1) [. . .] Finds that the 'Request for an Examination of the Situation' [. . .], does not fall within the provisions of the said paragraph 63 and must consequently be dismissed; [. . .].'	NA
62.	Vienna Convention on Consular Relations, 1998	Discontinued by Paraguay.	NA
63.	Request for Interpretation of the Judgment of 11 June 1998 in the Case concerning the Land and Maritime Boundary between Cameroon and Nigeria, 1999	'(1) [. . .] Declares inadmissible the request for interpretation of the Judgment of 11 June 1998 [. . .];'	NA
64.	Ahmadou Sadio Diallo, 2010	'[. . .] (2) [. . .] Finds that, in respect of the circumstances in which Mr. Diallo was expelled from Congolese territory on 31 January 1996, the Democratic Republic of the Congo violated Article [. . .]; [. . .] (7) [. . .] Finds that the Democratic Republic of the Congo is under obligation to make appropriate reparation, in the form of compensation, [. . .]'	Declaratory Compensation

(8) [. . .] Decides that, failing agreement between the Parties on this matter within six months from the date of this Judgment, the question of compensation due to the Republic of Guinea shall be settled by the Court, and reserves for this purpose the subsequent procedure in the case.'

Judgment on Compensation

'(1) [. . .] Fixes the amount of compensation due from the Democratic Republic of the Congo to the Republic of Guinea for the non-material injury suffered by Mr. Diallo [. . .];'

65. LaGrand, 2001

'[. . .] (3) [. . .] Finds that, [. . .] the United States of America breached its obligations to the Federal Republic of Germany and to the LaGrand brothers [. . .];

[. . .] (6) [. . .] Takes note of the commitment undertaken by the United States of America to ensure implementation of the specific measures adopted in performance of its obligations under [. . .];

and finds that this commitment must be regarded as meeting the Federal Republic of Germany's request for a general assurance of non-repetition

Declaratory Guarantee of non-repetition declaration made by USA Specific performance

(continued)

No.	Case Name and Parties	Judgment of the Court	Type
		(7) [...] Finds that should nationals of the Federal Republic of Germany nonetheless be sentenced to severe penalties, without their rights under Article 36, paragraph 1 (b), of the Convention having been respected, the United States of America, by means of its own choosing, shall allow the review and reconsideration of the conviction and sentence by taking account of the violation of the rights set forth in that Convention.'	
66.	**Legality of Use of Force, 2004**	*'Finds that it has no jurisdiction to entertain the claims made in the Application [...].'*	NA
67.	**Legality of Use of Force (Serbia and Montenegro v. Canada), 2004**	*'Finds that it has no jurisdiction to entertain the claims made in the Application [...].'*	NA
68.	**Legality of Use of Force (Serbia and Montenegro v. France), 2004**	*'Finds that it has no jurisdiction to entertain the claims made in the Application [...].'*	NA
69.	**Legality of Use of Force (Serbia and Montenegro v. Germany), 2004**	*'Finds that it has no jurisdiction to entertain the claims made in the Application [...].'*	NA

No.	Case	Decision	
70.	Legality of Use of Force (Serbia and Montenegro v. Italy), 2004	'Finds that it has no jurisdiction to entertain the claims made in the Application [...].'	NA
71.	Legality of Use of Force (Serbia and Montenegro v. Netherlands), 2004	'Finds that it has no jurisdiction to entertain the claims made in the Application [...].'	NA
72.	Legality of Use of Force (Serbia and Montenegro v. Portugal), 2004	'Finds that it has no jurisdiction to entertain the claims made in the Application [...].'	NA
73.	Legality of Use of Force (Yugoslavia v. Spain) 1999	The Court concluded that in this case it manifestly lacked jurisdiction.	NA
74.	Legality of Use of Force (Serbia and Montenegro v. United Kingdom) 2004	'Finds that it has no jurisdiction to entertain the claims made in the Application [...].'	NA
75.	Legality of Use of Force (Yugoslavia v. United States of America) 1999	The Court concluded that in this case it manifestly lacked jurisdiction.	NA
76.	Armed Activities on the Territory of the Congo, 2001	Discontinued by the Democratic Republic of the Congo.	NA
77.	Armed Activities on the Territory of the Congo (Democratic Republic of the Congo v. Uganda) 2005	'(1) [...] Finds that the Republic of Uganda, [...] violated the principle of non-use of force in international relations and the principle of non-intervention; [...] (5) [...] Finds that the Republic of Uganda is under obligation to make reparation to the Democratic Republic of the Congo for the injury caused; [...].'	Declaratory Reparation

(continued)

No.	Case Name and Parties	Judgment of the Court	Type
78.	**Armed Activities on the Territory of the Congo (Democratic Republic of the Congo v. Rwanda) 2001**	Discontinued by the Democratic Republic of the Congo.	NA
79.	**Application of the Convention on the Prevention and Punishment of the Crime of Genocide, 2015**	*'[...] (2) [...] Rejects Croatia's claim; (3) [...] Rejects Serbia's counter-claim.'*	Claim rejected
80.	**Aerial Incident of 10 August 1999, 2000**	*'Finds that it has no jurisdiction to entertain the Application [...].'*	NA
81.	**Territorial and Maritime Dispute between Nicaragua and Honduras in the Caribbean Sea, 2007**	*'(1) [...] Finds that the Republic of Honduras has sovereignty over [...]; [...] (4) [...] Finds that the Parties must negotiate in good faith with a view to agreeing on the course of the delimitation line of that portion of the territorial sea located between the endpoint of the land boundary as established by the 1906 Arbitral Award [...]'*	Declaratory Specific performance
82.	**Arrest Warrant of 11 April 2000, 2002**	*'[...] (2) [...] Finds that the issue against Mr. Abdulaye Yerodia Ndombasi [...], constituted violations of a legal obligation of the Kingdom of Belgium towards the Democratic Republic of the Congo, [...]; (3) [...] Finds that the Kingdom of Belgium must, by means of its own choosing, cancel the arrest warrant of 11 April 2000 and so inform the authorities to whom that warrant was circulated.'*	Declaratory Specific performance

83.	Application for Revision of the Judgment of 11 July 1996 in the Case concerning Application of the Convention on the Prevention and Punishment of the Crime of Genocide, 2003	*'Finds that the Application submitted by the Federal Republic of Yugoslavia for revision, under Article 61 of the Statute of the Court, of the Judgment given by the Court on 11 July 1996, is inadmissible.'*	NA
84.	Certain Property, 2005	*'[...] (2) [...] Finds that it has no jurisdiction to entertain the Application [...]'*	NA
85.	Territorial and Maritime Dispute, 2012	*'(1) [...] Finds that the Republic of Colombia has sovereignty over the islands [...];'*	Declaratory
86.	Armed Activities on the Territory of the Congo (New Application: 2002) (Democratic Republic of the Congo v. Rwanda) 2006	*'Finds that it has no jurisdiction to entertain the Application [...].'*	NA
87.	Application for Revision of the Judgment of 11 September 1992 in the Case concerning the Land, Island and Maritime Frontier Dispute (El Salvador/Honduras: Nicaragua intervening) (El Salvador v. Honduras) 2003	*'Finds that the Application submitted by the Republic of El Salvador for revision, [...] is inadmissible.'*	NA
88.	Avena and Other Mexican Nationals, 2004	*'[...] (4) [...] Finds that, [...] the obligations incumbent upon it under that subparagraph; [...]* *(9) [...] Finds that the appropriate reparation in this case consists in the*	Declaratory Specific performance Guarantees of non-repetition

(continued)

No.	Case Name and Parties	Judgment of the Court	Type
		obligation of the United States of America to provide, by means of its own choosing, review and reconsideration of the convictions and sentences of the Mexican nationals referred to in subparagraphs [. . .]; (10) *[. . .] Takes note of the commitment undertaken by the United States of America to ensure implementation of the specific measures [. . .];* *and finds that this commitment must be regarded as meeting the request by the United Mexican States for guarantees and assurances of non-repetition; [. . .].'*	
89.	**Certain Criminal Proceedings in France,** 2010	Discontinued by the Republic of the Congo.	NA
90.	**Maritime Delimitation in the Black Sea,** 2009	*'Decides that starting from Point 1, as agreed by the Parties in Article 1 of the 2003 State Border Régime Treaty, the line of the single maritime boundary delimiting the continental shelf and the exclusive economic zones of Romania and Ukraine in the Black Sea shall follow the 12- nautical-mile arc of the territorial sea of Ukraine around Serpents' Island [. . .]'*	Declaratory

91.	Dispute regarding Navigational and Related Rights, 2009	'(1) As regards Costa Rica's navigational rights on the San Juan River under the 1858 Treaty, in that part where navigation is common, (a) [...] Finds that Costa Rica has the right of free navigation on the San Juan River for purposes of commerce; [...] (5) [...] Rejects all other submissions presented by Costa Rica and Nicaragua.'	Declaratory No reparation
92.	Status vis-à-vis the Host State of a Diplomatic Envoy to the United Nations, 2006	Discontinued by the Commonwealth of Dominica.	NA
93.	Pulp Mills on the River Uruguay, 2010	'(1) [...] Finds that the Eastern Republic of Uruguay has breached its procedural obligations [...] and that the declaration by the Court of this breach constitutes appropriate satisfaction; [...].'	Declaratory Satisfaction: declaration of breach
94.	Certain Questions of Mutual Assistance in Criminal Matters, 2008	'[...] (2) [...] (a) [...] Finds that the French Republic, [...] failed to comply with its international obligation [...], and that its finding of this violation constitutes appropriate satisfaction; (b) [...] Rejects all other final submissions presented by the Republic of Djibouti.'	Declaratory Satisfaction: declaration of breach Rejects specific performance, cessation or guarantee of non-repetition
95.	Maritime Dispute, 2014	'(1) [...] Decides that the starting-point of the single maritime boundary delimiting the respective maritime areas between the Republic of Peru and the Republic of Chile is [...];'	Declaratory

(continued)

(continued)

No.	Case Name and Parties	Judgment of the Court	Type
96.	**Aerial Herbicide Spraying, 2013**	Discontinued by Ecuador.	NA
97.	**Request for Interpretation of the Judgment of 31 March 2004 in the Case concerning Avena and Other Mexican Nationals, 2009**	'[...] (2) [...] *Finds that the United States of America has breached the obligation incumbent upon it under [...];* (3) [...] *Reaffirms the continuing binding character of the obligations of the United States of America [...] and takes note of the undertakings given by the United States of America in these proceedings;* (4) [...] *Declines, in these circumstances, the request of the United Mexican States for the Court to order the United States of America to provide guarantees of non-repetition; [...].'*	Declaratory Rejects Guarantees of non-repetition
98.	**Application of the International Convention on the Elimination of All Forms of Racial Discrimination, 2011**	'[...] (2) [...] *Finds that it has no jurisdiction to entertain the Application [...].'*	NA
99.	**Application of the Interim Accord of 13 September 1995, 2011**	'[...] (2) [...] *Finds that the Hellenic Republic, by objecting to the admission of the former Yugoslav Republic of Macedonia to NATO, has breached its obligation under Article 11, paragraph 1, of the Interim Accord of 13 September 1995; [...].'*	Declaratory
100.	**Jurisdictional Immunities of the State, 2012**	'(1) [...] *Finds that the Italian Republic has violated its obligation [...]; [...]*	Declaratory Specific performance

		(4) [. . .] Finds that the Italian Republic must, by enacting appropriate legislation, or by resorting to other methods of its choosing, ensure that the decisions of its courts and those of other judicial authorities infringing the immunity which the Federal Republic of Germany enjoys under international law cease to have effect; [. . .].'	
101.	Questions relating to the Obligation to Prosecute or Extradite, 2012	*'[. . .] (4) [. . .] Finds that the Republic of Senegal, [. . .], has breached its obligation under Article [. . .];* *(6) [. . .] Finds that the Republic of Senegal must, without further delay, submit the case of Mr. Hissène Habré to its competent authorities for the purpose of prosecution, if it does not extradite him.'*	Declaratory Specific performance
102.	Certain Questions concerning Diplomatic Relations, 2010	Discontinued by Honduras.	NA
103.	Jurisdiction and Enforcement of Judgments in Civil and Commercial Matters, 2011	Discontinued by Belgium.	NA
104.	Whaling in the Antarctic, 2014	*'[. . .] (2) [. . .] Finds that the special permits [. . .] do not fall within the provisions of [. . .];* *(7) [. . .] Decides that Japan shall revoke any extant authorization, permit or licence granted in relation to JARPA II, and refrain from granting any further permits in pursuance of that programme.'*	Declaratory Specific performance

(continued)

No.	Case Name and Parties	Judgment of the Court	Type
105.	Certain Activities carried out by Nicaragua in the Border Area (Costa Rica v. Nicaragua) 2015 joined with Construction of a Road in Costa Rica along the San Juan River (Nicaragua v. Costa Rica)	'(1) [...] *Finds that Costa Rica has sovereignty over the 'disputed territory', as defined by the Court in paragraphs 69–70 of the present Judgment;* [...] *(5) (a)* [...] *Finds that Nicaragua has the obligation to compensate Costa Rica* [...];' Judgment on Compensation '(1) *Fixes the following amounts for the compensation due from the Republic of Nicaragua to the Republic of Costa Rica for environmental damage caused by the Republic of Nicaragua's unlawful activities on Costa Rican territory:* [...].'	Declaratory Compensation
106.	Request for Interpretation of the Judgment of 15 June 1962 in the Case concerning the Temple of Preah Vihear, 2013	'[...] (2) [...] *Declares, by way of interpretation, that the Judgment of 15 June 1962 decided that Cambodia had sovereignty over the whole territory of the promontory of Preah Vihear, as defined in paragraph 98 of the present Judgment, and that, in consequence, Thailand was under an obligation to withdraw from that territory the Thai military or police forces, or other guards or keepers, that were stationed there.*'	Declaratory

107.	**Construction of a Road in Costa Rica along the San Juan River, 2015** Proceedings joined with Certain Activities carried out by Nicaragua in the Border Area (Costa Rica v. Nicaragua) on 17 April 2013	*'(1) [. . .] Finds that Costa Rica has sovereignty over the 'disputed territory' [. . .]; (5) (a) [. . .] Finds that Nicaragua has the obligation to compensate Costa Rica for material damages [. . .];'* <u>Judgment on Compensation</u> *'(1) Fixes the following amounts for the compensation due from the Republic of Nicaragua to the Republic of Costa Rica for environmental damage caused by the Republic of Nicaragua's unlawful activities on Costa Rican territory: [. . .].'*	Declaratory Compensation
108.	**Obligation to Negotiate Access to the Pacific Ocean, 2018**	*'(1) [. . .] Finds that the Republic of Chile did not undertake a legal obligation to negotiate a sovereign access to the Pacific Ocean for the Plurinational State of Bolivia; [. . .].'*	Declaratory
109.	**Question of the Delimitation of the Continental Shelf between Nicaragua and Colombia beyond 200 nautical miles from the Nicaraguan Coast**	Note: Judgment on the merits is pending. By Judgment of 17 March 2016, the Court found that it had jurisdiction to entertain the First Request put forward by Nicaragua.	NA
110.	**Alleged Violations of Sovereign Rights and Maritime Spaces in the Caribbean Sea**	Note: Judgment on the merits is pending. By Judgment of 17 March 2016, the Court found that it had jurisdiction to entertain part of the request put forward by Nicaragua.	NA

(continued)

No.	Case Name and Parties	Judgment of the Court	Type
111.	**Questions relating to the Seizure and Detention of Certain Documents and Data, 2015**	Discontinued by Timor-Leste.	NA
112.	**Maritime Delimitation in the Caribbean Sea and the Pacific Ocean, 2018** Proceedings joined with Land Boundary in the Northern Part of Isla Portillos (Costa Rica v. Nicaragua) on 2 February 2017	*'[…] (2) […] Finds that the Republic of Costa Rica has sovereignty over the whole northern part of Isla Portillos, […]; […] (3) […] (b) Finds that the Republic of Nicaragua must remove its military camp from Costa Rican territory; […].'*	Declaratory Specific performance
113.	**Obligations concerning Negotiations relating to Cessation of the Nuclear Arms Race and to Nuclear Disarmament (Marshall Islands v. India) 2016**	*'(1) […] Upholds the objection to jurisdiction raised by India, based on the absence of a dispute between the Parties; (2) […] Finds that it cannot proceed to the merits of the case.'*	NA
114.	**Obligations concerning Negotiations relating to Cessation of the Nuclear Arms Race and to Nuclear Disarmament (Marshall Islands v. Pakistan) 2016**	*'(1) […] Upholds the objection to jurisdiction raised by Pakistan, based on the absence of a dispute between the Parties; (2) […] Finds that it cannot proceed to the merits of the case.'*	NA
115.	**Obligations concerning Negotiations relating to Cessation of the Nuclear Arms Race and to Nuclear Disarmament (Marshall Islands v. United Kingdom), 2016**	*(1) […] Upholds the first preliminary objection to jurisdiction raised by the United Kingdom of Great Britain and Northern Ireland, based on the absence of a dispute between the Parties; (2) […] Finds that it cannot proceed to the merits of the case.'*	NA

116.	**Maritime Delimitation in the Indian Ocean**	Note: judgment on merits is pending.	NA
117.	**Dispute over the Status and Use of the Waters of the Silala**	Note: judgment is pending.	NA
118.	**Immunities and Criminal Proceedings**	Note: judgment on merits is pending.	NA
119.	**Certain Iranian Assets**	Note: judgment on merits is pending.	NA
120.	**Land Boundary in the Northern Part of Isla Portillos, 2018** Proceedings joined with Maritime Delimitation in the Caribbean Sea and the Pacific Ocean (Costa Rica v. Nicaragua) on 2 February 2017	*'[. . .] (2) [. . .] Finds that the Republic of Costa Rica has sovereignty over the whole northern part of Isla Portillos [. . .] (3) [. . .] (b) Finds that the Republic of Nicaragua must remove its military camp from Costa Rican territory; [. . .].'*	Declaratory Specific performance
121.	**Application of the International Convention for the Suppression of the Financing of Terrorism and of the International Convention on the Elimination of All Forms of Racial Discrimination**	Note: judgment on merits is pending.	NA
122.	**Application for Revision of the Judgment of 23 May 2008 in the Case concerning Sovereignty over Pedra Branca/Pulau Batu Puteh, Middle Rocks and South Ledge**	Discontinued by agreement of the Parties.	NA
123.	**Jadhav Case, 2018**	*'[. . .] (3) [. . .] Finds that, [. . .], the Islamic Republic of Pakistan breached the obligations incumbent upon it under that provision; [. . .]*	Declaratory Specific performance Reparation in the form of specific performance

(continued)

No.	Case Name and Parties	Judgment of the Court	Type
		(6) [. . .] Finds that the Islamic Republic of Pakistan is under an obligation to inform Mr. Kulbhushan Sudhir Jadhav without further delay of his rights and to provide Indian consular officers access to him [. . .]; (7) [. . .] Finds that the appropriate reparation in this case consists in the obligation of the Islamic Republic of Pakistan to provide, by the means of its own choosing, effective review and reconsideration of the conviction and sentence of Mr. Kulbhushan Sudhir Jadhav; [. . .].'	
124.	**Request for Interpretation of the Judgment of 23 May 2008 in the Case concerning Sovereignty over Pedra Branca/Pulau Batu Puteh, Middle Rocks and South Ledge, 2018**	Discontinued by agreement of the Parties	NA
125.	**Arbitral Award of 3 October 1899**	Note: judgment is pending	NA
126.	**Application of the International Convention on the Elimination of All Forms of Racial Discrimination**	Note: judgment is pending	NA

127.	Appeal Relating to the Jurisdiction of the ICAO Council under Article 84 of the Convention on International Civil Aviation	Note: judgment is pending	NA
128.	Appeal Relating to the Jurisdiction of the ICAO Council under Article II, Section 2, of the 1944 International Air Services Transit Agreement	Note: judgment is pending	NA
129.	Alleged Violations of the 1955 Treaty of Amity, Economic Relations, and Consular Rights	Note: judgment is pending	NA
130.	Relocation of the United States Embassy to Jerusalem	Note: judgment is pending	NA
131.	Application of the Convention on the Prevention and Punishment of the Crime of Genocide	Note: judgment is pending	NA

Bibliography

A BOOKS

Amerasinghe CF, *Jurisdiction of Specific International Tribunals* (Martinus Nijhoff, 2009)

Amr MSM, *The Role of the International Court of Justice As the Principal Judicial Organ of the United Nations* (Kluwer Law International, 2003)

Boas G, *Public International Law: Contemporary Principles and Perspectives* (Edward Elgar Publishing, 2012)

Boczek BA, *International Law: A Dictionary* (Scarecrow Press, 2005)

Brownlie I, *System of the Law of Nations – State Responsibility Part 1* (Oxford University Press, 1983)

Bulto TS, *The Extraterritorial Application of the Human Rights to Water in Africa* (Cambridge University Press, 2014)

Cheng B, *General Principles of Law As Applied by International Courts and Tribunals* (Cambridge University Press, 2006)

Couvreur P, *The International Court of Justice and the Effectiveness of International Law* (Brill/Nijhoff, 2017)

Crawford J, *The International Law Commission's Articles on State Responsibility: Introduction, Text and Commentaries* (Cambridge University Press, 2002)

   Brownlie's Principles of Public International Law (8th edn, Oxford University Press, 2012)

   State Responsibility: The General Part (Cambridge University Press, 2014)

de Brabandere E, *Investment Treaty Arbitration As Public International Law: Procedural Aspects and Implications* (Cambridge University Press, 2014)

de Visscher C, *Aspects récents du droit procédural de la Cour internationale de Justice* (A. Pedone, 1966)

Forlati S, *The International Court of Justice: An Arbitral Tribunal or a Judicial Body?* (Springer, 2014)

García Amador FV, Sohn LB and Baxter RR, *Recent Codification of the Law of State Responsibility for Injuries to Aliens* (Martinus Nijhoff Publishers, 1974)

Gardiner RK, *International Law* (Pearson Education Limited, 2003)

Gray CD, *Judicial Remedies in International Law* (Clarendon Press, 1990)

Guo R, *Territorial Disputes and Conflict Management: The Art of Avoiding War* (Routledge, 2012)

Bibliography

Kaczorowska A, *Public International Law* (Routledge, 2010)

Kolb R, *The International Court of Justice* (Hart Publishing, 2013)

Lamn V, *Compulsory Jurisdiction in International Law* (Edward Elgar Publishing, 2014)

Lauterpacht H, *The Development of International Law by the International Court* (Cambridge University Press, 1982)

The Function of Law in the International Community (Oxford University Press, 1933)

Leckie S and Huggins C, *Conflict and Housing, Land and Property Rights: A Handbook on Issues, Frameworks, and Solutions* (Cambridge University Press, 2011)

Lefeber R, *Transboundary Environmental Interference and the Origin of State Liability* (Kluwer Law International, 1996)

Mann FA, *Further Studies in International Law* (Oxford University Press, 1990)

Martha RSJ, *The Financial Obligation in International Law* (Oxford University Press, 2015)

Martin FF, Schnably SJ, Wilson R, Simon J and Tushnet M, *International Human Rights and Humanitarian Law: Treaties Cases and Analysis* (Cambridge University Press, 2006)

Matheson MJ, *International Tribunals and Armed Conflict* (Martinus Nijhoff Publishers, 2012)

Noortmann M, *Enforcing International Law: From Self-help to Self-contained Regimes* (Ashgate Publishing, 2005)

Pronto A and Wood M, *The International Law Commission 1999–2009 Volume 4, Treaties, Final Draft Articles and Other Materials* (Oxford University Press, 2010)

Quintana JJ, *Litigation at the International Court of Justice: Practice and Procedure* (Brill/Nijhoff, 2015)

Ripinsky S and Williams K, *Damages in International Investment Law* (British Institute of International and Comparative Law, 2008)

Rosenne S, *The Law and Practice of the International Court 1920–2005*, vol 1 (Martinus Nijhoff Publishers, 2006)

The Law and Practice of the International Court 1920–2005, vol 2 (Martinus Nijhoff Publishers, 2006)

Sabahi B, *Compensation and Restitution in Investor-State Arbitration: Principles and Practice* (Oxford University Press, 2011)

Schwebel SM, *Justice in International Law: Selected Writings of Judge Stephen M. Schwebel* (Cambridge University Press, 1994)

Shelton D, *Remedies in International Human Rights Law* (Oxford University Press, 2015)

Sornarajah M, *The Pursuit of Nationalized Property* (Martinus Nijhoff Publishers, 1986)

Tammelo I, *Justice and Doubt: An Essay on the Fundamentals of Justice* (Springer-Verlag, 1959)

Wang G, *International Investment Law: A Chinese Perspective* (Routledge, 2015)

Weisburd M, *Failings of the International Court of Justice* (Oxford University Press, 2016)

Wellens K, *Negotiations in the Case Law of the International Court of Justice: A Functional Analysis* (Routledge, 2014)

Bibliography

B CHAPTERS IN COLLECTIVE BOOKS AND COURSES OF THE HAGUE ACADEMY OF INTERNATIONAL LAW

Ajibola B, 'Compliance with Judgments of the International Court of Justice' in M Bulterman and M Kuijer (eds), *Compliance with Judgments of International Courts* (Martinus Nijhoff Publishers, 1996)

Barboza J, 'Legal Injury: The Tip of the Iceberg in International Responsibility' in Maurizio Ragazzi (ed), *International Responsibility Today: Essays in Memory of Oscar Schachter* (Brill/Nijhoff, 2005)

Barker J, 'The Different Forms of Reparation: Compensation' in James Crawford, Alain Pellet and Simon Olleson (eds), *The Law of International Responsibility* (Oxford University Press, 2010)

Bedjaoui M, 'An International Contentious Case on the Threshold of the Cold War' in Karine Bannelier, Théodore Christakis and Sarah Heathcote (eds), *The ICJ and the Evolution of International Law: The Enduring Impact of the Corfu Channel Case* (Routledge, 2012)

Brownlie I, 'International Law at the Fiftieth Anniversary of the United Nations. General Course on Public International Law (Volume 255)' in *Collected Courses of the Hague Academy of International Law* (Martinus Nijhoff Publishers, 1995)

'Remedies in the International Court of Justice' in Vaughn Lowe and Malgosia Fitzmaurice (eds), *Fifty Years of the International Court of Justice: Essays in Honour of Sir Robert Jennings* (Cambridge University Press, 1996)

Constantinides A, 'The Corfu Channel Case in Perspective: The Factual and Political Background' in Karine Bannelier, Théodore Christakis and Sarah Heathcote (eds), *The ICJ and the Evolution of International Law: The Enduring Impact of the Corfu Channel Case* (Routledge, 2012)

Crawford J, 'Flexibility in the Award of Reparation: Role of the Parties and the Tribunal' in Rüdiger Wolfrum, Maja Seršić and Trpimir Šošić (eds), *Contemporary Developments in International Law: Essays in Honor of Budislav Vukas* (Brill/Nijhoff, 2016)

'The International Court of Justice and the Law of State Responsibility' in Christian J Tams and James Sloan (eds), *The Development of International Law by the International Court of Justice* (Oxford University Press, 2013)

Couvreur P, 'The Effectiveness of the International Court of Justice in the Peaceful Settlement of International Disputes' in AS Muller, David Raic and JM Thuranszky (eds), *The International Court of Justice: Its Future Role after Fifty Years* (Martinus Nijhoff Publishers, 1997)

d'Argent P, 'Compliance, Cessation, Reparation and Restitution in the Wall Advisory Opinion' in Pierre-Marie Dupuy et al (eds), *Common Values in International Law: Essays in Honor of Christian Tomuschat* (Kehl, 2006)

'Reparation and Compliance' in Karine Bannelier, Theodore Christakis and Sarah Heathcote (eds), *The ICJ and the Evolution of International Law: The Enduring Impact of the Corfu Channel Case* (Routledge, 2012)

de Aréchaga EJ and Tanzi AM, 'International State Responsibility' in Mohammed Bedjaoui (ed), *International Law: Achievements and Prospects* (Martinus Nijhoff Publishers, 1991)

Fiedler W, 'Damages' in LindaJ Pike (ed), *Encyclopedia of Disputes Installment 10* (Elsevier, 2014)

Graefrath B, 'Responsibility and Damages Caused: Relationship between Responsibility and Damages' in The Hague Academy of International Law (ed), *Collected Courses of the Hague Academy of International Law vol 185* (Brill/Nijhoff, 1984)

Gray C, 'The Different Forms of Reparation: Restitution' in James Crawford, Alain Pellet and Simon Olleson (eds), *The Law of International Responsibility* (Oxford University Press, 2010)

Lekkas S and Tzanakopoulos A, '*Pacta sunt servanda* versus flexibility in the suspension and termination of treaties' in Christian J Tams, Antonios Tzanakopoulos and Andreas Zimmermann (eds), *Research Handbook on the Law of Treaties* (Edward Elgar Publishing, 2014)

Merkouris P, 'The Advisory Jurisdiction of the Permanent Court in Practice: A Tale of Two Scopes' in Christian J Tams and Malgosia Fitzmaurice (eds), *Legacies of the Permanent Court* (Martinus Nijhoff Publishing, 2013)

Miles CA, *Provisional Measures before International Courts and Tribunals* (Cambridge University Press, 2017)

Pellet A, 'Some Remarks on the Recent Case Law of the International Court of Justice on Responsibility Issues' in P Kovacs (ed), *International Law – A Quiet Strength. Le droit international – une force tranquille. (Miscellanea in memoriam Geza Herczegh)* (Pazmany Press, 2011)

Rasulov A, 'The Doctrine of Sources in the Discourse of the Permanent Court of International Justice' in Christian J Tams and Malgosia Fitzmaurice (eds), *Legacies of the Permanent Court of International Justice* (Martinus Nijhoff Publishing, 2013)

Riedel E, 'Satisfaction' in Linda J Pike (ed), *Encyclopedia of Disputes Installment 10* (Elsevier, 2014)

Schleker C, 'Reparations' in DP Forsythe (ed), *Encyclopedia of Human Rights, Volume 1* (Oxford University Press, 2009)

Schneider ME, 'Selected Other Cases' in ME Schneider and J Knoll (eds), *Performance As a Remedy: Non-monetary Relief in International Arbitration*, ASA Special Series No. 30 (JurisNet, 2011)

Shaw MN, 'A Practical Look at the International Court of Justice' in Malcolm Evans (ed), *Remedies in International Law: The Institutional Dilemma* (Hart Publishing, 1998)

'The International Court, Responsibility and Remedies' in Malgosia Fitzmaurice and Dan Sarooshi (eds), *Issues of State Responsibility before International Judicial Institutions* (Hart Publishing, 2004)

Sperduti G, 'Restitution' in LindaJ Pike (ed), *Encyclopedia of Disputes Installment 10* (Elsevier, 2014)

Stern B, 'A Plea for Reconstruction of International Responsibility Based on the Notion of Legal Injury' in Maurizio Ragazzi (ed), *International Responsibility Today: Essays in Memory of Oscar Schachter* (Brill/Nijhoff, 2005)

Tams CJ, 'Law-making in Complex Processes: The World Court and the Modern Law of State Responsibility' in Christine Chinkin and Freya Baetens (eds), *Sovereignty, Statehood and State Responsibility – Essays in Honor of James Crawford* (Cambridge University Press, 2015)

Tomka P, 'The Special Agreement' in Nisuke Ando, Edward McWhinney and Rüdiger Wolfrum (eds), *Judge Shigeru Oda: Liber Amicorum* vol 1 (Kluwer Law International, 2002)

Tomuschat C, 'International Crimes by States: An Endangered Species?' in Karel Wellens (ed), *International Law: Theory and Practice: Essays in Honour of Eric Suy* (Martinus Nijhoff Publishers, 1998)

'Article 36' in Andreas Zimmerman, Christian Tomuschat, Karin Oellers-Frahm and Christian J Tams (eds), *The Statute of the International Court of Justice – A Commentary* (Oxford University Press, 2012)

Van Aaken A, 'Primary and Secondary Remedies in International Investment Law and National State Liability: A Functional and Comparative View' in Stephen W Schill (ed), *International Investment Law and Comparative Public Law* (Oxford University Press, 2010)

White G, 'The Use of Experts by the International Court of Justice' in Robert Yewdall Jennings, Vaughn Lowe and Malgosia Fitzmaurice (eds), *Fifty Years of the International Court of Justice: Essays in Honour of Sir Robert Jennings* (Cambridge University Press, 1996)

Wittich S, 'Punitive Damages' in James Crawford, Alain Pellet and Simon Olleson (eds), *The Law of International Responsibility* (Oxford University Press, 2010)

'The PCIJ and the Modern International Law of Treaties' in Christian J Tams and Malgosia Fitzmaurice (eds), *Legacies of the Permanent Court of International Justice* (Martinus Nijhoff Publishing, 2013)

C ARTICLES

Barthe-Gay C, 'Réflexions sur la satisfaction en droit international' (2003) 49 *Annuaire Français de Droit International*

Bejesky R, 'The Evolution in and International Convergence of the Doctrine of Specific Performance in Three Types of States' (2003) 13:2 *Indiana International & Comparative Law Review* 353

Boisson de Chazournes L, 'Plurality in the Fabric of International Courts and Tribunals: The Threads of a Managerial Approach' (2017) 28:1 *European Journal of International Law* 13

Borchard E, 'The Declaratory Judgment – A Needed Procedural Reform' (1918) 28 *Yale Law Journal* 105, as cited in Juliette McIntyre, 'Declaratory Judgements of the International Court of Justice' (2012) 25 Hague Yearbook of International Law

Deman C, 'Cessation de l'Acte Illicite' (1990) 23:2 *Belgian Review of International Law*,

Dizgovin FR, 'Foundations of Specific Performance in Investor-State Dispute Settlements: Is It Possible and Desirable?' (2016) 28:1 *Florida Journal of International Law*

Gray CD, 'The Choice between Restitution and Compensation' (1999) 10:2 *European Journal of International Law*

Kammerhofer J, 'The Binding Nature of Provisional Measures of the International Court of Justice: The "Settlement" of the Issue in the LaGrand Case' (2003) 16 *Leiden Journal of International Law*

Llamzon AP, 'Jurisdiction and Compliance in Recent Decisions of the International Court of Justice' (2005) 18:5 *European Journal of International Law*

McIntyre J, 'Declaratory Judgments of the International Court of Justice' (2012) 25 *Hague Yearbook of International Law*

Milano E and Papanicolopulu I, 'State Responsibility in Disputed Areas on Land and at Sea' (2011) 71 *Houston Journal of International Law*

Musgrave TD, 'Comparative Contractual Remedies' (2009) 34:2 *University of Wollongong Australia, Law Review*

Nikièma SH, 'Compensation for Expropriation' International Institute for Sustainable Development – Best Practices Series (2013)

Orakhelashvili A, 'Peremptory Norms for International Wrongful Acts' (2003) 3:1 *Baltic Yearbook of International Law*

Parish MT, Nelson AK and Rosenberg CB, 'Awarding Moral Damages to Respondent States in Investment Arbitration' (2011) 29:1 *Berkeley Journal of International Law*

Ratner ST, 'Compensation for Expropriation in a World of Investment Treaties: Beyond the Lawful/Unlawful Distinction' (2017) 111 *American Journal of International Law*

Reisman WM, 'The Enforcement of International Judgments and Awards' (1969) 63 *American Journal of International Law*

Schreuer C, 'Non-pecuniary Remedies in ICSID Arbitration' (2004) 20:4 *Arbitration International*

Shelton D, 'Righting Wrongs: Reparations in the Articles on State Responsibility' (2002) 96 *American Journal of International Law*

Tams CJ, 'Recognizing Assurance and Guarantees of Non Repetition: LaGrand and the Law of State Responsibility' (2002) 27:2 *Yale Journal of International Law*

Tcheuwa JC, 'Communauté internationale, guerre et responsabilité: réflexion autour de la responsabilité internationale des états' (2005) 58:1 *Revue Hellénique de Droit International*

Tomka P, 'The Role of the International Court of Justice in World Affairs: Successes and Challenges' with Special Reference to OAS Member States and the Pact of Bogotá (Lecture Series of the Americas, 10 April 2014)

Tranel AM, 'The Ruling of the International Court of Justice in Avena and Other Mexican Nationals: Enforcing the Right to Consular Assistance in U.S. Jurisprudence' (2005) 20:2 *American University International Law Review*

Uchkunova I, 'Provisional Measures before the International Court of Justice' (Brill/Nijhoff, 2013) 12:3 *The Law & Practice of International Courts and Tribunals*

Wittich S, 'Compensation' in *Max Planck Encyclopaedia of Public International Law* (2008) vol 1

Yearbook of Institute of International Law – Session of Hyderabad 2017, vol 78, Deliberations

Zyberi G, 'The International Court of Justice and Applied Forms of Reparation for International Human Rights and Humanitarian Law Violations' (2011) 7:1 *Utrecht Law Review*

D WORKS OF THE INTERNATIONAL LAW COMMISSION AND DOCUMENTS OF THE UNITED NATIONS

ILC, '2001 Articles on Responsibility of States for Internationally Wrongful Acts', UN Doc A/56/83 (2001)

'Draft Articles on Responsibility of States for Internationally Wrongful Acts With Commentaries' (2001) II:2 YBILC

ILC Report, 'Draft Articles on Diplomatic Protection', Official Records of the General Assembly, Sixty-first Session, Supplement No. 10, UN Doc A/61/10 (2006)

Gaetano Arangio-Ruiz, 'Preliminary Report on State Responsibility' UN Doc A/CN.4/416 & Corr.1 & 2 and Add.1 & Corr.1 (1988) II:1 YBILC

United Nations General Assembly Resolution 1803 (XVII) on 'Permanent Sovereignty over Natural Resources' (1962)

Convention on Consular Relations, United Nations, *Treaty Series* (1963) vol 1, 596, p. 261

Convention on the Prevention and Punishment of the Crime of Genocide, United Nations, *Treaty Series* (1951) vol 78, p. 277

Index

agreement, special
  cooperation, 44
  delimitation, 37, 39
  judgments, declaratory, 41, 43
  notification, 22, 26, 37
  performance, specific, 57
  procedure, 22, 42, 45
  remedies, 2, 12, 22
  resolution, dispute, 38
application, unilateral
  compensation, 115, 117, 121
  judgments, declaratory, 22, 41
  political, 42
  procedure, 22, 44
  remedies, 44, 99
  requests, 100
  seizure, 43
  territorial, 40
award
  amount, 127, 130
  cessation, 65
  compensation, 108–109,
    131
  damages, 117, 120, 132, 159
  declaratory, 27, 57
  implementation, 25
  judgments, declaratory,
    145
  reparation, 131
  restitution, 87, 91
  satisfaction, 155
  tribunal, arbitral, 162
Azavedo, 147, 150

bifurcation, 139
Brownlie, 113, 165

compensation
  availability, 94
  damages, environmental, 89–90, 132, 135, 141
  damages, material, 40, 109, 113, 118–119,
    123–125, 129, 131, 160
  damages, moral, 5, 19, 109, 113, 118–119, 121,
    128–129, 131, 136, 140, 142–143, 157, 160,
    162, 164
  damages, non-material, 40, 129, 142–143, 148,
    154
  damages, punitive, 113, 132, 159, 162
  remedies, 5, 113, 138, 145
  reparation, 108, 112
  restitution in kind, 93
  substantiation, 116, 119, 121, 123, 125–126,
    128–129, 139, 141, 144, 163
compliance, 28, 53, 59, 73, 75–77, 79, 167, 169
Crawford, 2, 48, 66–67, 71–72, 165

declaration
  of applicable law, 25, 34
  compensation, 77, 121, 128
  of illegality, 25
  measures, provisional, 19
  non-repetition, 70, 72, 78
  performance, specific, 28, 52, 55–56
  of principle, 96
  remedies, coercive, 94
  responsibility, of, 23, 27, 35, 119
  restitution, 84
  of rights, 23, 25, 32–33, 38
  satisfaction, 146, 150, 152, 154–155, 162
  of title, 23
  wrongfulness, 116, 120
delimitation
  boundary, 32

283

284 Index

delimitation (cont.)
  disputes, 32, 38
  maritime, 32, 34, 40, 122
  principles,rules, 43
  territorial, 21, 32, 36, 38, 40, 42, 152
dictum, obiter
  compensation, 109, 113
  expropriation, 96, 105
  findings, principle, 150
  jurisprudence, 4
  reparation, 93, 138
  restitution, 82, 85, 87, 95–96,
    104
diplomacy
  mechanisms, 7
  relationship, 71–72, 79
  resolution, dispute, 39
dispositif
  cessation, 74, 78
  compensation, 10
  conduct, 27, 29
  damages, 159
  declaratory, 27, 56
  performance, specific, 51, 58
  restitution, 93

election, right of, 48, 54, 86–87
enforcement, 79, 166
equity, 91, 130, 142–143, 149, 158
evidence
  compensation, 117, 124, 129
  documentary, 78
  substantiation, 120, 128
  valuation, 126
experts
  appointment, 139
  compensation, amount, 6, 109, 137, 139,
    143
  nomination, 110
  valuation, 125
expropriation
  compensation, 116, 137
  concept, 98
  conditions, 97
  consequences, 97
  contextualization, 97
  determination, 97
  lawful, 96–97, 99, 136
  legality, 102
  qualification, 136
  remedies, 21

restitution, 93, 95–96
right, of, 98
unlawful, 96–97, 99, 102, 105–106, 115,
  136–137

faith, good
  negotiation, 58
  obligation, implementation, 76
force, use of, 27, 33, 35, 40, 56, 73

Gray, 2, 31, 66, 106, 165

Human Rights, European Court of, 3, 158
Human Rights, Inter-American Court of, 158

ILC Articles
  application, 6, 165
  Article 29, 47
  Article 30, 64, 68
  Article 31, 111
  Article 34, 85, 111
  Article 35, 83, 85, 90, 105, 148
  Article 36, 111, 114, 148
  Article 37, 148, 152
  Article 43, 86
  Article 48, 71
  Article 48(1), 67
  cessation, 64–65, 68
  commentary, 3, 62, 64–65, 67, 71, 76, 90,
    108, 113, 123, 129, 148, 152, 159
  compensation, 26, 108, 111, 113, 123, 129–130,
    154
  election, right of, 86
  framework, 7
  non-repetition, 62, 64, 68, 70–71, 76
  performance, specific, 47, 67
  remedies, 2, 8, 13, 19, 34, 166
  restitution, 83, 85, 90, 95, 105–106
  rules, basic, 3
  satisfaction, 146, 148–149, 152, 155, 159
  theory, 4
impossibility, material, 67, 83, 87, 89–90,
    96–97, 103, 117
indemnity, 85
injunction, 49, 52, 59
injury
  cessation, 62
  compensation, 124
  compensation, restitution, 148
  damages, material, 111–112
  damages, moral, 123, 129, 143, 149, 158, 163

Index

285

direct, 21, 36, 113, 130–131, 145, 159, 161
indirect, 113, 132
legal, 79
nexus, causal, 141
reparation, 40, 44
restitution, 92, 105
satisfaction, 150
International Law Commission, 2, 106, 112, 165

judgment, interim, 14, 16, 18
judicata, res, 23–24, 32
jurisdiction
  admissibility, 45
  agreement, special, 41, 44
  compensation, 124
  competence, 4–5, 9–10, 12, 14, 16, 23, 28, 30, 47, 82, 106
  inherent, 12, 50, 52, 55, 162
  judgments, declaratory, 30–32
  limitation, 36
  procedure, 22
  remedies, 5, 8–10, 12, 23, 45, 164
  reparation, 11, 50, 168
  restitution, 87
  scope, 47

Lauterpacht, 30, 169
law, civil, 54
law, common, 54

measures, provisional, 5, 8, 13–14, 16–19, 73

negotiation
  adjudication, 40, 167
  agreement, special, 43
  compliance, 169
  faith, good, 58
  judgment, implementation, 43
  judgments, 167
  order, 34
  process, 36, 44
  remedies, 79, 167
  settlement, dispute, 94
  subsequent, 38
non-repetition
  action, negative, 61
  apologies, 75, 155
  cessation, 6, 61–62, 64, 76
  clarification, 78
  compensation, 19
  development, 71

diplomacy, 71–72
discontinuance, 62
formal, 69, 76–78
implementation, 72, 75–76, 78–79
injury, 69
obligation, 69
remedies, 8, 61, 63, 69–71, 76–79
reparation, 63
requests, 69, 75, 77–78
restoration, 71
substantiation, 77

objection, preliminary, 5, 22, 26, 45
opinion, advisory, 30–31, 35
  binding, 32
  judgments, declaratory, 24, 29–30
  jurisdiction, 30
  restitution, 82, 89, 103

payment
  compensation, 53, 98–99, 111, 130
  damages, 112
  interest, 95
  money, 111, 121, 158
  reparation, 122
  restitution, 95, 137
  restoration, 133
  sum, 88, 92
peace, 1, 166
political
  conflict, 42, 57
  considerations, 166
  expediency, 167
  factor, 91
  implications, 167
  relationship, 7
  rights, 126
  sensitive, 42
  settlement, amicable, 168
proliferation, 3, 157, 163
proof, burden of, 109, 141, 143
property, 15, 56, 84
  compensation, 116, 120
  damage, 123, 125, 135
  damages, moral, 129
  harm, 115
  immovable, 89
  loss, 126
  nationalisation, 97
  seizure, 96–98, 136
protection, diplomatic, 130, 132

286 *Index*

quantum
 bifurcation, 139
 compensation, 11, 44, 128, 139
 damages, material, 127
 determination, 119, 142–143
 evaluation, 114
 evidence, 129
 expropriation, 137
 judgments, 120
 reparation, 122
Quintana, 59

relief
 abstractness, 31
 appropriate, 55
 cessation, 63
 declaratory, 7, 19, 21–22, 25, 27, 38, 44, 82,
  116, 153–155
 forms, 6, 45, 53
 injunctive, 53, 55, 62, 79
 judicial, 16
 monetary, 26, 46, 93, 149, 161
 performance, specific, 54–55
 of prayer, 2, 21, 44, 75, 82
 provisional, 15
 requests for, 37
 restitution, 81, 106
remedies, coercive, 20, 22, 24–27, 33–35, 38, 40,
  45, 59, 74, 94, 150, 166
responsibility
 compensation, 112, 116, 119,
  125
 declaration, 35–36
 determination, 26
 judgments, declaratory, 26
 of law, 39, 161
 mechanisms, 62
 opinion, advisory, 89
 remedies, 61
 reparation, 40, 104
 restitution, 95
 rules, 3
 satisfaction, 145, 151
 territorial, 36
restitutio in integrum
 cessation, 75
 compensation, 101
 remedies, 83
 reparation, 75, 99–100, 106
 restitution, 5, 83, 99–100
Rosenne, 167

satisfaction
 apologies, 29, 68, 149–150, 154, 159, 162
 articles, ILC, 6
 breach, obligation, 146
 breach, sovereignty, 29
 causality, 152
 cessation, 63, 68
 cessation, restitution, 61
 compensation, 44, 111
 compensation, restitution, 147
 damages, moral, 130, 145, 148–149, 158
 damages, non-material, 159, 161
 force, 63
 injury, direct, 131
 judgments, declaratory, 19, 25, 29–30, 45
 non-material, 154
 non-pecuniary, 148–149
 pecuniary, 19, 38, 148–149, 154, 159–161
 pecuniary, punitive, 159
 performance, specific, 61
 practice, tribunals, 160
 promise, 78
 relationship, diplomatic, 71
 reparation, 85, 112
 responsibility, 148
 violation, rights, 123
sovereignty
 breach of, 29
 delimitation, territorial, 39–40
 judgments, declaratory, 38
 relief, 37
 reparation, 131
 restitution, 38, 101–102
 rights, 32, 37, 40, 45, 98, 150
 settlement, dispute, 21, 36
 violation, 153, 161
status quo ante, restoration
 cessation, 65, 73, 75, 79
 compensation, 100, 135
 consequence, 102
 determination, 55
 establishment, 48
 full, 100–101
 impossibility, 99
 performance, specific, 48, 51, 60
 remedies, 62
 reparation, 93
 restitutio in integrum, 86–87
 restitution, 83–85, 100
Statute of the Court
 Article 36, 23–24, 30, 32, 46, 168

Index

Article 38, 23, 27, 166, 168
Article 40(1), 22
Article 41, 13, 15–16
Article 50, 139
Article 59, 23–24, 27, 167
Article 60, 29
Article 63, 24
Article 65, 30
competence, 9
decision, final, 29
dispute, legal, 32
experts, 139
force, binding, 23–24
function, 1
function, judicial, 23
judgments, declaratory, 23, 46
measures, provisional, 13, 16
opinion, advisory, 30

performance, specific, 59
remedies, 23
reparation, 55
seizure, 22

terminology
  compensation, 110, 121, 162
  performance, specific, 47–48, 58
  restitution, 89
Tomka, 64, 168

United Nations
  Charter, 167
  expropriation, 98
  member states, 167
  opinion, advisory, 103
  organ, judicial, 1, 165–166
  satisfaction, 160

CPSIA information can be obtained
at www.ICGtesting.com
Printed in the USA
LVHW082106070321
680817LV00005B/88